Beyond Karen: Emerging from the Depths of an Epic Epithet

Beyond Karen: Emerging from the Depths of an Epic Epithet

by Karen Willard Ribeiro

Cover art: an 1896 painting by the French artist Jean-Léon Gérôme:
La Vérité sortant du puits armée de son martinet pour châtier l'humanité
(*Truth coming out of her well armed with her whip to chastise mankind*)
Cover design by Victoria K. Chapman, Weyakin Designs

Names: Ribeiro, Karen Willard, author.
Title: Beyond Karen : emerging from the depths of an epic epithet /
Karen Willard Ribeiro.
Description: First trade paperback original edition. | Amherst, MA:
InnerFortune, 2021.
Identifiers: LCCN: 2021906940 | ISBN: ISBN: 978-1-7369774-0-8
Subjects: LCSH Racism--History. | Race awareness--United States. |
Racism--United States. | United States--Race relations. |
Women, White. | Self-actualization (Psychology) | Feminism. |
Perfectionism (Personality trait). | BISAC SELF-HELP/ Personal
Growth / General | BODY, MIND & SPIRIT / Inspiration & Personal
Growth | FAMILY & RELATIONSHIPS / Prejudice
Classification: LCC E184.A1 .R53 2021 | DDC 305.800973 --dc23

for Karens everywhere –
    May we all live in harmony

Contents

Author's Note

Hello. I would like to hug you for simply picking up this book. But, distance and the Coronavirus pandemic, mostly the pandemic, won't allow for that. You see, **Beyond Karen** has big ambitious dreams; she wants to reach people squarely in the heart, like an ancient harpsicord playing universal heart strings, or at least like a tuning fork that imparts a contented resonance and connection between you and the truly beautiful elements of life.

Beyond Karen wants to heal relationships both intimate and political. She wants to strengthen mother-daughter bonds that have frayed over everything from opinions about what is "appropriate" for a daughter to wear to a fervently reinforced message put out by gendered capitalism that mothers are old and out of touch. She desperately wants to put a hard stop to the social media insanity that is forever putting a wedge between us.

Writing the word "wedge" just now reminds me of the sweet human connection I felt with a grown man as I saw him walk along a sidewalk picking his wedgie. Don't we all have a bit "too much" to dislodge from that sticking point at the tops of our legs?

So, are you curious about this book's cover image? It is a public domain painting by French artist Jean-Léon Gérôme titled Truth coming out of her well, armed with her whip to chastise mankind! The cover photo was going to be a bold photo of my battered hand giving the middle finger (the injury you'll read about in the chapter *Life Is (a) Pain*). But then I received heartfelt feedback that it wasn't in concert with the vision of the book.

In the grand scheme of the 2020-21 "moment," with COVID-19 death and illness and job losses and natural disasters and political extremes to contend with, taking a deep dive into the dark "well" of

Karen name calling to write at least my own way out of it has been a way to take action and not succumb to the overwhelm. I am attempting to offer you a wide-angle lens on the ongoing tragedy of the commons, to Karens, to the curse of and on white middle-aged women.

I want to add another unique voice to the ongoing discourse about privilege and white culture (which is not at all exclusive to Caucasian people), and to encourage collective introspection within the white middle-aged community of women in the suburbs and beyond. In the writing of **Beyond Karen** I have been gently moved in the direction that I—a privileged white woman—need to be moved. I have again learned how intensely biased I still am about things as seemingly benign as time.

I hope to soon witness the emergence of a more care-full humanity that is as diverse and healthy as natural ecosystems were a century ago; a humanity in which mistakes are learned well and thus inform better choices in how we think, feel, speak, act and interact; a society made up of all people trusting one another. I share tentatively with the faith and hope that we can truly desire kindness and compassion towards one another, in all ways, despite any subconscious fear, jealousy, and bitterness we may have not yet confronted in ourselves.

Perhaps by the time this book is published, society will have gotten beyond Karen, the meme, the trope, the epithet. The power motives to keep alive a frenzy of distraction which serve to neutralize societal disruption are strong but fickle—like a hound dog's attention span. Even if the meme were to fade into the Internet's archives, due to the distastefulness of its use, boredom, or a new name taking over—after all, as you will read, the use of my given name Karen as a pejorative took over for the name Becky—the Karen phenomenon is a symptom of a social illness that has been around for a very long time. So, we breathe deeply and affirm goodness as best we can.

My tangible hope with this book is to bring even a slight level of solidarity between people acting like the Karens named through various forms of media, people doing the online policing, and people who may have abandoned these forms of media altogether because of the divisive "entertainment" factor that thwarts[1] solidarity. I celebrate the strong-spirited people among us—those willing to confront "Karen" behavior in themselves and in others, steadfastly doing this important work with as open a heart and mind as possible. I hope that my words can support young women and girls, very familiar with the sting and bullying power of this name and other names that hurt the spirit, to *not* call others a Karen, to not succumb to the pressure to pay hurt forward, and to feel fortified by a perspective about deep female solidarity that their mothers and auntie's also wish for them.

At one point in the editing process, I removed everything personal from the book and took a purely journalistic approach because, as I have observed generally, no one wants to know you until you've helped them better understand themselves. I did not intend for this book to be about me, but in the writing of part one, part two was coming through alongside it, reflecting back to me the ways in which I have consciously attempted to extricate "Karen" beliefs and constructs from myself.

This book attempts to delve into the phenomena about the Karen meme with personal reflections and things I have learned for better or worse. It may be unavoidable for my stories to sound like I am defending myself as an Anti-Karen given my goal of charting a course for emerging **Beyond Karen**. My continued attempts to understand and undo white bias and offer up these learnings felt important, so here they remain.

When you notice themes repeating themselves in anecdotes, my personal stories, or analyses I offer, please be curious about what is emerging within your own mind-body. None of our journeys of unfolding and emergence are linear as much as we may still want them to be. Irritations along the spiral staircase, as Karen Armstrong has so beautifully named this circuitous process, give us the edge against which we may feel and grow. Like the often-used analogy of a grain of sand caught in an oyster, the more attention we give this irritant, with

---

[1] A thwart is a strut or support from one side of a boat to another. The irony between thwart as a "support thing" and to thwart as a "force of opposition" is the sort of tension readers will experience throughout Beyond Karen the book, and in the ongoing efforts to move beyond the name-shaming of self and others.

repeated attempts at self-soothing, the more likely we are to wind up with a precious pearl—of wisdom.

Throughout the book you'll find this infinity symbol ∞ at various points when I felt I needed a reminder to take a deep breath. I hope you find them helpful.

Despite the finite nature of all trends—even ones as potent as Karen—I do hope that the stories in this book have staying power and continue to provide insight to all readers including Karens and the people who name them, long after Karen (and this author) has died.

This book was written out of a vision for how "we" can do better for ourselves and each other. I firmly believe that whenever any among us can see "a better way forward," that person should be able to ask for and receive attention, respect, and consideration, even if many of their insights are familiar, especially if they are not. The weaving we each do of the various facets of life is the unique view that can spark inspiration for another, personally or systematically.

Beyond Karen is for all who have been silenced or stunted by rules that feel arbitrary and exclusionary, for all who vacillate between feeling like they are too much and also not enough, for all who understand what "gaslighting" (and other crazy-making behaviors) feels like deep in their bones, for the emergent and the over-the-top who yearn for equanimity. It is dedicated to our collective healing through listening and setting clear context in our conversations with each other every day. Small steps that go the distance, heart-felt actions and kind words that affect positive change, and beliefs and behaviors that ensure a livable future for all life.

Part One:

Nonfiction Activism

What Is a Karen?

Karen is more than a birth name; it is a behavior or set of behaviors deemed harmful. It is a bad and emotionally unfiltered behavior. It is a type of overpowering and entitlement behavior that made many middle-aged women famous against their will in the summer of 2020. I have been slow to come to understand Karen, at a level that means something; I began with research, I added quite a bit of journaling to the mix, and over time, I have come to reckon with my "Inner Karen."

Karening is the act of saying what you think to whomever you are speaking with, regardless of time, space, circumstances, and context— no matter how potentially triggering or explosive your words may have on them. Being a Karen is unfiltered speaking, acting, and thinking whereas filters are emotional tools that we either have the skills to use, or we don't.

Because Karen went viral countless times in the summer of 2020, we all know her or have an opinion of her. Questioning this opinion may bring critical insights into our unconscious biases about skin color, about genitalia, about power and authority, about impunity and entitlement, about consent and respect and agreements, and the very subtle interplay of thoughts, words, and actions.

With this Karen frame of reference, we might all—women, children, and men—elevate our consciousness, narrow the gaps between us (gaps in perception that cause emotional pain), and allow for the emergence of rules of engagement, i.e. politics, that are essential, derived with and from the essence of nature—physically, emotionally, spiritually, and biologically—so that no species elevates itself above another even as it learns the art of being together with crude tools such as words, actions, and thoughts.

A Wikipedia entry "Karen (pejorative)" was created in April 2020 and by July 2020 this entry had received hundreds of revisions. On May 9, 2020, this Urban Dictionary definition of Karen appeared:

The stereotypical name associated with rude, obnoxious and insufferable middle aged white women.

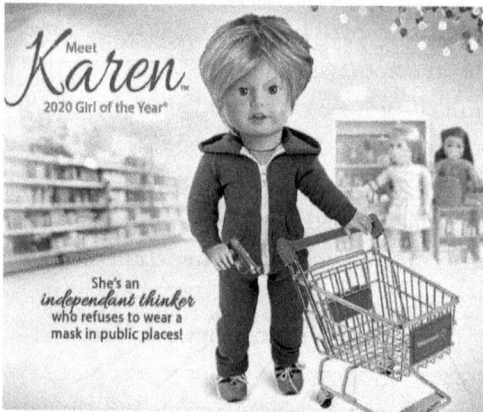

Meet *Karen.*™
2020 Girl of the Year*

She's an
independant thinker
who refuses to wear a
mask in public places!

Karens have been described as the typical over-entitled Western woman on steroids; to some, they are the most obnoxious examples of white privilege and white supremacy multiplied by several thousand percent. Karens have been defined as a mutated subspecies descended from the Soccer Mom, with traits like short tempers, bad haircuts, and vehicles that are unnecessarily large. If the viral meltdowns of the summer of 2020 weren't occurring alongside every level of emotional trauma due to COVID-19 and policemen murdering people of color, many Karen behaviors could have been chalked up to "normal" rude and wrong behavior that could come from anyone with unexamined social conditioning having a bad day.

In July 2020, a Google search for "Karens" returned *hundreds of millions* of responses, hundreds of thousands of "news" articles, and a petition[2] to stop using this meme had begun circulating. Throughout the summer of 2020, the Wikipedia of "Karen (pejorative)"[3] was updated almost daily.

---

[2] https://www.change.org/p/daily-mail-to-stop-the-use-of-karen-to-describe-racist-women-in-the-tabloids?source_location=topic_page
[3] https://en.wikipedia.org/wiki/Karen_(pejorative)

Referring to the Karens in May 2020, The Atlantic author Kaitlyn Tiffany, writes[4], "No meme better captures the fraught feelings of this moment, from coronavirus to all the looting America has done to people of color." This article is what got me, ironically I guess given my name Karen, angry enough to try and do something about it:

Amid the coronavirus pandemic, "Karen" has been adopted as a shorthand to call out a vocal minority of middle-aged white women who are opposed to social distancing, out of either ignorance or ruthless self-interest. It is the latest evolution of a long-standing meme. In The New York Times last year, the writer Sarah Miller described Karens as "the policewomen of all human behavior," using the example of a suburban white woman who calls the cops on kids' pool parties. Karens have been mocked for being anti-vaccine and pro– "Can I speak to your manager?" They are obsessed with banal consumer trends and their personal appearance, and typically criminally misguided, usually loudly and with extreme confidence.

I'll bet my entire life savings that she's standing there because she's waiting to talk to the manager

Quoted in this article is meme researcher and professor at Kansas State University Heather Suzanne Wood. About Karens she says their defining essence is "entitlement, selfishness, a desire to complain," and that "a Karen demands the world exist according to her standards with little regard for others, and she is willing to risk or demean others to achieve her ends."

---

4 https://www.theatlantic.com/technology/archive/2020/05/coronavirus-karen-memes-reddit-twitter-carolyn-goodman/611104/

Tiffany continues her brilliant explanation as to why the popularity of Karens has skyrocketed at this moment in time: inconsistent guidance from political leaders, conflicting social-distancing mandates among states, and turmoil in the streets such that we are left rudderless, policing one another's behavior.

Because we all love making others laugh (but have widely differing opinions of what is funny) the Karen meme became the summer's internet darling for helping others boost their social media platforms at the most base level.

Many podcasters and bloggers who have dug a little deeper into the roots of the Karen meme unearth the policies and regulations that have led to very real structural inequalities like housing and education and access to food and much more.

"Karen began as a Black meme used to describe white women who tattle on Black kids' lemonade stands," the community organizer Gwen Snyder tweeted. "White boys stole it and turned it into code for 'bitch.'" Perhaps a few of these white boys could feel the raging heat of intersectional injustice heading their way and chose to redirect it to white women?

One of the most succinct posts[5] I read about Karen, comes from Eric Shapiro, Content Editor for a small publication in Milpitas, California:

Flat-out: The left is *crushing* it with this "Karen" thing.

---

[5] https://milpitasbeat.com/flat-out-the-left-is-crushing-it-with-this-karen-thing/

I'm proud of us, frankly. For the uninitiated (if this article can penetrate the rock you're hiding under), a Karen is an entitled Caucasian woman, generally of suburban origin, with an inclination toward lording over others in an authoritarian manner, be it calling the manager or calling the cops. Right at this moment, the word is in its absolute prime, and we'd all be wise—amidst a frightening, uncertain world—to enjoy the fun while it lasts. … Karen takes down not whiteness per se, or privilege per se, or even white women or people of affluence per se. What it does instead, like mansplaining, is take down a mode of behavior, a strain of activity, an extant state of being.

All of which, unlike white skin itself, can actually be checked and corrected.

Great job, everyone. And *funny*, too.

According to Washington Post author, Hank Steuver, the most "captivating character on our screens this summer is Karen, and she's

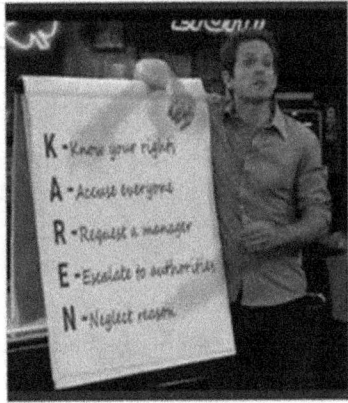

K - Know your rights
A - Accuse everyone
R - Request a manager
E - Escalate to authorities
N - Neglect reason

The children at my son's elementary school have started referring to me as a "Karen," and mocking my chic hairstyle. Is there anything I can do in the way of legal action to prevent this? I am deeply offended.

Let me speak with your task manager

everywhere."[6] He's not wrong when he writes, "Several times a day, Instagram and Twitter feeds serve up another galling, sad and often intensely satisfying segment of a reality series we can just go ahead and call 'Karens,'[7] in which women (almost always white, almost always of a certain demeanor) make the mistake of policing, harassing or discriminating against their fellow humans in public."

As soon as one Karen flames out across the Internet, another apparently more unhinged Karen rises in her place. One watches the video of the mask-defiant Karen in Dallas who angrily hurls the contents of her grocery cart to the floor[8], then, only hours later, one sees the terrifying video of a Karen and her husband (the male version of a Karen, sometimes known as a Kevin[9], has lately been termed a Ken) defiantly guarding their St. Louis manse[10] from passersby marching in a protest Sunday. This barefooted Karen, wearing a black-and-white striped shirt and the regulation capri-length Karen pants, is waving a pistol; her husband, in his schlubby pink polo shirt, brandishes a semiautomatic rifle [against their perceived threat by the Black Lives Matter protesters walking by]. (... in today's context there is no mistaking that they are Ken and Karen America.)

The list of Karen descriptors I found in one short moment looking for them on mainstream media, includes:

A racist bitch,
A tiny pistol packing nutcase,

[6] https://www.washingtonpost.com/entertainment/tv/whos-the-most-galling-captivating-character-on-our-screens-this-summer-its-karen—and-shes-everywhere/2020/06/30/f806a64c-ba44-11ea-80b9-40ece9a701dc_story.html
[7] https://www.washingtonpost.com/lifestyle/style/karens-try-to-make-unequal-power-structures-work-for-them/2020/05/29/31adc68a-8a3b-11ea-8ac1-bfb250876b7a_story.html?itid=lk_inline_manual_2
[8] https://nypost.com/2020/06/29/dallas-karen-tosses-food-during-mask-meltdown/
[9] https://www.instagram.com/p/CB_VBYHh51s/
[10] https://www.washingtonpost.com/nation/2020/06/29/st-louis-protest-gun-mayor/?itid=lk_inline_manual_5

A rude, entitled middle-aged woman,
The act of shaming immigrants publicly,
The act of lording one's privilege over another,
A day drunk whore,
Someone who speaks before she thinks,
An uneven bob haircut on a blonde,
A douchebag,
A Halloween costume,
Kate Gosselin,
JK Rowlings,
Ellen DeGeneres,
Whoopi Goldberg's neighbor,
A ruthlessly self-interested know it all,
A Republican,
A toilet paper hoarder,
Trump.

Whew. Just a little bit of research can be a lot to process. Over months I have come to accept my "Inner Karen" and wish to reflect for a moment in this "Emerging from the depths of an epic epithet" adventure on what I have distilled. We all have one waiting to be annihilated.

One way that my Inner Karen comes out is while sitting in parking lots and spaces where I'm parked in my car near other people in their cars, invariably in warmer weather when I can hear the engines laboring unnecessarily or in cold weather when I can see the greenhouse gas exhaust rising, when I can feel the weight of the wasted fossil fuels—the blood of my mother earth extracted by brutal force, with devastating, murderous, and irreversible consequences of seemingly endless extinctions, through shady and greedy machinations of money—burning not just in this air I breathe but in my body, my heart, my mind ready to explode like these tired engines laboring unnecessarily and these greenhouse efforts rising exhausted. This description of what I feel may seem like a bit "extra" or "over the top" but if I go as deeply as possible into my emotional reactions as I sit in my car in these moments, not idling, this is what lies at the roots of my feelings.

I have compassionately confronted people idling over the years more times than I can count—men and women, mostly men; young and older, mostly older; people of color and white, mostly white. Sometimes I am thanked because the person truly didn't know they were idling or that there were consequences to their idling they didn't consider. In these moments, I know that I've taken a small and important step toward progress. In these moments I feel that the anxiety I had to overcome, in order to choose to step up to this other person's vehicle (nowadays with a mask and the added intensity of our collective and visceral fear of each other), was worth it.

And then sometimes after I have tried to engage with another human being about a very sensitive subject, right in the heat of a moment where my intention to help is most likely going to be misconstrued as being bitchy, bossy, holier-than-thou, entitled, and self-righteous, I see emotional reactions which indicate that my efforts have pushed this human being slightly further over their edge, which in turn pushes me slightly further over my edge. It is all I or anyone can do in these moments to breathe and trust that this interaction will not have devastating, life-threatening, or otherwise irreversible consequences.

The middle-aged white hetero cis woman demographic is the most trusted demographic on the planet. When those of us in this demographic don't act trustworthy—when we are racist, sexist, classist, and act with impunity, immaturity, and impatience, we break that trust and, potentially, bring down the rath of others' ire.

No, it is not okay to let that bitchy, bossy, holier-than-thou, entitled, and self-righteous anger boil over into any form of abuse leveled on another being, including social media shaming. It is okay to do our best to choose to step up and overcome our anxieties about the act of compassionately speaking our truths to each other—in the heat of a moment when we are at risk of going over our emotional edges—with the intention of resolution and reconciliation.

∞

From my white personal experience, being made invisible by forms of gaslighting (discussed in depth in A State of Enough) or silent judgment has hurt worse than being confronted rudely because a verbal adversary is someone I can contend with and find ways to become more skillful from experience. Being talked over is the bigger part of Karening that has had more deeply painful consequences than confrontation as it carries with it a near absolute implicit judgment that I am a lesser human being. And from my experience, men have been Karens to me far more frequently than women. And because men still make bottom line major media decisions, we lately seem to see far more representation of women talking over others and expressing hurtful unconscious bias than men.

Like bigger hurricanes that get assigned female names so that people continue to think worse of women, or be less afraid of their intense winds and rains as conventional wisdom goes, the behavior of ignorantly talking over others has been given female names, most virally Karen. This implies that women talk over others more than men.

It is impossible to know if my experience of being talked over, which has contributed to my behavior of talking over others (which has been and continues to be carefully monitored so that I learn to not do this), speaks to others' experiences of being talked over. But the research and experiences shared in **Beyond Karen** are offered not to blame shift but to help balance the perspective and elicit greater personal reflection on the notions ascribed to Karen behavior.

As we all do more personal reflecting, we will collectively build compassion for one another. As we build compassion, we discover that hurt people hurt people. And we all hurt.

Rise and Fall

The story has just begun.

Let's take a brief pause for a deep breath. You can place your hand on your chest to feel its rise and fall as re-spiration enters and exits the body, fills it and empties, expands it and contracts. The breath will carry you through the rest of this book (and, of course, the rest of your life); this simple act of breathing has tremendous potential for transforming the body and mind when intentionally noticed. Mindful breathing can get us beyond Karen.

Here is my favorite breathing song. I sing it to myself when I notice my emotions becoming unstable, when I need to walk slowly and have words to accompany each step, or to "the universe" sometimes while I am driving alone (read left to right as you inhale and exhale).

INHALE word	EXHALE word
In	Out
Deep	Slow
Calm	Ease
Smile	Release
Pre-	sent
Mo-	ment
Wonder-	full
Mo-	ment

Isn't it wonderful that such a thing as breathing songs exist? Ok, back to the story.

White, middle-aged women, generally, have risen closer to the
"power" and are presumably more visible in the world than women of
color. I contend that this representative power is not desirable or real,
that our worship of money has us searching desperately for our very
souls.

What is representative power? Is it more than legislative? Is it
positionality and influence? Is it authoritative, ascribed, assumed?

White, middle-aged women have recently gone from being
overrepresented in television commercials to being underrepresented
through what may be described as either a corrective affirmative action
or an opportunistic "cover your ass" move to avoid getting sued
("your" being the mainstream media advertisers or content producers).
These previously "empowered," previously overrepresented middle-
aged women were very much on the younger side of middle-aged and,
generally, thin, and seemingly flawless. We all know that women on
the older side of middle-aged have long been underrepresented in
mainstream media and if they have "power" they also have stories
worth reading.

As an aside it is important to hope that we all have some
familiarity with the inequity that exists throughout the world with
respect to compensation for labor and what constitutes wealth.
According to Women Occupying Wall Street, women,
disproportionately women of color, do 66% of the world's work, earn
10% of the world's wages, and own 1% of the world's assets. (I
reinforce this again later in the book). The economic study of racial
disparity is important.

The representative rise of people of color also feels important. I
imagine the fall of white people is painful for those affected, especially
if they feel alone in it all. This rise and fall, like shallow breathing,
speaks to the opportunistic fickleness of our mainstream media.

I also contend that a reason for this fall, particularly for some of
the white middle-aged women who have gotten too close for comfort
to this "power" and may have been canceled as Karens (or a similar
label), is that they have stopped being complicit and are choosing to
use their power for good (and good isn't so profitable). Challenging
the foundation of white culture by choosing to act in alignment with

higher values instead of playing by these unwritten rules, is, to the bigtime money brokers, on par with sedition. Research Roger Ailes.

Back to breathing.

How does Karen epitomize the present state of political discord? She, if I may grossly overgeneralize, is a tumbleweed of ideas blowing with the wind, lacking rootedness to her own embodied opinions. Instead of having a lifelong experience of discussing situational and circumstantial cause and effect and reflecting on what that all means to her, instead of truly sitting with and dialoguing about the feelings evoked by life unfolding as it does, with others she feels safe around, she listens to those with assigned authority tell her what's what—to the point where she may not even realize she is lacking some of the fundamental developmental skills of critical reasoning.

The intensity of another's emotions can catch us by surprise and be a shock to our physical system. This shock can lead us to experience our own emotional intensity and make us feel we need to do something fast. If we take that urgent feeling and train ourselves to translate it into intentionality, we can attend to our breathing first and foremost, which can lead us toward our most compassionate thoughts, words, and actions in any moment. And as we practice emotional transformation with others, we become skillful with our own emotional intensity.

I am an emotionally intense person. I can be a lot for others less familiar with emotional intensity to bear and feel compassion towards. This doesn't mean it is not worth the effort to try and witness my energy. Those who do put in the effort, generally find a refreshing level of honesty and depth that can inspire growth in their capacity for being vulnerable. Being vulnerable is one of my superpowers and I look forward to a new era in which we humans of all genders, ethnicities, and skin colors, especially white-minded or "colonized" Americans who have struggled through what to others looks like long and hard "troubled teen" years, embrace vulnerability as an authentic language of connection.

Trauma in the body has a unique and volatile frequency. Similar but different to the frequency with which love resonates in the body, stored trauma seeks resonance in order to resurface. This resonance can be activated unexpectedly by a word or phrase spoken in just the right tone, or by a look—a flash across another's face that could be interpreted with meaning that may or may not have been intended. The resonance that traumas seek, in order to be held in safety and heal, is a powerful driving force.

If we do not actively pursue supports and learn how to breathe through emotional triggers, we may never arrive at that safe place the trauma needs to find wellness. The more skillful we get at noticing and breathing away these unexpected activations—skillfulness best developed in community with others such as mindfulness practitioners or peers who gather intentionally to name and witness each other as we work through feelings and emotions, like 12-step programs and other groups of anonymity—the less intense they become.

If we suppress the natural desire to heal emotionally, over time old and repeat traumas build in intensity, perhaps into desperation. Desperation leads to rash behaviors and hasty actions that could eventually lead one to have a public meltdown, or at least believe half-true narratives—like "life sucks" and "it's not worth it"—which keep us stagnant. And complicit.

Still breathing.

Still breathing.

It is my most sincere hope and wish that as we in white Western society finally begin to honestly and courageously face our feelings, our culturally programmed opinions and judgments about race and skin color, and the deep seated humanity-denying impacts it has had on generations of people of color, we likewise open ourselves up to face the disturbing impacts of the multi-millennial sex and gender biases which have perpetuated atrocities globally against the fairest, sweetest, most authentically alive among us. And these atrocities, like sex trafficking, female genital mutilation, rape, social media stalking and intimidation, continue to assail women worldwide. This is the greatest shame of humanity. There is absolutely no justification whatsoever for any of this abhorrent barbarism.

The lawmaking, and subsequent application of laws, that operates within a degenerative, unjust, and complicit culture of "othering" and dehumanizing people who view the world in a different—often more meaningful and robust—way than that ascribed by white Western society, is fraught with inevitable explosive emotional repercussions. Each time I ponder the fact that human beings continue to be caged in cells, incarcerated and debased as they are instead of held in community by mature adults who could help them understand and make amends for their actions, particularly in America, I find it truly hard to fathom.

If I think back to my own interactions with police, I am transported to something like the "twilight zone," a surreal out-of-body state I did not consent to, an entirely different reality. More on that later.

What is on me, my responsibility, what is on you, what is on every human being who claims to want peace and harmony in the world, is the active development of skillfulness in bearing reality—not hiding from it or being in any way complicit in the hiding, falsifying, or the diluting of reality. What is not on me or you, is the responsibility to educate the ignorant despite the fact that it is most likely in my or your best interests, ultimately, to do so.

Being human is complicated. We are an amalgamation of short- and long-term relationships with other humans and other species (including plants) and we all have unique and ever changing, often conflicting short- and long-term aspirations. Hearing each other clearly is always the challenge.

So I have, in my experience of reflecting on society and being vulnerable in it, in finding that the only way to alleviate pain and heal from it is to feel it deeply and desire its dissolution in the body-mind, landed upon a few notions about humanity that I would like to share here in this chapter about rising and falling and in this book about human beings struggling in relationship with one another both publicly and privately. These are just a few humanity rules that we learn in life but feel hurt by when they are not followed. These are offered as a resource to consider as we encounter microaggressions that trigger us into experiences we weren't expecting.

Macro Agreements.
1. Humans are kind and compassionate to each other.
2. Humans take good care of their bodies and minds.
3. Humans think, speak, and act with good intentions.
4. Humans behave responsibly.

Micro Agreements.
1. Police officers keep peace and ensure the safety of people.
2. Men (and women) respect each other's personal and emotional boundaries.
3. Parents think about, speak with, and act towards their children with good intentions.
4. Everyone recycles and only consumes what they need so that they behave like responsible stewards of the earth.

These are pretty powerful agreements that we often make (or are made for us) subconsciously. Another is that it is okay to dump our emotions on others, particularly our intimate partners, family members, and co-workers. It is never okay to dump emotions on another—unless we have made an explicit agreement with them and they have agreed to witness us process our feelings.

Lately I have been thinking that if I live closer to more people, I will feel less desperate for more community than I already have the privilege to enjoy. The reasons I long for deeper community have emerged out of a complex web of emotional experiences. The most succinct way to describe this longing—the reason why I am writing a book about white middle-aged Karens and their public demonstrations of emotional dysregulation, credited by some as having deflected the nation's attention from racial injustice as it heated up in 2020—is because the shame of white complicity hurts so much.

Some people feel shame more acutely than others. All people cope with shame differently. Some of us deny and block the sensation of shame so well that we believe we are immune to it. We may instinctively seek formal impunity or exemption from consequences through professions like policing and security offices. We may not realize that such efforts to avoid feeling the shame of whiteness directly, and often dramatically, perpetuates our complicity in racial injustice.

What leads me and my body-mind to check out, to give up? What can get me to stop caring about what matters? The repeat smacks in the face (figurative but just as painful to my heart) that my thoughts (hopes), words and actions (attempts to reconcile conflicts and injustices) are just not enough.

A smack in the face can be anything from a legislative bill stuck in limbo for decades—especially a climate bill like carbon pricing while the planet is burning, or a bottle bill to motivate people to reduce their streams of toxic waste—to a subtle joke, smirk, or distraction by a lover at the very moment you need them to simply breathe the pain of reality alongside you, to stand with you again and again, reaffirming your partnership so that at least one thing in this world is safe and secure.

Aren't we alike in this desire for one sure, safe, and secure relationship? If we humans have DNA that is 99% similar to each other, couldn't the things that unites us be our need for our lives to be of service and to be in sync with—to breathe each day with—at least one other person? What if we could all show up this way for each other?

Truth rides along the rise and fall of the breath; it always has, and it always does, if we are able to feel it. Truth emerges as a thought, a feeling, a word, a next right step to take, to follow.

If we stay true to the self and love the goodness within, we can bear the emotional winds blowing all around us. This sounds airy fairy because it is. Thank God for that.

Life has so much rhythm ... and it is pretty noisy.
Feeling is the art form.

A Few Karens

I have no particular methodology for introducing to you (if you are not already familiar with) the prominent Karens on social media, other than the desire to offer a wide range of characterizations. I am no "expert" on Karens; I have not done exhaustive research or interviewed people for unique content. I'm trying to not be that person.

There are so many Karens, from the first and most famous, Central Park Karen and other Cop Calling Karens, to the myriad social misfit or misdemeanor Karens. Each Karen has a story and I do not know it; what I do know is that there is a reason for their shame. And it's complicated.

There is Kidz Bop Karen, Uber and Lyft Karen, Costco, Walmart, Target, and Trader Joe's Karen, Coronavirus Karen, Black Karen, Canadian Karen, Tiny Pistol Karen (who is half of the "Ken and Karen" duo) and Gun-Wielding Karen, OG [Old Guard] Karen, Detroit, San Francisco, and Tennessee Karen, Insane Karen, Angry Karen, and Crazy Karen, Mega Karen, Blue Lives Don't Matter Karen, Max Level Karen, Farmers Market Karen and a whole lot more you-name-it Karens. There are people staging video freakouts to be able to name someone Karen and to get named Karen; and actual women named Karen are stepping off social media altogether.

Twitter, Instagram, Facebook, and YouTube are the platforms from which the following Karen content has been curated. The following is a brief overview of the Karens that stood out to me among the many threads of discussion and articles I read about Karens in the short period between May and July 2020.

Kidz Bop Karen

One early November day in 2019, a certified conflict prevention and reconciliation manager (according to Laura W.)[11], was cut off by a Lyft driver while driving with her husband and children down NYC's West Side highway. "Karen" gave the Lyft driver the middle finger, and passenger Chelsea Klein gave a thumbs up in return. "Karen" stopped in the middle of the road and went up to the Lyft driver's window. The driver apologized repeatedly but passenger Klein's "calm down" admonishment to "Karen" led "Karen" to verbally abuse Klein which was captured on video and posted to Klein's Instagram[12] (the feed has since been removed). This tirade led her to be dubbed "Kidz Bop Karen" because she told both people in the vehicle that her kids couldn't hear her yelling since they were listening to Kidz Bop.

Some of the comments in Klein's Instagram feed include:

"I'm so upset he [Lyft driver] didn't roll the window up and slowly squash her rotting pink peach face", "this is what my sleep paralysis demon looks and sounds like", "Go home Karen, it's Tuesday and you're drunk again", "OMG she's MARRIED Can you imagine that poor beta male at home?", and a whole lot more general anger.

The one person attempting to support "Karen" said, "As hilarious as this was, I hope this woman [Klein] does something about the negative exposure you got her. She clearly has issues and you took advantage of it to get views on YouTube and followers on Instagram."

---

[11] https://www.youtube.com/watch?v=FyeOL8yGx3Y
[12] https://news.yahoo.com/woman-filmed-viral-kidz-bop-173052354.html

The author of this comment was summarily attacked as a "clown of a human being" and the thread went off into weird Democrat bashing.

Lauren Karmo, campus editor of *The Oakland* [University] *Post*, in a November 20, 2019 post with the tags Satire and Showcase, writes: "Kidz Bop Karen is just another misunderstood, unfortunate victim of the kids today. Back in her day, she didn't have to worry about getting recorded and exposed on the internet for her crack headed, asshole ways, she could just go about her business in peace. But instead, she's been singled out and targeted for no reason by entitled millennials that just don't get how hard it is to be a stay-at-home mom on the nice side of town."

And perhaps because it can be hard to discern satire even in a piece specifically defined as satire, here is a comment, ironically, by a woman named Karen:[13]

- Firstly, I'd make sure I knew Karen was a boomer (she's not.)
- Secondly, if I didn't want people making broad sweeping generalizations about my generation (KBK is a known millennial defender, but thanks for all those bitchy jabs) I'd be careful not to make them about other (wrongly identified) generations.
- Thirdly, no minivan.
- Fourthly, I'd maybe use my cognitions reasoning skills and recognize I have one side of a story and not be so judgey. But hey—who am I to say?"

The point here isn't to choose any particular comments about this or other Karens, it is to demonstrate that people get really emotional about other people's experiences. They weigh in hard about them as if they knew the people involved, and the level of bitterness directed at not only the guilty party but also the commenters in these threads

---

[13] November 21st, 2019 8:58 AM

reminds me of modern-day stoning that might have killed a woman accused of adultery thousands of years, or maybe just decades, ago.

Big Box Store Karen, Florida Karens, and Zombie Karen

It would be quite a feat to identify all the various women (and a few men) dubbed Karen due to a scene they'd caused in public retail stores, from Costco, Walmart, and Target to supermarkets and pharmacies. The descriptor of what a Karen is kept expanding to include more and more attributes of these people becoming unglued, dysregulated, or—as this NIH study[14] might define the behavior—having an "emotional cascade" in public.

Costco Karen, according to Newsweek[15], coughed on a man's camera as he filmed her and her companion while they were being asked by an employee to wear their masks properly. She had her mask below her nose and her partner had his dangling from his ear. The person posting the video got many hundreds of comments which, being that comments are today's new currency, reinforced his behavior.

In May 2020, Coronavirus Karen apparently spent 20 minutes refusing to wear a mask and boldly telling a clerk at Trader Joes about "many researchers who say we shouldn't breathe our own CO2." She later posted a video for social media viewers about her sore throat that got better as she boosted her immune system.

One video montage that was aired on the Stephen Colbert Show in July 2020 takes a hit at these big box store Karens, along with a segment of Florida Karens, and Zombie Karen. The reference in the video to the "devil's law" is from a young Latinx woman in West Palm Beach, FL. Oddly enough, the only reference to this "law" I could find was a play written by a man in the about the legal rights of women in the early 1600s—an era defined by elite hierarchy as reigned by James I whose "Jacobean" era in England was wedged between that of the Elizabethan and Caroline (for Charles I). Why this ancient play is still referenced at

---

14 https://www.ncbi.nlm.nih.gov/pmc/articles/PMC2791094/

15 https://www.newsweek.com/i-got-covid-woman-coughs-man-costco-after-he-asks-her-wear-mask-over-nose-1526477

all is an important question. Another: How is it that this woman came to use it?

Here are the Stephen Colbert Show video lyrics set to a remake of Dolly Parton's song *Jolene*[16]:

> Karen, Karen, Karen, Karen, I'm begging of you please just wear a mask.
> You go on rants at Trader Joe's,
> Sit on the ground at the Costco,
> Say wearing masks is the devil's law.
> You wreck displays at Target Stores,
> You throw good cold cuts on the floor,
> And please stop talking 'bout your drawers Karen [this particular Karen said *"I don't wear a mask for the same reason I don't wear underwear; things gotta breathe"*]
> Karen, Karen, Karen, Karen, I'm begging you please don't lick that glass*.
> Karen, Karen, Karen, Karen, please just wear a mask you, big dumbass."

Here is the "devil's law" testimony:

> You literally cannot mandate somebody to wear a mask knowing that that mask is killing people. And we the people are waking up and we know what citizen's arrest is because citizens arrests are already happening, okay. And (while pointing at everyone in the audience) every single one of you obeying the devils' law are going to be arrested. And you, doctor, you are going to be arrested for crimes against humanity.

Accusing a doctor of "crimes against humanity", as if he was purposely trying to kill people by enforcing mask wearing when this is presented by his industry experts as the safest measure possible,

---

indicates that this woman was emotionally dysregulated. But why? Can we get that side of the story?

And the reference* to the glass licking has nothing to do with wearing a mask; it is about a woman labeled "Zombie Karen" after a July 2, 2020 video posted on Twitter (@whosalex) captured her antics after being denied entry to a local bar in Houma, Louisiana.

The Karenovirus is responsible for 3 managers being fired this month alone

Fifteen Karen Memes That Will Terrify Anyone In...

She decided to run full tilt into the window and then start licking it. The person behind the camera called this a scene from the movie *I Am Legend* about a plague turning humans into zombies.

Some of the comments in the thread in this post about Zombie Karen include:

"Trump and Pence were the first Karens. An[d] then it spread to their MAGA fans",

"Folks, this is NOT normal. Remember when life once was normal, at least somewhat", "Oh my gawd when is there gonna be a vaccine for the Karenovirus", and "to the rest of the world: We're so sorry for all this."

Can we pause for just a moment and imagine what set of circumstances it would take for any of us to be so emotionally unwell as to behave this way? It does appear in this Stephen Colbert Show video that "Zombie Karen" was likely extremely intoxicated or perhaps mentally unstable. The potential for psychic break is very real. And it is beyond sad that millions of people are depressed to the point of lethargy and apathy. It is abominable that we are putting mental unwellness on display for social credit.

Before social media got so amped up—back in the old days about 10 years ago when it was just Facebook and Twitter—opinions and interactions made sense to me. Now it seems like engaging in social media can be as much a spectator sport as a cock fight.

"Another Karen spotted in Florida this week even purposely coughed on a woman who had been filming her harass workers at a Pier 1 Imports. The victim, Heather Sprague, is immunocompromised as a result of a brain tumor. "I think I'll get really close to you and cough on you then, how's that?" the Karen says. 'Asshole.'"

According to this NY post article,[17] "A Karen attempted to shame a Starbucks employee who refused her service for not wearing a mask. After posting footage of the employee on Facebook, a monumental backlash ensued. The internet responded by raising more than $57,000 (other sources quote $78,000) for the harassed employee."

St. Louis Ken, Karen and Other Gun-Wielding Karens

Since the June 20th incident[18] in St. Louis, Missouri when a white middle-aged couple named Mark and Patricia McCloskey—apparently afraid of a group of Black Lives Matter protesters walking past their

---

[17] https://nypost.com/2020/06/27/starbucks-barista-receives-57000-in-donations-after-karen-shames-him/

[18] https://www.complex.com/life/2020/07/st-louis-ken-and-karen-couple-face-felony-chargers-for-pointing-guns-at-peaceful-protester ; https://www.bbc.com/news/world53588201

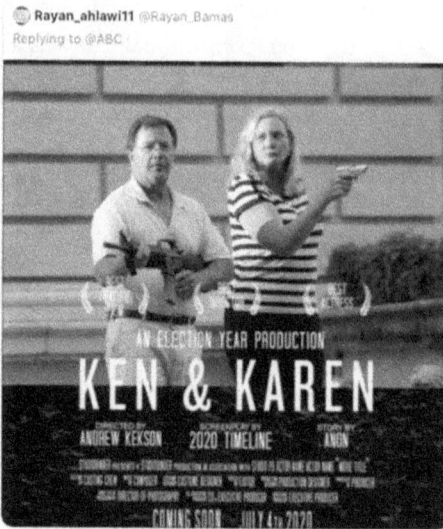

home, brandished guns and waved them at the protesters—a number of similar incidents have taken place where white women and men, labeled Karens, have pulled out guns in public to threaten African American men and women.

One Baton Rouge, Louisiana example, "teacher went berserk in frustration over flooding, pulled gun and now facing school investigation," has to make one wonder what caused this woman to have a psychological break. Within days of the Karen and Ken gun incident, "Chipotle Karen" went viral. In this article[19] Michelle Rennex writes, "As more and more 'Karens' pop up in the media for their increasingly more dangerous and targeted actions, people found that reducing them to a comedic term downplays what they do. Pulling a gun on innocent black people isn't the same as complaining to the manager when you don't get your way."

Also, by turning problematic and dangerous white women into memes as quirky Karens trivializes their actions and desensitizes people to them. While we laugh at how sensitive, overdramatic and nosy these white women are, it ignores the real problem at hand: Racists are dangerous and what they do to minorities is not normal, nor is it OK.

[19] https://www.theroot.com/lawyer-for-michigan-couple-who-pulled-gun-on-black-fami-1844348022?utm_campaign=TheRoot&utm_content=1594482558&utm_medium=SocialMarketing&utm_source=twitter

Domino's Pizza Karen

A July 2020 BBC article announced that Domino's Pizza[20] had to apologize for running a promotion in Australia and New Zealand offering free pizza to "nice Karens." In my local area, a dairy farm ice cream shop decided to give away ice cream to anyone named Karen on a particular day. I thought that was fantastic and promptly got myself over there for a cone and a selfie. This kind of promotion seems entirely benign to me. In fact, the apology that Domino's ran got them just as much, if not more, publicity than the promotion itself. Quite a strategic win-win.

Here is an excerpt of the Domino's apology[21]:

We are sorry.

Our post came off the back of a number of situations in Victoria, Australia which received international media coverage, including in New Zealand. A person who decided they didn't have to follow the mandate and wear a mask and took it out on retail workers; a person who breached a COVID-19 checkpoint, potentially endangering others; a person who was bored walking in her neighbourhood. These examples were widely known, and publicly commented on: Bunnings "Karen", Checkpoint "Karen", and "Karen" from Brighton.

We wanted to bring a smile to customers who are doing the right thing—Karen the nurse, Karen the teacher, Karen the mum.

In New Zealand, because it lacked this important context, people interpreted this in a different way than we intended. We appreciate how this has happened and have listened—we've removed this post.

We want you to know that we are always listening and learning and when we get it wrong, we fix it.

We are sorry.

---

20 https://www.bbc.com/news/world-asia-53589897
21 https://www.facebook.com/DominosNZ/posts/10157760919412462

It is important to note the coincidence between folks in New Zealand not understanding the Karen context and the very low incidence rates of COVID-19 due to a well-managed response to the pandemic. In America we have such mistrust in what we see online, in the news, and in video because we know the technology exists to edit everything.

A few years ago, I was interviewed by a local media station about political performance art I was involved in and by the time it was broadcast, my words had been switched around and a completely divisive and inaccurate segment was spliced in. These are the subtle media manipulations that are so ubiquitous that we can't all collectively address them one by one; the system that rewards alternative facts must change.

A BBC article[22] by Ashitha Nagesh related to the above apology interests me because it doesn't perpetuate vitriol alongside the various accounts of Karen behavior; it moves the reader to think beyond Karen by posing the question, "So, when is a Karen not a Karen?" and the writer gives readers an example of the anti-racist human shield protesters in Portland, Oregon called the Wall of Moms Bloc.

I appreciate the straightforward reporting in this article and would like to further investigate another question Nagesh poses, "Why are Americans so angry about masks?" She answers this question by saying, "The refusal of some people to acknowledge the risks associated with the virus, and to be shielded from these risks by their white privilege, has also been seen as 'Karen' behaviour." Yes, and let's ask ourselves, "why is this so?"

Various pundits rail against "privileged conservatives" or "Republicans" for not wearing masks and there is plenty of finger pointing and name calling going on well beyond the Karens. I believe the Karen phenomenon is part and parcel of a multiple systemic issues behind the debate to mask or not to mask. This fomenting of confusion rests squarely on the current administration's lack of leadership. With respect to mask wearing, House Judiciary Chairman Jerry Nadler had to go out of his way during the July 2020 hearing questioning Attorney

---

[22] https://www.bbc.com/news/world-53588201

General William Barr's excessive use of police force, in cities like Portland Oregon, to specifically call out three republican members of his committee (Jim Jordan, Andy Biggs and Mike Johnson) for refusing to wear masks[23]. If Americans have lost faith in our leadership, even if we are unable to admit this, we are understandably going to have a hard time overcoming skepticism about the science behind the coronavirus. The mistrust has been cultivated for decades.

Arwa Mahadi, writer for The Guardian, agrees: "Yes, people who refuse to wear face masks are selfish. Yes, they're putting lives in danger. But do they deserve to be vilified and publicly shamed? I don't think so. Not just because public shaming is often ineffective but because they're not the biggest villains here: the people who truly deserve our anger are the public figures and authorities—everyone from the US's surgeon general to representatives of the World Health Organization—who, until fairly recently, told us that masks were useless if not dangerous, before doing a U-turn and insisting we all wear one[24]."

If a Karen is someone who has largely abdicated to external experts (bosses, reporters, medical professionals) her inner authority for most if not all of her life, she may be at risk of psychological whiplash from all the flip flopping that has taken place on the highest levels with regards to this global pandemic.

Central Park Karen

When I think about the quintessential Karen that I learned about as I began writing this book, the woman who was choking her dog on a leash, the woman who proceeded to call the cops and make false accusations of "an African American assaulting her," the woman filmed by said man with a camera on his birding hat, wanting her to follow the rules of Central Park, I recall seeing Amy Cooper in a messy and nonlinear state of emotional dysregulation.

---

[23] https://www.cnn.com/world/live-news/coronavirus-pandemic-07-29-20-intl/h_34c156a8a28f358908b8861be2fa4849

[24] https://www.theguardian.com/commentisfree/2020/jul/22/shaming-people-who-refuse-to-wear-face-masks-isnt-a-good-look

Amy Cooper's racist accusation was the proverbial straw that broke the camel's back in the movement for black lives. Tensions were so high with Derek Chauvin and his complicit fellow officer's murder of George Floyd that Christian Cooper's video of this Central Park[25] incident was seen about 45 million times. Her unconscionably racist action had to be called out. She became the Karen poster child as the intolerance of white supremacy—or as poet Nikki Giovanni calls it, white cowardice—and law enforcement overreach was boiling over like a massive methane explosion across America. She lost her job and her dog and has received unknowable amounts of psychic hatred. The employer disavowed itself from her. That was all well and good. But for her ignorance and really bad timing, she deflected heat off and became a viable scapegoat for Derek Chauvin and the murder he committed.

What, if anything, would be different if our American media were less pariah like? Are we unable to want for Amy and Christian to reconcile this emotionally intense experience while holding the pain of police brutality? Despite the ordeal and the fact that details of this ongoing trial are obscure, Chris Cooper is reported[26] to have formally stated that, "bringing her more misery just seems like piling on."

25

https://twitter.com/melodyMcooper/status/1264965252866641920?ref_src=twsrc%5Etfw%7Ctwcamp%5Etweetembed%7Ctwterm%5E1264965252866641920%7Ctwgr%5E&ref_url=https%3A%2F%2Ftime.com%2F5857023%2Fkaren-meme-history-meaning%2F

[26] https://www.nytimes.com/2020/10/14/nyregion/amy-cooper-false-report-charge.html

Why Amy Cooper's name was said so frequently and with such disregard is my question. What is it about throwing an emotionally unwell woman (or anyone for that matter) to the wolves? Are we that much in need for a sacrificial lamb when all the countless efforts to obtain police accountability do little more than reinforce the truth of corruption?

I guess for some there may be satisfaction in canceling someone easy to take down, holding their arrogance in check. Perhaps there was a sense of closure that at least the pawns in Amy's chess game were all taken, and maybe her queen. But let's hold the pain of reality with those willing to face their demons, knowing that we have a sea change upon us.

How can we shorten the time between gross and intolerable infractions and their reconciliation—without washing over the consequences of pain and suffering? How can we balance perspectives even as the emotional intensity of unexamined biases and subsequent experiences of truth-telling continues to rise?

A few weeks after Central Park Karen flooded social media, the name of an old white man in "the villages"—one of the largest white retirement communities in Miami-Dade Florida, who shouts, alongside his golf buddies, "white power" at a white supremacist party—went undisclosed even after this "Fifty Shades of Whey" tweet[27] was retweeted by the former President? How could the media be held accountable for balanced reporting standards? Or for calling out the white cops murdering Black people for that matter; why aren't these names broadcast with the same frequency as Amy's or other "Karens?"

It is beyond hard to hold that question alongside the racial tensions that continue unabated. We may be reading books to unlearn some of our biases in the privacy of our homes, but we are not yet seeing the paradigms shift at a level commensurate with the needed healing in the spaces, like mainstream media and other established institutions, that are absurdly complicit.

---

[27] https://www.nbcmiami.com/news/local/officials-confirm-man-shouting-white-power-in-video-shared-by-trump-is-retired-miami-firefighter/2255236/

If we were able to hold this question, which comes down to representative gender imbalance, might we also be able to question what it was that got Amy so wigged out that she felt assaulted by a man simply videotaping her, so much so that she completely failed to consider her dog's safety?

Nick Nugent wrote a story titled, *In Defense of Karen*[28], where he offers another side to the story:

> Chris could have contented himself with the private shame he imparted, even if Amy only persisted in protesting that the off-leash parts of the park were either closed or too dangerous. But Chris's actions moved the battle into new territory. He stated, "Look, if you're going to do what you want, I'm going to do what I want, but you're not going to like it." Such words could easily have been interpreted as menacing, especially after Chris lured Amy's dog to himself with the offer of treats he had kept in his pocket "for just such intransigence."
>
> It's beyond disheartening that we now think it acceptable to record private citizens in order to present them as objects for recreational stoning, even when their actions are inappropriate, as was the case here. For a nation that supposedly eschews shaming, we've certainly turned it into a celebrated art form.
>
> Make no mistake about it, Amy's actions were beyond the pale. She rightly deserves criticism and consequences for her behavior, albeit from the right people and in the right proportion. But we should also acknowledge that Chris's actions threw gasoline onto the fire and that he deserves his own fair share of criticism. To do so does not detract from Amy's wrongs or somehow excuse her racist conduct. But it does help to explain them and thereby potentially help us all avoid similar behavior in the future. So, let's criticize both parties. We can all be jackasses under the right stresses. But let's curb our enthusiasm to broadcast other people's sins. Cameras can point in both directions.

I include Nugent's excerpt here for balance. I also absolutely believe that Amy Cooper's egregious sin of falsely accusing Chris Cooper of assault in her 911 call, which she came to her senses and recanted in person when the police arrived at the scene, deserves punishment. I wish that everyone would learn that police "forces" first emerged as "slave patrols" and have deep and ugly roots that need to be examined honestly and fully. And I believe that it is *because* we have yet to collectively atone for our racial sins that we find it hard to evaluate both sides of an emotionally hot, racially charged event.

A woman in her early 30s named Candace Owens also came to Amy Cooper's defense on Instagram and was summarily shamed, called out, and named Black Karen. From what one can read online about Candace, it seems her far right Republican fiscal perspective and lack of empathy for others leads her to take initiative for others who are being similarly insensitive. She raised over $200,000 for Michael Dykes, the owner of a cafe that was boycotted by protesters after he called George Floyd a thug. GoFundMe then "suspended the account associated with Candace Owens and the GoFundMe campaign ... because of a repeated pattern of inflammatory statements that spread hate, discrimination, intolerance and falsehoods against the black community at a time of profound national crisis."

Taking an anti-position against something trending as virally as Central Park Karen can win people large followings on social media. But maybe Candace was genuinely angry at Chris Cooper for filming Amy Cooper without her permission. Is it even possible to differentiate between genuine opinions and social media ploys for attention these days?

As we know, Amy was fired from the Franklin Templeton investment firm two days after the incident and forced to surrender her cocker spaniel to the Abandoned Angels shelter she'd rescued it from due to the outrage over her choking the dog on its leash. Amy was prosecuted for Falsely Reporting an Incident and could face up to a year in jail. Her arraignment was October 14, 2020 and then the case was postponed twice. Her misdemeanor charge was ultimately dropped on February 16, 2021 with Christian Cooper not attending the hearing. It was important to hold Amy Cooper accountable and she completed

Critical Therapy Classes which included racial bias instruction. Meanwhile Roger Stone went free on seven counts of felony charges including lying to Congress, obstruction, and tampering with witness evidence—even after posting to his Instagram a picture of U.S. District Court Judge Amy Berman Jackson appearing to be in the crosshairs of a gun, who presided over his case. When will we experience accountability in mainstream media?

Here is the apology that Amy Cooper wrote:

I reacted emotionally and made false assumptions about his intentions when, in fact, I was the one who was acting inappropriately by not having my dog on a leash. When Chris began offering treats to my dog and confronted me in an area where there was no one else nearby and said, "You're not going to like what I'm going to do next," I assumed we were being threatened when all he had intended to do was record our encounter on his phone. He had every right to request that I leash my dog in an area where it was required. I am well aware of the pain that misassumptions and insensitive statements about race cause and would never have imagined that I would be involved in the type of incident that occurred with Chris. I hope that a few mortifying seconds in a lifetime of forty years will not define me in his eyes and that he will accept my sincere apology.

After reading these and other cancel culture[29] or shame-induced apologies, I reflect on the nature of apologizing. It is much too easy for a woman to say, "I'm sorry." For generations women have apologized for speaking at all and I still, regularly, hear many women throw apologies around as if they are trying to excuse their very existence. I used to be one of these women but somewhere along the line, thanks to my choice to attend a variety of women's conferences from the late

---

[29] https://www.youtube.com/watch?v=_3MccCsSuU0 - Cancel Culture Fuels Intolerance, Sky News in Australia

90s to early 10s, I have dramatically limited the "baked in" apology factor in my life.

Apologies have wonderful power to reconcile when they are personally initiated and not forced. I believe that Amy Cooper was right to apologize for her racist threat to Christian Cooper and I would have loved to have seen a heartfelt apology by her posted online so the 45 million people who got riled up by her Karen video could have a sense of the reconciliation. But what about Derek Chauvin? There is video evidence that he knelt on George Floyd's neck for nearly 9 minutes, where is his apology? Supposedly police officers are not allowed to apologize even if they would want to. Yet one female officer in Springfield, Massachusetts was fired for liking a post her niece put up on Facebook about defunding the police in a different state, even after the officer formally apologized of her own accord.

We must not only emerge from the epic epithet that is Karen, we must also emerge from white supremacy; together.

Dear Karen

If you were to write to 'Karen,' what might you say?

What does this subject of social media shaming evoke in your mind and body? Ask yourself if you are thinking any of these things:

- I just keep to myself and don't meddle in others' business, so this doesn't really apply to me.
- The Karen shaming is no big deal, it's the "same shit different day" sort of thing.
- This is outrageous and upsetting on so many levels and I don't want to deal with one more upsetting thing right now, thankyouverymuch.
- It upset me to watch all the Karen stuff going on but it's over now.
- Karen behavior is never going to end and there's nothing I can do about it.
- These women are a scourge on society and they deserve to be shamed—this is how we hold entitlement accountable.
- Now that the dust has settled a bit, it is time to reflect on what this behavior means and how we can all learn from it.

Maybe you find there is a bit of truth and resonance to all these statements.

Having given you an overview of some of the more widely circulated Karens, I would like to share a few of my own Dear Karen letters that I wrote as I continued to immerse myself in and contemplate the implications of Karen—from the period between Memorial Day and the Fall of 2020:

My first "scratching the surface" thoughts:

Dear Karen,

It must have come to your attention by now that our first name is a meme. But if you haven't already heard this, brace yourself. This could be hard to hear.

As you probably know, a meme is a graphic and written representation of a trend that packs an impressive punch. It is one of the most effective and affective forms of media, a conveyance of a message delivered straight to the subconscious mind. Brilliant, huh? If you like card games, there is one called What Do You Meme that you can play to get acclimated.

Anyway, this Karen meme is a whopper. It is an epic epithet, like a swear word, for some of the most despicable characteristics a human can have. If you are a person of color, you might laugh this off like one would about a white Brad or a Chad, a Steve or another benign male meme name. If you are an elderly woman, you might never appreciate the far and wide reach of a meme. And if you are a young woman with the name Karen, you may be doing your best to suppress your anger—or you may already be pissed off—like me.

It took me a couple weeks to feel angry about Karen the meme. It was May 2020, five months into the year I had dubbed The Year of Truth[30] in my Inner Fortune blog. One of my Karen Facebook friends sent out a message to all of her friends named Karen announcing what she had heard about our name. It was a short thread. There were a few people who didn't know about it, like me, and one who didn't know what a meme was. Karen referenced a couple of hashtags and when I looked

---

[30] https://innerfortune.com/2020-the-year-of-truth/

at them, I did not find the solace and community I was looking for—which is perhaps just like a "Karen" to seek constant reassurance and comfort. The first one, #ProudToBeKaren, is related to the Karen nation of people in an area of Burma (Myanmar), as it should be, and the second one #AskAKaren, had a few interesting and inoffensive memes, a genuine sharing about things that people wanted to help others learn.

Where is the balanced perspective to this Karen naming commotion? I haven't been able to find it. I am aware that people of color use our first name frequently to refer to white women who call the manager or the cops about the slightest thing, completely oblivious to the potential job loss or life-threatening impact that call may have, a critique I think is fair. There are a few theories about how being a Karen really became a global trend; they all seem interrelated, like unique storms that all converged to break the levee suppressing political correctness.

Come to think of it, I really appreciate the convenience of having one word, one thing, to hold all the pain and suffering that a person of color might feel around white people's ignorance. And with a Karen being the epitome of an air head or a person with her head in the sand about reality, anyone who is "asleep at the wheel" of life can expect to crash. But why **our** first name?

That's a big question. For starters, suburban white middle-aged women are a big part of The Problem (of systemic oppression and racism) because ...

- we might talk about the sad state of the world instead of what actions we are taking to address it,
- we're more likely to talk about the vacations we are planning instead of our big carbon footprint,
- it seems suburban white middle-aged women complain about lazy husbands or the bad service from "hired help"—for landscaping, (re)decorating and house cleaning, child rearing, etc.—instead of actually mowing lawns, scrubbing toilets, listening to

children, or realizing that privileged luxury costs much of the world their dignity.

What are Karens to do? White women with big opinions earned those opinions by getting educated, marrying the "right" guy with a good job and a good family, moving to the town with the best educational prospects for their children, sacrificing wants and needs—if they'd even had any wants or needs that they could have clearly articulated—for these men and children, and they probably do a lot to volunteer for their communities to "do their part" and "give back!" And while these are admirable points, a hard truth about most of this "American Dream" is that the dogged pursuit of the dream leads to insulating oneself from reality, becoming numb and zombified, and perpetuating the figurative or literal walls around oneself—which is The Problem.

Karens are always trying to fix problems, with their networks and assumed powers of influence, rather than trying to understand the scope of the problems—the roots, causes and effects, the pain and suffering. Though, can one who hasn't suffered at the scale of a root problem like hunger, houselessness,[31] chronic unemployment, physical violence, truly understand—viscerally embody and feel—the pain and suffering it carries?

Well, I guess that's all for now. If you have any ideas on what we might do as a community to address this, please let me know. I am now writing a book called **Beyond Karen** and am thinking about the ways that I practice being a good human being. It's all I know how to do at the moment.

With Love,
Karen

---

[31] note: no one is without a home, but many are without a house. Without a house one makes their home in the community of others.

And then I wrote this "letter" to myself shortly after Independence Day:

Karen,

I'm afraid **Beyond Karen** sucks, that readers will expect the sociological breakdown and explanation from a professor, an "expert." I am afraid that too many people find affiliation by taking down easy prey—by being Karens themselves—that being vulnerable on purpose and sharing distilled stories of pain and suffering will not be heard with the intent that they are offered but will instead give predators' ammunition.

There are way too many examples of women who have felt their hearts were in a good place but then exposed their ignorance about a thing so blatantly that their heartfelt intentions got trampled with a big "fuck you, Miss Know It All." This is the force of voice suppression in a nutshell. Is that OK? I don't know. I have largely escaped these forces from the little bubble of my present life. It's like God has been protecting me from over exposure, keeping my life small and condensed in order to be able to feel things intensely enough to learn from them, to take the hard knocks at a scale that is healable.

[When I think of the epitome of hard knocks, what comes to mind is] The Central Park Five—a gut wrenching story of five innocent African American and Latinx teenagers in the right place at the wrong time, sacrificial lambs for the woman DA who had no regard for the truth or their humanity, so evil she was willing to destroy them in order to get the media off her back. Is the shame of Central Park Karen enough to atone for something so vile as this?

Can the OG [Old Guard] Karens ever be shamed enough to get them to wake the F up to the truth of at least some of the pain and suffering that plantation mistresses, a.k.a "Miss Anns," have caused in America due to their evil complicity? Their turning of blind eyes to the soul crushing travesties and multi-generational trauma leveled on innocent African American families, stolen from their land, survivors of the most inhumane, unbearable, unspeakable conditions imaginable? Can any of us possibly fathom being shackled to the body of dead family and community members, being suffocated by the claustrophobia and noxious smells and the toxic excrement flowing all around in a space already so hot and humid as to be unbreathable? No, none of us can. And some people feel so entitled as to refuse to wear a simple mask to help stop the spread of the coronavirus?

Let's be honest, aren't we all feeling claustrophobic and ready to have a panic attack about the whole thing? What if this pandemic is causing descendent African American doctors, nurses, and any first responder wearing so much PPE to possibly be feeling ancestral emotions of their great great great great grandparents? What explains this lack of compassion? What is the role of shame in this moment? I have shame stories. But who would want to read another person's shame stories? Don't we hate TMI [too much information]? Isn't an unprocessed, dysregulated white woman already perceived as The Problem? The shame stories I could tell have been ruminated over plenty, but have they been resolved? I'm not so sure.

I think back to the attempt a friend of mine named Sarah and I made together to look at the effects of misogyny in our lives and how quickly our vulnerabilities—her vulnerability that came at me like Methuselah's snakes when I interrupted her during a meticulously planned phone call we'd had. I felt I was being a supportive #metoo kind of listener. The shock of her anger went off inside me like dynamite, exploding into a depth of shame I didn't know was in me. I drove home in a literal downpour that came out of nowhere, matching my intense sobbing for 20 miles, leaving me so wrecked I could not pull the weight of my soggy flesh out of the soggy car. The trust and respect she and I had established with each other by virtue of having and sharing deep trauma stories was not even enough to do this work together. If this is my truth, what the hell makes me think that hurling my life out to the wolves isn't going to get me eaten alive? Is this willful and ignorant disregard for my incredibly resilient family? I sure as hell hope not.

I feel like this is one of those times, one of those things that I am being guided to do by some higher authority, one of those your-life-will-be-a-waste-of-flesh-if-you-don't-do-this moments. I just pray that whatever ignorance I expose is received with kindness, one that allows others to look at their own with compassion and forgiveness. If shame is the medium du jour, who am I to question it?

All my best, Karen

Lastly, after I began intentionally nourishing the creative writer side of myself to help get through the Presidential debates by writing a weekly story on medium.com, I felt moved to compose yet another Dear Karen letter (as well as a story the day Joe Biden was officially proclaimed the 46th POTUS called "White Women Must Cross This Bridge"[32]):

Dear Karen,

Please trust your sweet heart and read this letter...

I watched a news feature this past week about the demonstrations of intolerance over the utterly broken, corrupted, dragged out judicial process that the Taylor family and the Louisville community is enduring after Breonna Taylor's murder. Then I noticed this sign being held by one of the men in the crowd seeking justice:

This is a big statement. The sign holder has every right to hold it and want others to read it and feel the weight of the message.

Cops Are Just Karens With Guns. Wow.

---

[32] https://innerfortune.medium.com

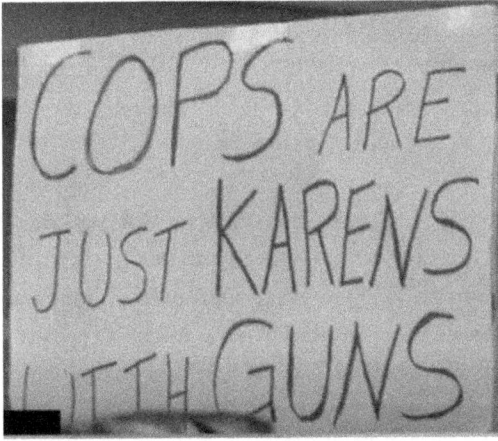

A few months ago I started writing you a letter. I ended up writing a whole two-part book actually—one part about Karens and the memes about Karens in the media, along with my interpretation of root causes of "Karen" behaviors, and one part about ways I have personally wrestled with these root causes in order to do my best to not be a pretentious ignorant bitch.

The goal of this whole effort was to try and reconcile the multifaceted conflicts I observe or "cognitive dissonances" (things that we hear or see that can't fully register in our brains because our beliefs or lived experience is the opposite). And I felt these conflicts so keenly that I assumed the vast majority of my fellow Americans were also observing and feeling them.

Maybe the vast majority of us are indeed feeling intensely conflicted (or utterly bullshit) about our access—or lack of access—to power, our life's potential—or lack thereof, and the forces at play behind all of it; forces which we can only bring into our consciousness when we are not already overloaded by them; forces which ultimately come down to the longstanding effects of misogyny and racism.

I wanted (still want?) to believe, Karen, that even if you are the sort of person acting in ways that have turned my name and the name of other middle-aged women into an epic epithet, that you might actually be willing to read my gut wrenching stories, my valiant effort stories, and my achieving balance stories. I want to believe that all the people who could be called "Karen"—so hard hearted about the effects of misogyny and racism as to continue to perpetuate hateful beliefs of white supremacy and to perpetuate, with unexamined white behaviors, evil upon our black and brown and native brothers and sisters—might be willing to look deeply and find within the courage to change and make amends.

I wanted, and still want, to believe Karen, that after you had read these stories about the ways I've (or anyone has) gone from being a terrified and traumatized young person to an open-eyed, open-hearted advocate for change who leads by simple example, that you too might be inspired to face the demons which bind you to a complicit and dysregulated persona—one who may be so traumatized and terrified that you cannot see her or the ways she behaves. It's hard to know if you would.

Dear Karen, my friend, I know how hard it is to be conflicted about reality and to feel as if you are only safe in your little bubble of society; to do your best to believe you can close your eyes to the hard truths behind all your comforts—from home ownership and job security to the organic food and supplements in your diet. I know how impotent you can feel when you've mustered the courage to advocate for change and ended up feeling as if you were just standing naked in the cold. But keep at it. It matters. And naked is okay.

I sense how strong the forces are to keep you quiet and in your little bubble. And I get how exhausting it is to rise up, to keep learning, to keep trying. But unless you wake up to the truth about these forces at play—no, at war—in order to keep you silent and complicit and in your small insignificant life, we as a nation may truly be fucked.

I hope that statement is just the right balance of offensive and motivating so that you, "Karen," can hear what I, Karen, am saying. I am not interested in shaming you like the hundreds of journalists representing the power brokers who operate the levers of the military-industrial complex. I want nothing more than to help you feel like you are not alone. We all feel small and insignificant under the weight of our current imbalance of power reality.

All the ways you may feel crazy actually do have explanations. The gaslighting that goes on in business and in day-to-day conversations— that make you think you're the only one who sees what's going on because no one else is willing to name it—is a result of centuries of white Christian heteronormativity.

Trust that even though there is an amazing unknowable higher power sustaining all life, all species, all 8+ billion of us humans, (including the 328,239,523 of us in the United States), this higher power has been minimized, along with our spiritual growth potential, by its deep association with the worship of the white male Patriarch.

I'm not asking you to turn your back on what you know to be God or on any of the white male figures in your life. In fact, 97 out of 100 of them may be just as terrified and traumatized by the cognitive dissonance as you are. But you may be quite a bit more comfortable using your voice than they are.

So please, I beg you, please **feel** what is going on before you speak. Let your heart break wide open with the pains of injustice happening everywhere, but most acutely right now in Louisville and Kenosha with the soul-sapping trials of injustice leveled upon Breonna Taylor's and Joshua Blake's family and community, and the progressive places where people have been feeling truth together for a long time.

Trust that this fight for justice is not just real, it is righteous. And lastly, trust that for better or worse, we all are in this together.

Okay... maybe you already trust all this to be true... now what? You've read articles and actual books made out of paper to educate yourself, you may have even initiated a few civil conversations. Congratulations. Seriously take a moment to feel good about that. Having conversations about the subjects that polarize, divide and alienate, may be the most courageous action we can take right now.

Let's keep doing that.

Well, after watching the embarrassment of the [then] current POTUS' half of the Presidential debate last night, for the short period of time that I could bear to watch his excruciating, impetuous behavior, I have to say just one more thing, about this man, the ultimate Karen: please do not vote for him. And if you struggle with that notion, please go outside for a long while and breathe; reflect on what you think and feel about the world, not about what your family or colleagues think and feel. Reflect on what is true.

Thank you and best wishes,
Karen Willard Ribeiro

I have shared these three letters with you to illustrate the transformation I am going through as I write this story over time. Please know that I know that every time I write the word "you/your" or "we/us/our" in this book, particularly when I am sharing an insight as I have experienced it, I am also writing to myself, to learn and practice, to envision all of us in this societal transformation together.

Everything that feels like emergent truth grips us with inner light, inner sunshine, bright insight, and the desire to radiate with the world. I (and obviously other Karens) have often emerged hastily, from a mind space or mental frame of reference—rather than from an embodied, integrated, deeper Truth with a capital T space, or spirit-based frame of reference—for decades ... or centuries. I am learning to emerge out from generations of white culture and its impact. And I am doing my best to widen the aperture of the different lenses through which I see the world and everyone in it.

Name Calling

The period in America between Memorial Day and "Interdependence" Day was none like I have ever seen. Even if someone was trying to avoid the media, they couldn't help hear about the riots after George Floyd was murdered[33], the anger, the rising up in the streets. This was the moment that catalyzed courage and action from a million "points of light[34]," a moment which has challenged the forces which have been rocking Americans to sleep for decades, and a moment in which retaliation by extreme means (such as public shaming) are desperately deployed to distract Americans from this light of truth and keep them in their stupor of selfishness.[35]

This rising up in the streets, this tidal wave of action, has the power to branch off through the estuary of various media channels in two very distinct directions: one, a natural cycle of information in which a message finds a receptive audience through a clear, unimpeded medium, and is able to be fortified by feedback that wends its way back to the messenger like water returns to the sea; or two, an artificially manufactured cycle of information in which an original message is manipulated by an unscrupulous media, and is then dammed up with media trolls employed to distort and deny natural feedback from completing its due course. In this second scenario, the flow of information is more like a series of babbling brooks from which the unwitting can hose each other at will.

---

[33] DailyKos reports these were started by Aryan Cowboy Brotherhood member Mitchell Carlson: https://www.dailykos.com/stories/2020/7/28/1964542/—Umbrella-Man-finally-identified-as-a-member-of-a-white-supremacist-group-and-biker-gang

[34] http://www.thebigwiki.com/wiki/george-h-w-bush

[35] selfishness was made a "virtue" by the neoliberal Ayn Rand in 1964: https://en.wikipedia.org/wiki/The_Virtue_of_Selfishness;https://www.revolutionarymisfit.com/on-ayn-rand-and-neoliberalism/

Prior to learning about the Karen meme, the only experience I had of being a Karen in any way other than the name I was born with, where my name was even a "thing," took place in the summer of 2013. This year the film *Monsters University* came out and my sister-in-law loved it. Kindergarten teacher Karen Graves would tell her students, "Please don't call me Karen." This is what my sister-in-law said every time she heard someone call my name for at least two years afterwards. Silly me, I thought it was because the teacher wanted her students to call her Ms. Graves instead of using her first name.

Deborah Cameron, a feminist linguist and professor of language and communication at Oxford University, says[36] that because popular girls' names change more rapidly than boys', female names are often a reliable indicator of age and generation, as well as sometimes class and race. "Perhaps this type of [middle-aged, white] woman is considered an acceptable butt for jokes about annoying women because she's 'generic,' there's no race or class angle," she says. As for why middle-aged white men feature less often in these jokes, Cameron says male names carry less social information because parents' choices tend to be more stable over time. She also notes sexism could be a factor.

An epithet is a commonplace description of a thing—like making a letter L on your forehead to call the person you're looking at a Loser—and a slur is a profane or derogatory and emotionally charged version of an epithet. Usage is not at all straightforward. A slur like WTF is a more palatable acronym for swearing, while a word like queer, which

[36] https://www.newstatesman.com/science-tech/internet/2018/01/karen-sharon-becky-and-chad-how-it-feels-when-your-name-becomes-meme

caused untold emotional wreckage in the past, has been boldly reclaimed by the community it formerly shamed. Racial and physical handicap slurs are never okay. I'm not sure if Karen is an epithet or a slur at the moment of this writing, but I've chosen to err on the side of optimism. The UK think tank Demos found[37] that 10,000 racial or ethnic slurs a day, or one in 15,000 tweets, were posted on Twitter in a nine-day period of 2012. Half of these were "white boy" and casual use of such slurs was about 5-10%. There was a statistically insignificant use of racial slurs intending to cause harm or violence. This may lead one to assume that the frenzy whipped up with hashtags like #KarenGoneWild are simply for the entertainment value capable of alleviating boredom, particularly during this unprecedented global social distancing and sheltering in place. Did you know you can even generate your own epithets on websites like PorkJerky.com and FantasyNameGenerators.com?

Geoffrey Nunberg and Lynne Gerber, social scientists from UC Berkeley, are featured in a Spring 2014 Cal Alumni magazine article[38]: *You Can't Say That! Is It Time to Write the Epitaph for Epithets?* In it Nunberg explains:

> Redneck [had been] largely employed as a term for poor, rural white people from ... the Deep South. It was a synonym for "white trash," and wholly derogatory. But now its most common usage is by right-wingers either as a badge, or as an accusation—This is what the liberals think of us. Redneck is employed about 20 times more often in the premier conservative political journal, National Review, than in liberal organs such as The Nation and The American Prospect. In ordinary conversation, liberals use "redneck," but I suspect not as often as working-class southerners who are reclaiming the word.

I love this excerpt because for a long time, "redneck" was one of the running epithets used in my home to describe my son Nathan. And he's

[37] http://www.demos.co.uk/files/DEMOS_Anti-social_Media.pdf?1391774638
[38] https://alumni.berkeley.edu/california-magazine/spring-2014-branding/you-cant-say-it-time-write-epitaph-epithets

someone who has no issue with the label, he just doesn't resonate with it anymore. Gerber, the above-mentioned article's co-author, turns the heat up a bit on the subject of epithets by sharing an expert opinion about the potential hidden meaning of obesity: "Unlike race and gender, obesity is widely perceived as a matter of volition. So to be fat can be seen as consonant with being morally bankrupt ... unacceptable biases can be justified when presented sub rosa as fat phobia."

Name calling is a reactive mechanism for shifting our intense emotion onto another, usually one we subconsciously perceive as an easy target. Unless we are confident in whatever sliver of ourselves is being singled out by another wielding a name in our direction, name-calling can really sting. Plenty of big boned beauties love their outside-the-range-of-"normal" weight, but if we're not one of them, being called "fat," or "redneck," or "Karen," depending on the level of sensitivity we may feel about it at any moment in time, can be much more than a criticism or a joke or a wakeup call.

With all the perceived anonymity of a computer screen in front of us, do we feel invincible, beyond reproach in our name calling? Would we say to one's face what we are about to click and post? I'm all for a bit of harmless banter, but in a snap, even face to face, light banter can get heavy. Don't we owe it to each other to err on the side of caution; to not inflict more trauma on each other; to love thy neighbor?

The time and space it takes to heal trauma and build skills may be the gift that the world has been given with the COVID-19 pandemic. Are we able to take that time and space to heal? Or are we too stressed about our financial, interpersonal, political, socio-cultural instability— too distracted by media streams—to heal the old hurts? These distractions are truly seductive, and the old hurts are so very easy to brush off as insignificant. In fact, the thought of choosing to dredge up "old hurts" may sound absolutely ludicrous. But the subconscious mind, full of unprocessed emotions like fear and anger and unresolved issues, may act up in places where we least expect it—like in the supermarket or another public space.

What if the best time to hit "send" and publish something is when the body-mind is in balance, not coming from an extreme perspective. We are not always in balance, and taking harmful actions leads to more imbalance, personal suffering and a struggle to regain balance. What would it be like if we really built the skills to understand each other—and we realized that we are all interconnected—and that when one of us is suffering, we all suffer?

The severity of Karen behavior, in the extreme form it has come to describe, must not be minimized. As Ruby Hamad, author of *White Tears/Brown Scars: How White Feminism Betrays Women of Color*, reported for the New York Times[39], "Feeling afraid and being in danger are not necessarily the same thing. Historically speaking, when white people are afraid it is usually people of color who get hurt. Contrary to myths of black rapist hordes preying on innocent white damsels, it was the sexual degradation of enslaved and colonized women that was a defining feature of settler colonialism. European colonizers, and then American slave owners, built their societies not only on lands stolen from Indigenous populations, not only through capitalist exploitation of forced labor, but also on the abused bodies of black, Indigenous and brown women."

If we are to learn to see each other more deeply than hair, more deeply than the color or thickness of our skin, we need to welcome the wisdom of new frameworks and social models into our consciousness, into our day to day behaviors.

I think having insufficient models of discerning truth is the heart of suffering. When we suffer, without models of how to be in pain, how to hold pain in our body and mind, we pay it forward. We even hurt the ones we love because we want someone else to absorb our pain, someone who "gets us" or can listen enough to help us feel heard. We all need to be compassionate with the roots of pain and suffering in ourselves and each other, we can learn how to not be the causes of it.

I sometimes imagine what it would have been like had I grown up alongside women like Patrisse Cullors, Opal Tometi and Alicia Garza, the three founders of Black Lives Matter and members of its wider coalition M4BL, the movement for Black lives. These women were entirely ready to rally the nation upon hearing about the shooting murder of Trayvon Martin by the acquitted George Zimmerman, of

---

[39] https://www.nytimes.com/2020/05/27/opinion/amy-cooper-central-park-racism.html

Eric Garner, choked to death, like George Floyd, by a cop with complicit, "trained bastards[40]" by his side. These women are still leading a massive movement out on the front lines, and from behind the scenes, serving a racial revolution, exploring resolution, reconciliation, and change that we need to see in the world right now. Women leaders like these three inspire me because they seem immune to the ego pressure of so much visibility. Maybe ego immunity is a byproduct of the willingness to keep digging into the roots of suffering until the travesties stop?

In one website named flu-trackers,[41] I found an interesting and respectful thread that got pretty deep into the roots of the Karen name calling. Here are a few insights that were shared:

- Sharon S: This is not acceptable. I am in the middle aged / senior white woman category. How is it ok to ever refer to me "a Karen"? We cannot hope to be a more cohesive society if we are adding stereotypes to our culture.

- Mary W: Actually, we have seen this 'attitude' all along with this pandemic. It has been a technique used to degrade the severity of the COVID-19. We have seen it with the resistance of wearing masks, the "it's only the flu", "it'll be over soon", and hundreds of deliberate COVID-19 hacks that have been occurring in the United States. I wonder "who" would be so devious to attack the health of people, and why.

- Emily: The bullying and worse of women, especially older women, has been a gambit of opportunistic cowards for far longer than I have been alive. It also shuts down reasonable debates, but so does assuming that differences of opinions about mask wearing and disease impacts are coming from dark motives.

---

[40] https://medium.com/@OfcrACab/confessions-of-a-former-bastard-cop-bb14d17bc759 and a corollary article: https://medium.com/@lucasfava_78933/should-i-say-all-cops-are-bastards-cb8bf0292669
[41] https://flutrackers.com/forum/forum/health-humanitarian-issues/873596-it-is-not-ok-to-label-all-middle-aged-white-women-as-a-karen

- <u>Sharon S</u>: "The 'CAREN Act' (Caution Against Racially Exploitative Non-Emergencies) was introduced on Tuesday at a San Francisco Board of Supervisors meeting by Supervisor Shamann Walton. The ordinance's name is a twist on 'Karen,' the name social media gives people making racially biased 911 calls.

The name "Karen" is both racist and misogynist because it was a name popular in the 1950s for white female babies. It is like calling someone a "Mildred." That name conjures up a vision of an elderly white woman since that name has not been popular for white female babies since 1920s. It is racist, ageist, misogynistic to use the name CAREN (specifically to mimic "Karen") for a law against racism. We need less stereotyping—not more.

I was one of the first women professionals at a large aerospace company in the late 1970s. Women were not encouraged to speak up because the hold on progress was so tenuous that no woman wanted to call attention to herself. **It felt like we were sneaking into the party and it was important to try to be as invisible as possible while still excelling at the job** (my emphasis). In large meetings women did not speak up on important issues. That was done privately after the meeting.

And when we did start to exert some opinions (in the 80s) we were privately labeled "pushy", "aggressive", "demanding" for doing the same thing male co-workers did. Especially frowned on was any ambition to get promoted. Just lucky to be selected to wear a suit and be able to sit with the grown-ups at the decision makers' table once a month. The Karen messaging is wrong.

Reader, please take a moment to sit with these women's words, especially this last excerpt by the aerospace professional. Doing so can help us begin to appreciate the complexity of this "epic epithet." Because even though it may feel like a very low priority to reflect on the past, a past fraught with "issues" like women's invisibility, a past that society has "gotten over," the past is still very present in the lives of everyone who is middle-aged or older. And I contend that the younger children of these elders have energetically inherited, to greater or lesser extents, their related pain and suffering.

Before really looking into the details about Karens, I thought comically to myself that my middle-aged white face, with all its wrinkles might make a good representation of a Karen. I am a bit gaunt; my formerly plump cheekbones fell off my face one day maybe 10 years ago and I have enough stress wrinkles to make me want to hide from the camera, especially on web conference calls where I seem to be the only one my age that has a chicken neck like my mother had. Oh, the number of times I would see her hold her saggy skin back while standing in front of the mirrored medicine cabinet over the bathroom sink! My mother, to me, was her most beautiful at the end of her life, bald head and massive jowl. But, sadly, it took a body full of cancer from her bones to her brain for her to finally care less about her appearance.

It is true though; I do have a deeply grooved scowl and furrowed brow. I used to hold a smile even when driving because I can look like I am in a bad mood even when I'm completely peaceful. My daughter, who gets cocoa brown in the sun like her father and generally eschews sunscreen will not leave the house without it on her face because she is doing what she can to protect her face from wrinkles like mine. I can see where the phrase "resting bitch face" comes from.

Funny aside: I was in a centennial march celebrating women's suffrage in early 2020 when my friend Marilyn and I came upon a woman with a sign that said, "resisting bitch face." It had a big hole in the middle for her face and I asked if I could take a picture with her (and her sign). She assumed I wanted a picture with my face in the hole, which she gladly took, but I was simply proud of her for wearing a sign that I thought had said "resting bitch face!"

I am hearing my friend Alisa's voice in my head admonishing me for being so self-deprecating. She calls me fetching. It is entirely because of friendship like hers that I can be comfortably honest about most things that feel true.

Friendship and witnessing one another's stories is a solid antidote to shame, an incredible source of strength, and a way to avoid the pretentiousness, the pretending, that may undergird the name calling that many of us didn't grow out of in middle school. Maybe name calling stems from isolation. The more resonant I am with others, the less I care about smiling just because someone walked by and said he thought I was angry after a nanosecond glance in passing.

∞

After being on a three-day Zoom conference, I found a Zoom video chat between Cate Blanchett and Sarah Paulson in which I learned that Cate recommends using CBD oil for facial lines (I have since seen positive results!). This Zoom chat was timed to correspond with the completion of the Mrs. America series on Hulu. Cate stars as Phyllis Schlafly, the woman who shut down the momentum of the Equal Rights Amendment and threw her political clout, and the conservative throng of women behind her, to help get Ronald Reagan[42] elected.

As a middle school student, I knew that Ronald Reagan was full of beans (and not just jellybeans). Very uncharacteristic of me at the time, I somehow joined a school campaign to get out the vote for incumbent Jimmy Carter, who called Reagan a right-wing extremist. Little did I know at the time that Reagan had received Carter's Presidential debate briefing in advance of the debate (not just a copy, *the entire book* of President Carter's 69 questions and answers)[43]. And, through the Beacon Broadside, I learned of Daniel Luck's exposé of how Reagan became so popular politically: he was an FBI informant[44] reporting suspected communists in Hollywood in what he called the Hollywood Blacklist. He went against the grain of his liberal upbringing in order to be famous; he wasn't able to be the A-list celebrity actor from Illinois that he'd hoped to be, so he sold out his values and left an immeasurable wake of racial, environmental and judicial destruction. Wouldn't it be better for Americans to aspire to be honest and "average" B-students than an overzealous take-no-prisoners Alpha dog?

Also from Illinois, Phyllis Schlafly went against the grain. Not of her political upbringing, which was already conservative, but of her sex. She swam hard against the tide of the second wave of the women's

---

[42] Killer Mike, "Reagan" https://www.youtube.com/watch?v=6llqNjC1RKU

[43] https://www.ozy.com/true-and-stories/the-stolen-campaign-documents-that-helped-reagan-win-the-presidency/89685 /

[44] http://www.beacon.org/Reconsidering-Reagan-P1585.aspx

movement, the one more inclusive, more awake to gender and race, because, according to the Mrs. America series, she was pissed off about not having a voice among men commensurate with her sharp mind.

Sarah Paulson's character Alice behaves like a massive Karen to the hotel concierge at the Houston National Women's Conference in episode 8, where she later gets educated by the queer black woman sitting next to her. Alice has unwittingly ingested pot brownies which leads her to uninhibitedly belt out a stanza of This Land Is Our Land. She and Cate Blanchett were superb—as was the entire cast—and I was hoping this video chat was going to delve into the content of the series. It was lighthearted and friendly but apolitical.

Monica Hesse of the Washington Post reflects on Paulson's character[45]: "Forty years before the term "Karen" was coined to describe entitled white women's may-I-speak-to-your-manager life strategy, Alice is modeling some extraordinary Karening. She is confident that her dial-a-man tactic will work, as it always has before. "'My husband should be able to straighten this out," she tells the harried female clerk, after breezing past a long line of patiently waiting guests. "Shall we get him on the phone?'" She also summarizes the baseline of Blanchett's character: "Phyllis Schlafly's anti-ERA movement has a slogan: Stop Taking Our Privileges. She means the privilege of being taken care of ... It is white men's job to worry for them, to defend them, to create a society that benefits them."

Throughout **Beyond Karen** I explore gendered politics and feminism like this Mrs. America series as I believe there is so much history to unpack with the Karen epithet. For now, I will keep delving into reflections on name calling.

I think that the most critical aspect of being predisposed to name calling is entitlement. This may seem obvious. Watching, reading about, and researching others' interpretations of feminist history or other issues pertaining to social justice has made it clear to me that those who defend what they have (land, privilege, rights) are more inclined to label and disparage others who don't like the lack of access to the same

---

[45] https://www.washingtonpost.com/lifestyle/style/karens-try-to-make-unequal-power-structures-work-for-them/2020/05/29/31adc68a-8a3b-11ea-8ac1-bfb250876b7a_story.html

opportunities. However, those who defend what they love (land, privilege, rights) are more inclined to welcome others to join in and share in the experience.

∞

Before the weight of Karen descended on me, I was feeling surprisingly elated about this notion of being Karen—as if finally, all the stress in my life was for a higher purpose, a meaning. I have arrived at some grand destiny to be the butt of jokes, the grand dame of middle-aged cantankerousness, the name to represent the worst purveyor of public poisonousness, every cashier's worst nightmare, the goat of global gossip. All in the bright hope of ultimately shifting consciousness, of healing. Call me a Karen; I will listen to why you feel that way and will try not to take it personally!

I had felt for this brief moment like the deep consciousness-raising work I'd done in my life could somehow hold the weight of this name, at least the sardonic intention of it. But the ugly truth is that this false bravado is par for the course of what keeps us in the stupor of selfishness I mentioned and there is not one chance in hell that the ugly underbelly perpetuating this Karen epithet will suddenly disappear with a hefty dose of Non Violent Communication[46].

There are some poisonous posters out there who clearly have personal vendettas against the women they are naming Karen. When reading their words, a real gross energy seems to spill out from the screen. Would it be possible—even if these guys were surrounded by a large community of loving beings—for them to see their online ugliness? Truly hard to say.

While the following excerpt is similar to the content in many Karen articles I have read, I found two elements of a May 13, 2020 piece by Jeff Barg of the Philadelphia Inquirer that were unique at the time. Barg notes that Karen was the fourth most popular[47] baby name in the 1960s

---

46 https://www.cnvc.org/about

47 https://www.babynamewizard.com/voyager#prefix=karen&sw=f&exact=false

and that in 2017, it was 557th (it was 635th in 2018[48] and a friend of mine suggested that after all this name calling the name Karen could even go extinct). Barg also explored the not-okay subject of the k-word being compared to the n-word. After a bit of digging and exploring the trackbacks from one site to another, two things occurred to me:

1.   Some obscure organization called Journalist Excellence Worldwide[49] started the whole notion of Karen as the k-word by posting a poll on Twitter with this misleading statement: "Considering this is an equivalent of the n-word for white women, should it be banned on Twitter? If no, explain." Notice the presumption that these two are anywhere near equal and the use of the lowercase n? And, probably after rigging the results, this person or group managed to whet the appetites of a number of journalists salivating for more "social mention," more "kred."

2.   Barg, like so many other Karen-reporting journalists drooling over the likes and retweets and *visibility* their pieces are getting, is hypocritically perpetuating the same divisive, predatorial, shaming behavior he despises. With Barg it is more subtle, and I could be making this comment about any Karen piece, perhaps even this book if it didn't feel like such a mission of societal transformation, but it was in the reading of his piece that the thought of his complicity in the epic nature of this epithet occurred to me. Barg, presumably Jewish, is stirring up the pot by saying that "*astute observers* noted that there already is a k-word, and it's wildly anti-Semitic."[50] We all want to be smart, astute observers, don't we? But we don't have to rile up readers with emotional chaff—unless perhaps we are caught

---

[48] https://www.ssa.gov/oact/babynames/popularity_decrease.html

[49] https://twitter.com/journalistew/status/1246925471931076608 - 95.9% of 332,895 respondents said no.

[50] https://www.inquirer.com/opinion/karen-memes-slur-kate-gosselin-hate-speech-women-20200513.html

between a rock (being told by our boss to do this) and a hard place (our values).

Here is his pot stirring excerpt:

> When MAGA-capped zealots barreled up to Philadelphia City Hall last week and the state capitol in late April, demanding haircuts and eat-in dining and acute respiratory infections for all, their mascot was not Donald Trump or Sean Hannity or even that guy from Duck Dynasty, but Karen.
>
> You know Karen. She's the face of a thousand internet memes, the middle-aged white woman with the Kate Gosselin haircut, I'd-like-to-speak-to-your-manager charm combined with the I-don't-believe-your-science intellect of an anti-vaxxer. She is millions of American women who would call the cops on black children selling lemonade. And she has a new cause celebre: reopening America when she wants to, regardless of what medical professionals say.
>
> Actually, make that two new causes: She also wants you to stop using the "slur" Karen, thankyouverymuch.

Is this the kind of writing one wants to gain notoriety or visibility from? When I read these and other definitions of Karens, I feel sick, which seems like an appropriate response. Maybe it is an amazingly good thing that there could be one word that might be able to hold the complete and utter grossness of what's wrong with the world at the moment. If there could be one word to contain the complex, centuries-old troubles of silent complicity—at least in America and other colonizing countries—erupting in this societal moment, a collective public scrutiny of its root causes could potentially bring much needed healing.

Instinctively I feel badly for Kate Gosselin, the actress from the reality TV show Kate Plus Eight, who appeared to be the poster child Karen with a bad haircut. I've yet to watch her original show and *Women's Health Magazine* reports that she has a new one, Kate Plus

Date[51], coming out soon, years after her divorce from Jon, her previous co-star and father of their twins and sextuplets. I wonder what she endured as a result of the Karen wave. She has long hair now and I imagine few women going out of their way for the blond unevenly cut bob hairstyle since Karen became a trendy pejorative.

But a little curious digging about Kate got me thinking about a possible unreported connection between the surge in Karen labeling and a Reddit rant. Jon and Kate supposedly went through a hellish divorce and there have been custody battles with two of their children; *and* the Wikipedia definition[52] of Karen goes into detail about a venomous divorced man who launched a hate platform against his wife who took their house and two children:

One origin of the use of the term *Karen* as an Internet meme dates to an *anonymous* Reddit user, Fuck_You_Karen, who posted rants denigrating his ex-wife Karen, whom he alleged had "taken" both his children and, later, his house during divorce proceedings. The posts led to the creation of a subreddit in 2017, r/FuckYouKaren, to both compile a narrative and share memes about the posts. Since Fuck_You_Karen deleted their account, the subreddit refocused to memes about the stereotype in general rather than one specific woman.

Both partners going through divorce are in pain, the one initiating and the one resisting. Clearly this anonymous man, the presumed initiator of the slide behind the Fuck_You_Karen avalanche, had a vendetta against his ex. The people who are writing about the Karen meme as a way to let some bitch off the hook too easily—saying that the anonymity of being called a Karen isn't enough shame, enough punishment for the crime, that their real names need to be called out loudly, as if to say or imply that the woman should be thrown down on the sidewalk by her hair, face rubbed into the cement and body ground down under his boot—are also in their own way Karens, completely oblivious to their own emotional trauma that would have them point fingers at others who are triggering them (which leaves three fingers pointing back at themselves).

---

[51] https://www.womenshealthmag.com/life/a27890796/kate-plus-eight-now/
[52] https://en.wikipedia.org/wiki/Karen_(pejorative)

Back in May, Wikipedia reference to the Karen haircut only included Kate Gosselin, but by July Karen haircut references somehow included the stunning blond locks of Jenny McCarthy Wahlberg, a woman with a vast array of achievements to her credit.[53] It seems to me that this is an editing error because Karens are also supposedly anti-vaccinations and Jenny has simply taken a clear stand against improperly scheduled vaccinations.

As Karen has escalated to represent all things wrong with America during this pandemic, haircuts and vaccinations are no longer a thing we take for granted. Haircuts could be seen as perfunctory, surface, aesthetic, generally unimportant. Hair grows back. Yet haircuts have a lot to do with our ego and how we are seen in the world. Simply saying to oneself, "It doesn't matter what I look like" isn't usually true. We all want to feel good about ourselves.

Vaccinations have saved millions of people's lives since Edward Jenner developed the smallpox vaccine in 1796 and at the same time there are uninvestigated consequences of improperly scheduled vaccinations and their biodynamic interactions in children. It's complicated. The scientific community worked diligently on developing a vaccine for the Coronavirus to stop or at least slow the number of casualties in this present pandemic. And there are strong emotions on both sides of this complex issue requiring high level study and action.

The spaces where one can find an intense amount of online ugliness, perpetuating division and hate mongering, of dragging successful women like Jenny McCarthy down, has intentionally not been included in any resources or analyses in this book. While a great deal of Karen fodder exists on Reddit, I have intentionally chosen to not feature sources from this platform in my review of the Karen epithet because I find it to be so biased as to be utterly reprehensible. It may be responsible for the rise in toxic memes and has been investigated by the Southern Poverty Law Center[54] for having the "most violently racist content on the internet."

[53] https://en.wikipedia.org/wiki/Jenny_McCarthy
[54] https://www.splcenter.org/hatewatch/2018/04/19/day-trope-white-nationalist-memes-thrive-reddits-rthedonald

From Steven Rosenbaum at Media Insider, June 8, 2020: "Reddit prides itself on being an open community for average folks and hobbyists. But it's really nothing like that. It's a mostly unregulated Wild West stuck trying to balance an open-platform philosophy with the web's increasingly dark wave of hate speech, racist and sexist memes, and pornography."

[CEO and co-founder Steve] "Huffman, responding to the current racial protests, posted a blog that said in part that Reddit employees 'do not tolerate hate, racism, and violence, and while we have work to do to fight these on our platform, our values are clear.'

That was pretty disturbing to folks who know better, among them [former CEO Ellen] Pau, who wrote: 'I am obligated to call you out: You should have shut down the donald instead of amplifying it and its hate, racism, and violence. So much of what is happening now lies at your feet. You don't get to say BLM when **Reddit nurtures and monetizes white supremacy and hate all day long**.'"

If a whole media channel exists to perpetuate hate, and the writers and posters on this channel are both aware and oblivious to this perpetuation of hate, what is the ripple out effect, the wider impact in American society and the world of just this one channel alone? How many guys are paid (certainly more than the disgustingly low minimum wage many single moms are paid) to write pieces like this? What is the ulterior motive behind the slew of posts that perpetuate division and discord all across the internet?

And then, having intentionally researched opinion from the exact opposite direction, I found a breath of fresh air:

Brendan O'Neill, editor of Spiked, wrote an article that appeals to anyone "who still retains the ability to think independently," on June 25, 2020, *The Hatred For Karen's Is Out of Control: The ritualistic humiliation of white women shows how poisonous identity politics has become*. I include a fair amount of this article here because it is thorough, careful, and compassionate, and these are the skills we must all reacquaint ourselves with, being kind to ourselves and each other as we regain them.

It's 2020 and one of the most popular trends on the internet is the ritualistic humiliation of women. … And the hatred for them is off the scale. It has become a bloodsport. Mobs of the supposedly virtuous love nothing more than to hunt these women down, film them, post the content online, and then sit back and watch as the women's lives are destroyed by armies of Karen-haters. Women have lost their jobs, gone into hiding, issued desperate, Salem-like denunciations of themselves in a bid to save some shred of their reputation. Let's call it what it is: modern-day witch-hunting.

[But] the wheels might finally be coming off the Karen-hating juggernaut. The shaming ritual [of a white woman named "Leah"] took place in Seattle this time, when a black man called Karlos Dillard[55] followed the woman to her home after they allegedly got into an argument while driving their cars. Dillard says Leah stuck her middle finger up at him and called him a nigger. Leah says this didn't happen. It later transpired that Dillard has something of a history of hunting down 'Karens' and accusing them of saying things they didn't say.

…The new racialists of the regressive left and the identitarian movement would have us believe that the white woman has all the power. She is higher up than the black man on these people's ridiculous, politically illiterate, class-ignoring identity lists in which every racial and gender group is ordered according to whether they are privileged (bad) or oppressed (good). Even the fact that the woman is weeping is held up as proof of her privilege and power. She is, according to the new regressives, using her 'white women's tears' to signal her dominion over a black man who merely wants justice for the fact that she allegedly flipped him the bird. This is patent nonsense, and anyone who still retains the ability to think independently knows it is. The power in this chilling video lies entirely with the man wielding his camera phone as a tool of humiliation, of public shaming, akin to when someone in the 1600s

---

[55] http://www.edrants.com/when-is-a-karen-not-a-karen-the-cruelty-and-lies-of-karlos-dillard/ - this is a very thorough account of Carlos Gum, aka Karlos Dillard.

would point a finger at a woman and declare: 'I saw her cavort with the devil.'

It is this warped social-media appetite for spectacles of shaming, for being part of a virtual mob that takes to task an allegedly evil person, that bolsters and empowers people like Karlos Dillard. It is reported that he has a strange obsession with Karens and he is even selling anti-Karen t-shirts through his Instagram page. This speaks to the extent to which Karen-shaming has become a kind of industry. There are memes, there is branded clothing, and there are of course the videos of exposed and shattered Karens which are watched and shared millions of times. Dillard was able to reduce Leah to a weeping wreck desperately trying to remain anonymous because of this broader, entrenched and increasingly misogynistic culture of seeking out white women to revile and tear down.

Selling anti-Karen t-shirts? Who is paying this guy to behave this way? The link from O'Neill's piece[56] in the footnote goes into the history of Dillon's (his real name is Carlos Gum) "systemic misogyny" of targeting women with "an undeniably cruel, attention-seeking, and truth-bending thrust to his grievances." @Edrant adds, "one does need to ask whether the cold and compassionless act of revealing the personal details and doxing a terrified woman for a minor road rage offense is the act of a bona-fide Karen." He goes on to say, "Dillard's wanton cruelty is a serious setback to the impressive progress of the courageous Black Lives Matter movement. When the evidential details are manufactured or outright erroneous, as they clearly are here with Dillard, then it dissuades someone who is on the fence about joining a vital and necessary struggle that will lead to a better tomorrow." The site links to a restraining order[57] filed against Dillard and his criminal record.[58]

When I read about Carlos Gum, who O'Neill describes as a "Karenfinder General," I also learned that he believed Donald Trump

[56] https://www.spiked-online.com/2020/06/25/the-hatred-for-karens-is-out-of-control/
[57] https://twitter.com/TrueAnonPod/status/1275551275581489153
[58] https://pastebin.com/pnLihvQK

would help him get a business loan and help lift him up out of poverty. How many people are unable to face their broken heartedness over the lies this POTUS has told and continues to tell?

O'Neill's piece on the Karen phenomenon, for me, offered the most balanced perspective available—and it took me a number of reads at different stages of this exploration for that appreciation to settle in. He speaks to phrases that I, as a "progressive," did not know and had to work to hear, like "regressive left" and "identitarian movement." And when I let his words sink into my consciousness—words like, "Their thirst for tearing people down for doing or saying something wrong utterly overshadows the instinct to complain that any middle-class white woman might have," I am able to feel my white privilege guilt in a way that speaks to the companion rage I have about feeling as if I have been sold down the river by the community to whom I have attempted to dedicate my heart. It's worse than all the actual whiplash I have experienced in my life.

∞

Holding both sides of the Karen name calling is a lot to reflect on at the moment. And as fast as this thought or feeling rises, I hear the Kansas song, "all we are is *Dust in the Wind*" in my head knowing that ultimately, as with all things, this too will blow over. But I am done waiting for nature to take her course when she is being manipulated by countless emotionally dysregulated people in every facet of society. It is not just the greedy elite who believe they are entitled to more and more and more and more of everything. It is all of us who can no longer bear the trauma of a life full of so many "things that make you go hmmmm," so many experiences of cognitive dissonance, that our brains are simply no longer able to contain the compacted rubble of emotions we have suppressed for so long. And then I hear the voice of others, like Kuba Shand-Baptiste, saying[59] "No, Karen is not the equivalent of the N-word for white women—this isn't a debate worth having." No, Kuba, it is not

---

[59] https://www.independent.co.uk/voices/karen-n-word-racism-white-women-julie-bindel-coronavirus-a9453201.html

the equivalent of the n-word; that BS was manufactured to pit us against each other. But all of this is, most definitely, a discussion worth having.

The Truth currently emerging inside me (after having a good cry about it all and being hugged by my husband and my dog) is this: The perfect moment is the one in which you are consciously growing love instead of perpetuating hate. Let's do this!

The K- and F-Words

As I mentioned previously, there have been rumors about women boycotting the nefariously invented "Karen as k-word" and inflammatory comparisons of it to the n-word. Various online dictionaries have referenced Kaffir as the original k-word which the Oxford English Dictionary explains as deeply nuanced. Kaffir can be a racial slur or a religious insult, "a means of abusing and alienating those who are from a different ethnic background or of a different faith" and it can be a neutral description of non-Islamic, polytheistic people from north-eastern Afghanistan or the Nguni people from south-eastern Africa. It has its etymology rooted in the Arabic word Kafir, meaning infidel and translating to English as "non-believer." Through the Apartheid era in South Africa the word developed derogatory racial connotations and has been criminally banned there since 1976 due to "the unlawful, intentional and serious violation of the dignity of another."[60]

Interestingly, there is an entire ethnic group of people named Karen; a group of people who have been fighting the longest civil war on the planet, courageously resisting oppression by the Burmese in the Karen Conflict[61] since 1949. The nation of Karen (pronounced with the emphasis on the second syllable) is physically located in Myanmar (Burma) on the border of Thailand. I watched a presentation about the Karen culture by the Karen Organization of Minnesota, where approximately 12,000 of the 100,000 Karen refugees have resettled. Burma was a British colony from 1886-1946 but when Burma was given their independence on January 4, 1948, the Karen were not included.

---

[60] https://public.oed.com/blog/word-stories-kaffir/ and
https://en.wikipedia.org/wiki/Kaffir_(racial_term)#cite_note-joubertLaw-4
[61] http://gyaw.org/the-karen-conflict/

The Karen Revolution began January 3, 1949 and continues to this day in order to win recognition and their own political destiny. As in all armed conflict, the casualties are heinous. The Karen people have been used as human shields, forced to sweep and lay landmines, and subjected to "summary executions" and systematic rape. I learned that only the southern Karen, the Pwo and Sgaw, have written forms of communication and that their creation story, called the Golden Book Story, is about three brothers, the Karen, the Thai, and the White, and the White stole the book and ran away. When missionaries came to convert them with the bible, they believed. According to this KOM presentation, about 65% of the Karen are Buddhist, 20% are Christian, and 15% are Animist.

Learning about the atrocities that this nation of Karen have experienced has left me deeply saddened. I feel great empathy for their plight and incredible awe for their resolve.

Sitting with this information and reflecting on the many generations of people who have not lived without the tidal ebbs and flows of religious strife brings me back, as so many histories of oppression do, to the roots of capitalism and colonialism. Would these intense conflicts over differing spiritual perspectives exist and have existed regardless of the mechanisms for expressing greed and egoic conquest? Is it human nature to battle?

∞

In the stage of "reactionary" disbelief, before having learned of the k-word's real non-Karen origins, I wondered how it was possible that any name of my middle-aged era or any other, could be so singularly vilified, so vile. The realization of just how possible is simple actually; middle-aged white women have been deemed by the media to be a despicable demographic, for generations.

Just Google "middle aged women" and you'll see what I mean. Here is a smattering of the first few hits, or should I say punches in the face:

- "What's Wrong with Middle Aged Women"
- "12 Mistakes Middle Aged Women Make"

- "Yes, Middle Aged Women Do Want to Have Sex" (*don't all healthy adults?!*)
- "The Invisibility of Middle Aged Women"
- "Signs of a Mid Life Crisis"

Then, click "news." Doing this led me to a July 2020 interview[62] of Jenny Eclair by the Belfast Telegraph titled, "Middle aged women aren't invisible, they're just ignored." This title comes from a remark Eclair makes in the interview, "Middle aged women aren't invisible, they're just ignored when whatever cougar potential a woman had wears off." This is both depressing and something resonant, true to my experience. I hadn't heard of this Irish comedian prior to the Google search, and was particularly grateful for her last comment in the interview, "More attention should have been given to female comics back in the Eighties and Nineties, and that didn't happen. Opportunities are better now [*a comment she has to make because no one likes a complainer*]. Women feel more deserving of their place. It seems extraordinary how long people got away with all-male panel shows." Honestly, this brings up a whole bunch of old upset for me. I have too many memories about the world making very little sense to me as I took my initial steps out into the trails the second wave of feminists had blazed.

For a bit of humor, I turn to Ellen DeGeneres. I'm reading her book, **Seriously I'm Kidding**. Here's a fun joke about endorphins, which she says are "magical elves that swim through your bloodstream and tell funny jokes to each other:"

"Knock, knock ... Who's there? ... Little endorphin ... Little endorphin who? ... Little endorphin Annie." Ellen adds, "And then the endorphins laugh, and then you laugh. See? It's science."

Daria Lamb of the Institute for the Future, in a webinar titled, Future Forces Disrupting Sustainable Business, shared an interesting thought about a person's formative 14-24 years of age. She calls experiential events that happen during these years to have "outsized impact" or hold more weight than they would for others not that age. A middle-aged

[62] https://www.belfasttelegraph.co.uk/life/weekend/jenny-middle-aged-women-arent-invisible-theyre-just-ignored-39391761.html

woman today was in this formative 14-24 age range in the 1980s, an era, according to Oxford Research Encyclopedia, "marked by political conservatism and an individualistic ethos." For me, that was an era of corrupt leadership, a president who was a former FBI informant ratting out people with "communist leanings" and an unbridled free market of Reaganomics undoing decades of actual conservation.

Taking a deep breath here. Rolling my sleeves back up and digging back in.

A contributor to Forbes detailed the five most profitable[63] demographics to market things to:

1. The aging population—it creates oodles of opportunity for profiteering; just think of all the health care costs including nursing homes and pharmaceuticals,
2. The young adults— always a sure bet as they are the real drinking crowd, dating and getting married and buying lots of new housewares,
3. Immigrants,
4. The environmentally and socially responsible investor, and
5. The tech savvy.

The article fails to elaborate on the last three.

But middle-aged women are in between the young and the old (just *had* to point out that obvious fact). Are the "typical" middle-aged women—generally set up with housewares, wardrobes to their tastes, and other basics, i.e., a demographic not in need of more stuff and not particularly profitable—the most perfect demographic to demonize?

Here is a huge, mind-blowing statistic to underscore the effects of the patriarchy from Annalisa Merelli's report in Quartz: "A March 2020 United Nations report[64], which looks at gender inequality and attitudes towards women around the world, put a staggering number to it: Nearly 90% of all people—that is, both men and women—are prejudiced against women."

---

[63] https://www.forbes.com/sites/moneyshow/2019/09/24/how-to-profit-from-changing-demographics-around-the-globe/#41e6bd225ea0
[64] http://hdr.undp.org/en/GSNI

Take a moment to let that statistic sink in. 90% of people worldwide have at least one innate bias against women. It is a bit less than 90% for women and a bit more than 90% for men. So when the thought emerges, "this feels like a gender bias against women," trust your gut that it is most likely accurate.

Think about some of the celebrities under Karen attack. The most famous I've come across is Ellen DeGeneres. JK Rowling has also been dubbed Transphobic Karen due to her expressed fears about shared bathrooms (is she *entitled* to be afraid?), giving haters a whole bunch of fodder to spew on social media. Ellen is now being called "Talk Show Karen." There has yet to be any substance supporting the ire directed her way, other than her being difficult and demanding to work with (as opposed to any other talk show host or famous person?).

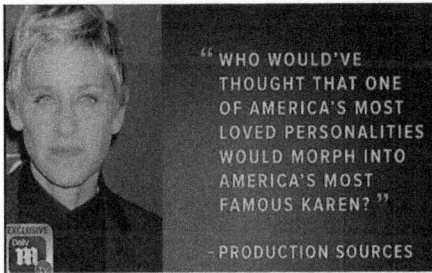

" WHO WOULD'VE THOUGHT THAT ONE OF AMERICA'S MOST LOVED PERSONALITIES WOULD MORPH INTO AMERICA'S MOST FAMOUS KAREN? "

-PRODUCTION SOURCES

Here are their apology letters[65], which seems to be a sick necessity in this cancel culture. In one article "an insider" reportedly says, "It's funny how history repeats itself. Many of us remember when Rosie O'Donnell was the queen of nice. Look how that turned out. She wasn't! Ellen is Rosie 2.0. Everyone now knows that she is not what she sold herself as. She's just mean, mean, mean.[66]"

How is this reporter not perpetuating the bigger of the two evils? I have tried to find anything of substance in Ellen's situation, but I can only surmise that, in the way that Trump had it out for Rosie, Ellen, the wealthiest comedian on the planet, must have upset the money.

Is this history repeating itself actually funny as this "insider" says? Humor is a great way to—as Emily Dickinson would say—tell the truth but tell it slant. I have wondered why one must tell the truth slant and

[65] https://nypost.com/2020/07/30/ellen-degeneres-on-toxic-workplace-allegations-i-am-sorry/?_ga=2.222225947.2068874433.1597596439-2115807192.1597596439 and https://www.bbc.com/news/uk-53002557
[66] https://meaww.com/upset-staffers-ellen-de-generes-call-her-talk-show-karen-amid-toxic-workplace-probe

use humor when humor can be expressed with such immaturity and lack of skill and I arrive at two ideas: one is that we could intentionally add humor to our children's educational requirements, like civics class, and the other is to protect comedians with impunity for educating the general public about things that leaders struggle to be courageous and vocal about.

Humor we find in shows like Saturday Night Live (45 years running) and Comedy Central, is deployed to soften the blow of hard truths—like the Drunk History episode[67] about Ronald Reagan that, in 2 minutes, captures

Black Jeopardy Remake (Karen's Potato Salad)

the gist of his ruthless fraudulence (decades after the fact)—and relatively benign annoyances like the Black Jeopardy episode[68] with host Keenan Thompson and guest Chadwick Boseman (RIP) as T'Challa spoofing Karen for bringing *her* potato salad to a barbecue in the category White People. But libel and slander of the nature Ellen DeGeneres has suffered, along with "insider" burglary[69] are emphatically *not* funny.

There are too many people speaking truth to power and getting assaulted, doxed, silenced virtually or for real for real. I have already spent too many hours of this one precious life researching ways in which honesty and integrity battles with ambition and fortune; the generality of this is for each of us to wrestle, or not. The ways in which women are being and have been attacked, and more specifically named Karen,

[67] http://www.cc.com/video-clips/981j4v/drunk-history-the-reagans--rise-to-power
[68] https://www.youtube.com/watch?v=hzMzFGgmQOc
[69] https://www.the-sun.com/entertainment/1311024/ellen-degeneres-mansion-robbery-inside-job-cops-claim/

are what remains front and center for me. I can analyze any number of Karens from various angles, which is relatively manageable.

Unpacking the gender bias (or "war on women") has evolved over decades and is best appreciated from a wider aperture. This level of consciousness raising takes everyone doing what they can from their vantage point and sharing their perspectives with curious inquiry.

∞

I am no lab scientist, but I am aware that there is more funding for erectile dysfunction—particularly one stream of $84 *million per year* funding from the Pentagon[70]—than there is for studying "the" menopause which affects 50% of the population. In fact, it wasn't until 2016 that the National Institute of Health even began to implement its new policy of Sex As a Biological Variable[71]. This is almost unfathomable so I would fully excuse you for glazing over as you read this fact. Stress today, Alzheimer's Tomorrow (according to this interesting article).[72]

Many sources corroborate a sex bias in medical research, and in my review of this evidence I found it quite interesting that there were very few areas in which there was an opposite bias with more women being studied; one of these areas is neuroscience. Could it be that the science of getting inside the heads of women—particularly by the same medical university (Johns Hopkins) that, without the consent of the African American woman whose cells they studied and continue to profit obscenely from 70 years later, invented cell cloning—is the holy grail of the oppression of women? Please read this New Science article[73] and Rebecca Skloot's 2010 book, **The Immortal Life of Henrietta Lacks**.

Any middle-aged woman *who has risen above the patriarchal pathology* is formidable. She has had access to education and has observed power up

---

[70] https://www.bbc.com/news/world-us-canada-40741785

[71] https://swhr.org/are-nih-policies-unintentionally-impeding-womens-health-research/

[72] https://www.studyfinds.org/stress-today-dementia-tomorrow-study-finds-middle-aged-women-most-at-risk/

[73] https://www.newscientist.com/article/2250449-genetic-privacy-we-must-learn-from-the-story-of-henrietta-lacks/#ixzz6Urc8HiHj

close even if she assigns it to herself vicariously through the men in her life. She understands the problems with the world and yet may have either bitten her tongue in order to sustain her security, rendering herself complicit, or she may have learned to speak her mind, suffered consequences like job loss or divorce, and has thus considers herself a force for change with a newfound level of confidence that is key as an agent for change.

A divorced woman might be profitable to marketers as she's back "on the market." But a well-adjusted employed "happy" woman who doesn't spend money to soothe her discomfiture, a woman who is immune to the marketing ploys to make her hate her face, her body, her hair, her nails, her house, her car, her job, her partner(s), her life—this is a woman outside the control of the market, off the grid or "matrix" if you will.

Cultural divides, class divides, and all the behavioral and environmental things that could define who we are based on where we've been are what make ALL of us unique; we have this in common. Even people living in the same household for most of their lives, a family unit in its broadest definition, live very different experiences based on all their unique and myriad conversations that develop into opinions and interests and visions.

I believe that people, particularly the middle-aged white women labeled as Karens, who are acting in really ugly and dehumanizing ways, are those who have been shut down, turned off, and are not just asleep to others and important aspects of reality, but also asleep to themselves, their truth, their nature, their unique voice, their light. And if we cannot see ourselves, we cannot see others. Conversely, when we can see ourselves, we can see others.

When I watch some of the videos of Karens screaming about their medical conditions and their legal right to not wear face masks or going ballistic about a public demonstration that doesn't seem to take into consideration the subset of people that she cares about, I see a woman in severe emotional pain who is unable to gauge the pulse of the wider space she is in or her place in it. Self-centeredness in the extreme is a psychological definition of narcissism. And according to healthdirect.gov in Australia, here are the causes:

- insensitive parenting
- over-praising and excessive pampering—when parents focus intensely on a particular talent or the physical appearance of their child as a result of their own self-esteem issues
- unpredictable or negligent care
- excessive criticism
- abuse
- trauma
- extremely high expectations

What would a group of Karens say? What would they vent about? That question made me look for the answer. I searched for "Karens unite" and got pretty angry with what I found, including sites dedicated to the hatred of Karen. I thought about including some of that incendiary content here but just as quickly let it go. THIS IS HOW TO GO **BEYOND KAREN**, KAREN (is my screaming necessary?). Devalue the physical-emotional anger rising up and replace it with objective curiosity. Tone down the foul and tune into the gentle.

There may exist a safe space for Karen sharing, a resource for proactively dissolving this hatred of Karens, but I didn't find one (and, naturally, I want to build one through **Beyond Karen**). To the contrary, the message conveyed through Google and the slew of sites I referred to previously seemed to indicate that no one would listen to a Karen or a group of Karens say anything because rogue women are the problem, they are to blame for everything that is wrong in the world, not just America, everywhere. But what this really translates to is, "keep your head down, be a good work-a-holic, mind your business, don't have any controversial opinions or you'll be ground into dust well before your time is up."

But maybe we have to swing wildly through these extremes for a while until we settle down to some semblance of rational community policing—online and beyond. If one is susceptible to shame, being called out, despite being a painful experience, could be considered a gift, a catalyst for a needed lesson to be learned in that moment, especially if the one writing the incriminating post does it with such intent. This virtual "calling in" instead of calling out, within the realm of cancel culture, is an expansive form of the boycott that includes public figures not just products and organizations.

Hatred is toxic and if we succumb to it on any level—as a hater or allowing oneself to be hated—we only end up wounding ourselves, our body-mind, in the process. Anger and fear are intense emotions that need to be attended to with care. The fact that it may be becoming safer to feel angry is a good thing in terms of consciousness raising. Acting impulsively on the anger is not. And yes, there is so much to be angry about and it may be nearly impossible to neutralize it in the moments it arises for anyone not familiar with mindfulness practices such as the ones teachers like Thich Nhat Hanh (and others) espouse, like cradling one's anger and attending to it as one would a crying baby. So we practice and we stay open to learning from our mistakes.

∞

When the first actions of looting broke out in south Minneapolis after George Floyd's murder by police officers (the one holding him down and the ones who did nothing) on *Memorial* Day, many people understood this as a natural response to the pent-up anger. That understanding is good; that understanding created communities which were capable of holding the anger and the people feeling it. It was palatable and reverberated out like a wave, like the viral power of media.

When we are out on the streets demonstrating what democracy looks like and yelling "if we don't get it, shut it down," we are not talking about shutting down anyone's life essence or even corporations as complicit as Black Rock. We, the people, are talking about shutting down corruption. How far *are* the reaches of corruption?

Interestingly I was able to find, by Googling, a paper by Michel Dion, on the *Philosophical connections between the classical and the modern notion of corruption: From the Enlightenment to post-modernity*[74], which finds "that the **classical notion of corruption** implies the degeneration of human relationships (Plato and Hegel), the degeneration of the body-and-mind

---

[74] https://www.emerald.com/insight/content/doi/10.1108/JFC-01-2016-0009/full/html

unity (Aristotle, Pascal and Thomas Mann) or the degeneration of collective morality (Cicero, Locke, Rousseau, Hume and Kant). The **modern notion of corruption** as bribery was mainly introduced by Adam Smith. Nietzsche (and Musil) looked at corruption as degeneration of the will-to-power. The classical notion of corruption put the emphasis on the effects rather than on the cause itself (effects-based thinking). The modern notion of corruption as bribery insists on the cause rather than on the effects (cause-based thinking).

If we (hypothetically) shut down behemoth corporations like Amazon, Google, Apple, Microsoft and all the Big Box stores, even though the large shareholders of these may all earn way too much money, who does it hurt? Obviously, the employees first and foremost; but allowing for the many new career paths that will reemerge as we rebalance our inputs and outputs to be more in line with the real needs we have for survival, they will be okay. Can we go without these corporations? We can get by without toilet paper. Really. But do we want to? We can grow our own food, but it might only feed us for a few days. We can store up supplies, even explosive gasoline, but, ultimately, the political levers that manage the supply chains of global goods are in just a few fat little hands.

I have a couple of very simple ideas about this, naturally, because even though tax law, algorithms and derivatives are designed to obfuscate checks and balances, good solutions are simple. The wealthiest men in the world are at the helm of the planet's crash course, we know this.

ONE:

What if no one human being could make more than the President of the country? Who needs more than $400,000? I expected this figure to be $300,000 because the last time I checked it was $250,000. Maybe the governmental cost of living adjustments are more generous, like the health insurance plans, for government officials than for most Americans? If no one could earn (including shares and bonuses) more than $400,000 per year, we might soon find that people in "high" places would be there because they wanted to be there and because they were capable and qualified to be there. More women would run things.

TWO:

Taking a deeper dive into the annual World Gross Domestic Product, we find it to be roughly $150,000,000,000,000, which is a lot of money. There are roughly 8 billion people, which is a lot of people. But, hypothetically not accounting for cost of goods, this would allow *EVERY* household of 4 people to earn $75,000 per year. Not bad.

Economies are struggling because "Main Street" (small business) is struggling. Big business (like the ones listed above) keep the stock market going, obscuring or obfuscating reality. Jeff Bezos is expected to become the world's first trillionaire if he hasn't already. It would take almost *32 years nonstop* just to count from one to one billion. What else could a large family (like America) do when Pop (like Jeff Bezos) is eating over 90% of all the food? Worker Ownership and Cooperatives are important models to follow.

On most days, objective curiosity in problem solving seems to me like an impossible expectation of the highest levels of media and political representation given the level of immaturity displayed day to day. The vehemence that is directed at powerful articulate women right now with hearsay and weak substantiation is an industry-wide embarrassment. Calling us Karens may be an impotent tactic, a last ditch shot in the dark to shut women up in general, and powerful women in particular. Our willingness to not fight back may be a way to subconsciously contain the rage within our bellies that has grown larger and more pregnant with no delivery in sight year after year.

After an extensive review of articles written about Karens I have concluded that several journalists who cover pop culture are doing their due diligence and covering trends with varying flavors of regurgitated content, but there are also throngs of media manipulators paid to simply spew garbage content and hate onto the world wide web. Who pays these drones is my question? Is it the same few organizations curating high level psychographic profiles, and if so, what is in it for them? Where does the buck truly stop?

A testimonial by Peter Phillips for a recent book, **United States of Distraction**, reads, "[It] challenges our hegemon-media's ideological mind control and the occupation of human thought. Huff and Higdon correctly call for mass critical resistance through truth telling by free minds. Power to the people!"

Peter Beinart, in an article (with excerpts below) for The Atlantic titled, *The New Authoritarians Are Waging War on Women* writes: "Besides their hostility to liberal democracy, the right-wing autocrats taking power across the world share one big thing, which often goes unrecognized in the U.S.: They all want to subordinate women."

WTF? YOU WENT FULL KAREN?

NEVER GO FULL KAREN

Drawing on Texas A&M political scientist Valerie Hudson's work, Beinart continues, "This political hierarchy appeared natural—as natural as adults ruling children—because it mirrored the hierarchy of the home. Thus, for millennia, men, and many women, have associated male dominance with political legitimacy. Women's empowerment ruptures this order."

It's easy to see how this [subordination of women] worked for Trump. He made Hillary Clinton—the first woman ever nominated for president by a major party—the personification of America's corrupt political system. But rather than credibly promise to cleanse America of corrupting financial interests, he promised his supporters—the majority of whom told pollsters that America had grown "too soft and feminine"—a government cleansed of the corruption of one particular villainess.

…In 2017, he [President Rodrigo Duterte] informed Filipino soldiers that because he had declared martial law on the island of

Mindanao, they could each rape up to three women with impunity. In 2018, he told soldiers to shoot female rebels "in the vagina," because that would render them "useless."

Duterte's anti-feminist crusade—like Trump's and [Brazilian President Jair] Bolsonaro's—has also featured the ritualized humiliation of powerful women. When Senator Leila de Lima demanded an investigation into Duterte's drug war, he vowed to "make her cry." The government then detained de Lima on drug-trafficking charges and leaked evidence supposedly proving, in Duterte's words, that she was "screwing her driver" like she was "screwing the nation." A congressman who would later become Duterte's spokesman joked that de Lima wanted to be detained at an army base "because there are many men there." Not even Duterte's female vice president, Leni Robredo—a member of a rival political party—has escaped his taunts. At a public event in 2016, he noted gleefully that the skirts she wore to cabinet meetings were "shorter than usual."

… [Hungary's Prime Minister promotes debt-free education for women if they chain themselves to the home by having three or more children and advertisements urging Poles to "breed like rabbits" while access to the morning-after pill has been banned are no different.] In late 2017, after Polish women protested draconian new restrictions on abortion, the government raided the offices of women's groups.

For women's-rights advocates, these sexist authoritarians pose a conundrum. Defeating them requires empowering women. Yet the more empowered women become, the more right-wing autocrats depict that empowerment as an assault on the natural political order. It's no coincidence that Bolsonaro and Duterte are fervent critics of female former presidents, or that women were among Duterte's and Trump's principal opponents. Christine Blasey Ford's allegations inspired women protesters to fill the U.S. Senate. Yet images of women yelling at male senators probably helped Republicans keep the Senate in the 2018 midterm elections.

...The new authoritarianism underscores the importance of an old feminist mantra: The personal is political. Foster women's equality in the home, and you may save democracy itself. This piece[75] is worth reading in its entirety. I agree with the final sentiment 100% and in forthcoming chapters I hope to convey the hard work that my husband Paul and I have done, since we began dating in high school, to evolve our individual and collective cultural constructs about roles, earnings, authority, and pretty much everything. Our scrupulous dedication to processing feelings, to exploring equality in thought, word and deed, has been challenging on many levels; and it has been entirely worthwhile.

An extreme of hate that leads anyone, especially political leaders like the "new authoritarians" in Beinart's article, to perpetuate this purposefully obscured and hidden war on women, reflects more than a lack of love and respect. We live in a culture of fear; most journalists cannot report Truth without putting their careers and their lives at risk.

TimesUp for real for real. The fomenting of hate online, or in politics, or through arbitrary bullshit rules[76] that are driving farmers and factory workers to suicide, may kill us all. We literally see the effects of rogue political leaders in the extreme of dry desert soils, denuded, raw and malnourished. In order to restore the soil it must be acknowledged, identified, named, and cared for over time. The expanse of time that the soil—or a community's dignity—has been abused must be restored and that is extremely challenging. Sometimes it feels impossible, especially if we are thinking in isolation.

I imagine that Karens are bottled up ready to explode from all the tamping down that women of my era have experienced—white, black, red, yellow, every color, every one. There are precious few release valves for this kind of pent-up energy and the wine drinking gossip parties are not part of the solution even though they are presented as the "perfect" way for white women to vent.

---

[75] https://www.theatlantic.com/magazine/archive/2019/01/authoritarian-sexism-trump-duterte/576382/

[76] https://www.business-humanrights.org/en/india-activist-vandana-shiva-links-monsantos-genetically-modified-seeds-to-farmers-suicides and https://www.youtube.com/watch?v=ns-kJ5PodJw

Let's go back to the non-tongue-biting Karen who spews racist hate and chews up waitstaff instead of her imperfectly cooked steak. If my former self—which would no doubt have become a Karen were it not for some divine intervention that moved me to a community of curious people trying to wake themselves up—was informed she was a Karen, through means such as shaming on social media or having lost her job or her dog, do you think she would have been able to say to herself, "whoa, this is a real wake up call, I need to change my ways and heal thyself" or do you think she would respond with a big "fuck you very much?"

If I pepper every sentence or so with the word fuck, I am emotionally dysregulated. If I have done this for a long time and it has become second nature, I will need a lot of support to change the behavior (starting with even wanting to change it).

If saying fuck is an occasional thing for emphasis, it's unlikely to be worrisome (even if my husband once had a list on the fridge to track my impropriety), after all it is a word of unparalleled impact. And if my use of F bombs increases with intensity and frequency randomly (or at certain times of the month) it could be a result of hormonal shifts and indicative of moments when I need to be more clear and direct about asking for what I need or it could simply be a result of all the bullshit I sense around me and not having enough sense of community to convince myself that what I see is real. It is not at all easy, or even safe, to ask for what we need, even if we've had lots of practice.

I do feel the beginnings of the shift toward safety in calling bullshit for what it is and hope and believe it is underway for real. But when I listen to interviews like the one Krista Tippett hosted on her show, On Being, with Resmaa Menakem and Robin DiAngelo and I hear the pain in Resmaa's voice when he says "black folk can't temporarily remove their skin like white folk can remove their signs," and "the news cycle hasn't told white people yet that they can now not give a damn again," I feel as if there is nothing to do but sit and marinate in the grief of it all.

If white and Black people can hold despair together, we can also hold hope together. Being honest about our despair together may be just as effective at boosting our emotional wellness as being active optimists together.

A State of Enough

Tens of millions of Americans participated in spontaneous Black Lives Matter protests in the *couple of weeks* after George Floyd's murder. New School professor Deva Woodly reported on July 3, 2020 that, collectively, civil rights marches in the 1960s had only turned out hundreds of thousands, not millions. Protesters remain on the front lines of change, telling legislative and political authorities, and anyone who might listen, that systemic oppression has got to change. The ultimate message of a protest is "We've had enough of the lies."

The criminal justice system rarely delivers justice. For most people of color it is a shell game of organized, calculated, systemic disenfranchisement. As Tamika Mallory, an organizer of the women's march, said to the media channel BeLatina, "We cannot look at this as an isolated incident. The reason buildings are burning are not just for our brother George Floyd," she said. "They're burning down because people here in Minnesota are saying to people in New York, to people in California, to people in Memphis, to people across this nation, enough is enough."[77]

At this moment, the word Enough continues to describe the boiling over of rage among Black Americans due to the injustices that have never let up since the first Africans were enslaved here and, like the subjugation of women, continue under ever more subtle forms of gaslighting and oppression.

Gaslighting is a term used to describe crazy-making behavior, and it comes from a 1938 movie with Ingrid Bergman as the wife of a man who turns down their gas lamp a tiny bit every day. When she starts to

---

[77] https://belatina.com/george-floyd-protests-long-overdue-antiracist-revolution/andhttps://www.democracynow.org/2020/6/1/tamika_mallory_speech_police_brutality

notice and question things by asking, "is it getting darker in here or is it just me?" The husband pretends to not notice even though he's the one turning the gas lamp down. The truly ugly side of this is, of course, the fact that the woman is the one questioning her sanity, making herself crazy, and the man continues to act as if he is innocent.

When a business or a nation is so profit driven that it perpetually cheapens the quality of its product or the lives of its citizenry while barely changing the branding or political rules of engagement, people can keep consuming and existing for quite some time before they hit a level of intolerance brought about by deteriorating health and wellness. Attempts to control corporate behaviors like "bait and switch" or to enforce civil rights legislation through regulations require political will. Political will seems to get more and more challenging to quantify and qualify and the practice of obfuscating justice grows more and more sophisticated.

So while I'm trying to weave together aspects of my life in solidarity with enraged women and men fed up with systemic oppression of women and men alike due to the deep, painful, lasting but not permanent effects of economic greed that have left our collective psyches weak and desperate for attention, I am celebrating the strength of the communities taking action by whatever means they must, to STOP the insanity, and draw attention, if there can still be hope, to end the epidemic macro and microaggressions that come through us and out of our damn divisive devices.

Tens of millions of Americans also became unemployed in the spring and summer of 2020. One early July report[78] noted 51 million people had filed for benefits as a result of the pandemic and that this figure didn't even include those who'd already exhausted their benefits and remained unemployed, adding shame and more overwhelm to the fear of illness and loss of loved ones.

As we pondered how much lower our spirits could sink as a nation, Alyssa Battistoni from the Boston Review put things in perspective:[79]

While the number of jobs had grown steadily for several years before COVID-19 hit, wages had not. The Western trajectory of industrialization appears to be exhausted: global markets are already crowded, leaving little room for "emerging markets" to develop. Even the phenomenal growth rates of China and India had begun to slow before the pandemic hit. There are reasons to think that capitalism is running out of "fixes"—there are fewer peasants to be converted to low-wage proletarians, fewer places for production to be outsourced, fewer sites (the moon?) from which to extract resources.

We feel as if we have had enough of "everything." We are depleted in body, mind, and soul. To break down this all-encompassing, overwhelming notion of "enough!" and to put a few dowels into this crumbling societal cake, here are some specifics:

- We have had enough of guns in schools,
- We have had enough of high level political gaslighting,
- We have had enough willful destruction of natural resources,
- We have had enough of media sensationalism,
- We have had enough of profiteering and the disgusting imbalance of power leading to houselessness, joblessness, and soul crushing apathy.

---

[78] https://www.forbes.com/sites/jackkelly/2020/07/16/51-million-americans-are-unemployedheres-the-story-of-the-job-seekers-behind-the-numbers/#600fc4006ac1
[79] http://bostonreview.net/class-inequality-politics/alyssa-battistoni-when-will-capitalism-end

These are huge topics that are on the hearts and minds of most of us, even if not consciously. From here we can *intentionally look for solutions* that others are championing at the moment, such as those mapped point for point to the previous five issues, detailed here:

- Loaded: A Disarming History of the Second Amendment, by Roxanne Dunbar-Ortiz,[80]
- Politifact statistics on the POTUS' lies[81] from the Poynter Institute,
- UN Environment Programme—how to give nature the urgent attention[82] it needs,
- Literature review of news media by Hendriks and Kleemans— Proving the Obvious,[83]
- Restorative Justice For All[84]—an ethos of understanding through dialogue.

If we are to explore solutions, they must come from a hopeful expectation, a vision for what is possible. We must search from this frame of mind, not from the frame of mind that has our guts in knots. If we stay together in hopeful expectation, we see that we have reached a tipping point where *at least* 3.5% of America is united and activated toward solutions in this very moment about all the concerns, the impacts, the human and interspecies, intersectional effects of the problems.

This 3.5% figure[85] is the one Jane Fonda cites in her Fire Drill Fridays as needed for a national movement to take hold; and it is the

---

[80] http://www.citylights.com/book/?GCOI=87286100460830

[81] https://www.politifact.com/personalities/donald-trump/

[82] https://www.unenvironment.org/news-and-stories/story/nature-can-still-heal-itself-if-we-give-it-urgent-attention-it-needs

[83] https://journals.sagepub.com/doi/full/10.1177/1931243117739947?utm_campaign=The+New+News+Consumer&utm_medium=email&utm_source=Revue+newsletter

[84] https://www.rj4all.info/Race-Power

[85] https://whatwillittake.com/covid-gendered/insights-from-jane-fonda/

same figure[86] that Erica Chenoweth, Harvard Kennedy School professor and co-director of Crowd Counting Consortium, says has been the peak participant level for unseating government leadership or a nation seeking independence. It might appear that we have absolutely hit this critical mass, but I believe we also need to be united on why things are the way they are as a critical mass in order for change to root.

Building critical mass around COVID safety is a fine example of solution-oriented leadership. We have learned that women leadership has fared much better overall at stopping the spread of the coronavirus; the countries led by women (13 of the 193 United Nations countries) are seeing some of the lowest cases of coronavirus and deaths.

These nations include:

Iceland (Katrin Jakobsdottir), New Zealand (Jacinda Ardern), Germany (Angela Merkel), Scotland (Nikola Sturgeon), Thailand (Tsai Ingwen), Finland (Sanna Marin), and Norway (Erna Solberg). Could it be that citizens of these countries, both men and women, have higher levels of natural immunity-stabilizing hormones like estrogen due to less media manipulation, less misinformation, and clearer communication?

We do not have to be hamstrung or suffocated by the oppressive antics of the wayward American administration. We do have choices. We can choose to feel positive in even the slightest way. Be glad to breathe, to have sensation in the body, to hold an object and really look at it, even a "scary" spider has so much to teach us about love and compassion. When we choose to *look in the exact opposite direction* of our fear, we can find a path forward.

I make this point about addressing fear because this chapter about the state of enough—the intolerance on both sides of the governing aisle and both sides of the economic coin—is about to get real. I will offer more insight about addressing fear in a bit (and the next chapter on emotional reeducation is chock full of ideas for bearing emotional intensity) because the act of consuming details that have emotional

---

[86] https://www.nytimes.com/interactive/2020/07/03/us/george-floyd-protests-crowd-size.html

intensity is best done while also learning techniques for bearing it. This is one take on the activist's approach to building the boat as it sails ahead.

∞

In the summer of 2020, enough people had grown sufficiently intolerant of Karen behaviors that their collective efforts to stop whatever they were doing and capture/share these Karen behaviors real time created the viral phenomenon; the social media shaming brought much needed sunlight to help disinfect and deodorize. In the chapter about name calling I skimmed the surface of the racist history Karen has when I referenced Ruby Hamad's book, **White Tears/Black Scars**. Now it is time to dig deep, get uncomfortable, and begin the healing so that we can take steps to go beyond Karen.

I'll start the discomfort with a reveal about the town I've lived in for twenty years. Amherst Massachusetts was named after Lord Jeffrey Amherst who, to me, will only be remembered as the man who gave blankets infected with smallpox to the indigenous Nipmuk and Pocumtuc peoples. He murdered them. The fancy Lord Jeffrey Inn situated in the town commons just recently changed its name. Pressure is on the mostly white town leadership to integrate racial justice goals into every municipal goal, as all towns should, naturally.

There are many thousands of carefully articulated petitions for change that cross the desks of the senators and representatives each year in just Massachusetts alone. The number of issues that deserve more attention than they are getting is enough to make even the most effective, efficient, dedicated public servant wish they could go to sleep for a hundred years. But public servants are elected to serve and all courageous voices seeking change agitate—call, email, rally, etc.—so that they do not turn a blind eye to the issues. This is what democracy looks like.

I have petitioned various decision-making bodies of our state and federal legislatures, mostly with regards to climate change, but I have also advocated on behalf of Indigenous peoples and mothers and about healthcare and other broad overarching concerns. You may be interested and upset to learn that as of summer 2020 the Massachusetts state seal continues to be an image of a Native American man with a threatening sword over his head. For the past 36 years the legislature has been petitioned to change this (among many other related things). Every excuse in the book has been made, including the cost of changing the seal that has been emblazoned on highways and bridges, but the seal has actually changed over the exactly 400 years since the colonizers landed in Plymouth and each time the sword returns over this man's head[87].

If the Washington R*dskins, thanks to years of pressure from Native activists and investors, can (finally) rid themselves of the "R word" and Mississippi can remove the confederate battle flag from its state flag (finally), Massachusetts can scrape itself off the low road and redesign its seal. One Native American man who testified for this—one of the last people in the room to testify instead of one of the first as he should have been given the fact that his tribe, the Massachuset (which means "by the range of hills"), has, as all tribes have, self-governing authority—suggested the seal depict the tree of life. He said this with a graceful frustration in his voice.

Why didn't women or men in my town speak up against Mr. Amherst's despicable act of stealing land by killing thousands of native peoples who had lived here for thousands of years with smallpox infested blankets? For the same reason why white women didn't rise up together to confront the men who were whipping their laborers like donkeys; they were complicit and wanted the land, the new lives, the American Dream more than they wanted justice. (by the way, after 146 years of animal-whipping cruelty, Ringling Bros. and Barnum & Bailey Circus closed for good in 2017).

This question of "why have white women struggled with cross-race solidarity" is a huge and complicated one that I hope many more people are considering due in part to what we are seeing on social media with the Karen shaming phenomenon. On the one hand it is an in-your-face reckoning of the colonial white woman's complicity in the subjugation and, in thousands of harrowing cases, the murder, of other people, of

---

[87] In January 2021 the Massachusetts Governor finally authorized the changing of the state seal!

Indigenous communities, of Black adolescents and men, of Asian American and Pacific Islanders, of strong, well-rooted people living simple lives. On the other hand it is, like the Coronavirus, one more thing that, at least for me, prompts deep seated anger to rise up and be felt with growing pains and hope for healing.

∞

There is a lot of truth in bumper sticker phrases and "Think, It's Not Illegal Yet" is one of my favorites. The one that comes to mind as I pause to make a distinction about gender and power is, "Absolute Power Corrupts Absolutely."

I often get frustrated with the "kid gloves" approach that the media and political influencers take when holding white men in power accountable. It takes a tidal wave of truth to hold morally bankrupt white men accountable. Yes, there are exceptions to everything one can assert, but it is not a stretch to say that, historically and presently, white men are more responsible for systemic racism than white women. Yet, because white women are more vulnerable and a hell of a lot less likely to inflict pain and suffering of the magnitude of those white men corrupted by power (I cannot even name these things they "order" others to do for money, but you know what they are), she'd be thrown under the bus before he would. Apologies to bus drivers everywhere.

So why did 19th century suffragettes, who had had enough of the subjugation of women, of losing "rights" to their property, including their children upon marriage, not unite across race in order to address this violence?

It has been a century since women won the right to vote. There is much one can learn about the tense relationships, the courage as well as the complicated complicity during this first foray into rebalancing the power dynamic that gave so much to white men and took so much from people of color, and, less obviously, from women.

In a blog on educationpost.org, ShaRhonda Knott-Dawson writes, "The suffragettes realized they needed to change their alliances from Black folks to Southern White women. Southern White women are a lot of things, but inconsistent in their hatred for Black people is not one of those things. And if the suffragettes wanted to partner with Southern White women, there could be no 'racial equality' stuff."

One tense relationship that I have been learning about is the one between Ida B. Wells and Frances E. Willard. According to biographer Paula Giddings, Ida B. Wells, a trailblazer who was unstoppable in her efforts to stop lynchings in and beyond her Memphis community, a child born into slavery who became a founder of the NAACP, "knew that in order to bring change, she needed to expose the truth: that too many white liberals were doing nothing to oppose these crimes against black Southerners. She was also pushing to gain financial and political backing from the British people."[88] According to historian Vicken Babkenian[89], Frances E. Willard, founder of the World Women's Christian Temperance Union and pioneer of the 8-hour workday, was a fierce opponent of the male-dominated statesman in Europe not taking action to stop the Ottoman Empire's massacre of Armenians, whose similar overseas fundraising efforts launched the first global American Red Cross relief effort.

But as Ida B. Wells had reported, there was plenty of inaction happening at home in America. This past Juneteenth, *99 years after the fact*, I learned about the Tulsa Oklahoma Greenwood race riots during her time in 1921, which were not unlike the People's Grocery riot in Memphis Tennessee (where a mob of white people lynched the three Black owners of the grocery store, her friends), responsible for her anti-lynching crusade. Lynching, she determined, was used to protect white economic power and to ensure a captive black labor force; it was "an excuse to get rid of Negroes who were acquiring wealth and property and thus keep the race terrorized[90]. Ida B. Wells-Barnett is also noted as saying[91]: "I'd rather go down in history as one lone Negro who dared to tell the government that it had done a dastardly thing than to save my skin by taking back what I said."

---

[88] https://www.npr.org/2011/03/25/134849480/the-root-how-racism-tainted-womens-suffrage

[89] https://armenianweekly.com/2019/09/18/frances-willard-armenias-angel-on-capitol-hill/

[90] https://items.ssrc.org/reading-racial-conflict/ida-b-wells-and-the-economics-of-racial-violence/

[91] https://www.americanswhotellthetruth.org/portraits/ida-b-wells

Wells knew what moral authority is; she knew that one must not turn a blind eye to injustice happening in front of them. And despite the fact that there were different human beings in churches worshipping the same God she worshipped, claiming to uphold the same values she upheld, proclaiming the gospel of love thy neighbor as thyself, these human beings, these *white* human beings, were perpetuating and feigning ignorance to the most god-awful things beyond the imagination.

How Could This Be Happening? For Wells to feel as if she was the "lone Negro" speaking truth about the everyday slurs that were oppressing the minds and bodies of her and everyone she cared about, the everyday acts of violence—both the nonverbal and verbal abuses as well as the calculated, collaborated, corroborated *murders* of her friends and family members (her parents, despite rising above the near insurmountable odds as slaves, despite having broken free of their dependency on *the master,* died when she was just 16 years old leaving Ida to raise her sisters and earn the money to support themselves by teaching)—she absolutely had to have had unparalleled faith and direct spiritual guidance to keep her going day after day.

The "moral authority" with which Frances Willard approached truth—the exhaustive pursuit of global temperance, which centered around abstinence from alcohol in order to protect the jobs of the men and the women and children in their home—might today alienate all those who are not Christian, or of the white, cis, heteronormative dominant paradigm. But how did this heteronormative dominant paradigm root itself so firmly in society as to effectively lobotomize white people of reason and a sense of righteousness?

Frances Willard was named the "uncrowned queen of American democracy," by British editor W.T. Stead, and her rallying cry[92] that brought hundreds of thousands to her side was the "everybody's war" between rum shops and religion. On the surface her indefatigable and passionate effort seems incredibly noble and her life's work, particularly in labor reform, supported a lot of people. But despite her *good intentions,* similar to those with which the world is paved, her white Christian

---

[92] https://franceswillardhouse.org/wp-content/uploads/HST391-2-wctu1.pdf

perspective could have never been the "one size fits all" approach to religion, to government, to education, to any aspect of life.

These two women approached truth from very different angles. Both were appreciated as "modern," as visionary, and both women had the incredible courage to go right into the fray, onto the front lines, attempting to educate and rally others to their causes. Both chafed over others' vested interests that kept them silent or impotent and both women sought to address the balance of power that subjugated their familiars. Both women achieved so much. Why were they not able to unite? A detailed Truth Telling presentation can be found online.[93]

There were (and still are) many white women who did much to uphold the supremacy of their race. Elizabeth Gillespie McRae details some of their stories in **Mothers of Massive Resistance: White Women and the Politics of White Supremacy**. Without these mundane, everyday acts, white supremacist politics could not have shaped local, regional, and national politics the way it did or lasted as long as it has. Here are some of the ways McRae details the insidious complicity of white women in the past which have led to the boiling-over rage bringing people to the streets today in the midst of a global pandemic with its epicenter in America:

They instilled beliefs in racial hierarchies in their children, built national networks, and experimented with a color-blind political discourse. [They were] censoring textbooks, denying marriage certificates, deciding on the racial identity of their neighbors, celebrating school choice, canvassing communities for votes, and lobbying elected officials.

This top-down white supremacist mindset of the 19th and 20th centuries, a mindset that was *made legal* by the Alabama state governing body in 1901 where it remains in force, has not yet been sufficiently challenged. Maybe the words of Theodore Roosevelt curated by Paula J. Giddings, Margaret Vandiver, and Manfred Berg as presented by the

---

93 http://www.willardandwells.org

Equal Justice Initiative[94] and the unfathomable stories EJI has documented of some of the 4,084 Black lives lost to lynching between 1877-1950 might be enough to shock us white people from our complicit slumber (and please know that I say this with great compassion for myself and for you as we relearn history together):

> By the start of the twentieth century, national leaders had learned to profitably employ popular white supremacist views and pro-lynching rhetoric. In 1906, President Theodore Roosevelt declared that "the greatest existing cause of lynching is the perpetration, especially by black men, of the hideous crime of rape." "Let [the black man] keep his hands off white women," the Memphis AvalancheAppeal editorialized, "and lynching will soon die out." "[If] it requires lynching to protect woman's dearest possession from ravening, drunken human beasts," white women's rights activist Rebecca Felton wrote in the Atlanta Journal in 1898, "then I say lynch a thousand a week if necessary."

Breathing deeply.

It may be easy to think that if we were alive back then we might have the moral courage of an Ida B. Wells. If we are not now out in the streets raging about racism as if our hair was on fire, it is unlikely that we would. I know I am not and am writing this book about the complicit white women now called Karens, who once looked the other way and perpetuated gross injustices with their silence, who are now being canceled for their supremacist behaviors, in order to build my moral courage.

In the racial reeducation work I am doing (and I highly recommend the 30-day challenge by the AntiRacist Table founders Lynn Turner and Kirsten Ivey-Colson), I find myself reflecting on a notion about fear of others who are more spiritual, more grounded in community, more elegant and refined than us—the subconscious jealousy that seems to exist underneath greed, scarcity-mindedness, and appropriation. I believe many of the indigenous communities that white men and

---

[94] https://eji.org/wp-content/uploads/2019/10/lynching-in-america-3d-ed-080219.pdf

women have continued to exploit for centuries—the people who lived in balance with the resources around them—tried to share their ways of living in balance even as they themselves were experiencing fear.

∞

Even though Willard added the anti-lynching crusade to her list of social reform campaigns once she had been better educated by Wells, her legacy was tarnished by her racist comments blaming immorality on black men's consumption of alcohol (over two hundred anti-lynching bills were introduced into the United States Congress in the twentieth century and none of them passed[95]). Alcoholism is a symptom of a societal problem, like the economic subjugation Wells spoke of. Willard claimed she was not a racist. Was she a high-profile Karen? Or was Willard one note away from a unified voice with Wells?

Are women ready to unite? How are women of color continuing to model for white women how to speak truth to power? Are white women listening? How are women of color turning their backs on white women because they have had enough of the failed attempts? Are women of color noticing?

Maria Popova, in a July issue[96] of her *Brain Pickings* newsletter dedicated to the legacy of Congressman John Lewis, writes, "How few of us are capable of such largeness when contracted by hurt, when the clench of injustice has tightened our own fists. And yet in the conscious choice to unclench our hearts and our hands is not only the measure of our courage and our strength, not only the wellspring of compassion for others, but the wellspring of compassion for ourselves and the supreme triumph of personhood." Let us take a collective moment together to breathe in and out that delicious truth. Repeatedly.

∞

My jaw is tight as I hold hard truths.

---

[95] https://medium.com/@backlinkshawarma/time-and-distance-overcome-dd605fe0f2f5
[96] https://www.brainpickings.org/2020/07/18/john-lewis-love-light-forgiveness/

What are the patterns of temporomandibular joint (TMJ) disorder, of clenching one's jaw and grinding one's teeth? 90% of the people affected by TMJ are women. Is the stress that leads one to pack it into her bones affecting women equally irrespective of race or are there racial aspects that could be studied and understood in order to support and alleviate this tension for all women? How does one's sense of agency and voice or lack thereof play into TMJ and a whole host of emotional-physical ailments? Unfortunately, the research done on most health issues for women are done on white women and *extrapolated* to women of color, just like for hundreds of years health research was done on men and *extrapolated* to women.[97]

We know what happens to a rubber band when it's stretched too tightly, it snaps. Many women I know are—or feel they are—holding so much, emotionally, physically, mentally or otherwise energetically, that they fear they could snap under the right circumstances. On a recent trip to the dentist, the hygienist who cleaned my teeth told me that in her 25ish years of experience she hasn't seen so many cases of TMJ. She said that although it primarily affects women, everyone is more stressed these days and that those who seem to be the most "chill" on the outside have the worst cases of teeth grinding and TMJ.

As an aside I was surprised to learn from this dental hygienist that brushing after meals can prevent diabetes. It made no sense to me; and because I didn't want to walk away thinking toothpaste was now being touted as a cure for diabetes, I asked for clarification. She said oral bacteria causes inflammation which leads the body to become diabetic. Removing bacteria reduces inflammation and reduces the risk of diabetes.

This explanation of bacteria-inflammation-diabetes is so clear and understandable it is motivating me to change my behavior. It is also no surprise that even dental bacteria can have such an impact on us when we are all so utterly inflamed about things that we don't even have the words to describe. At least it is a little refreshing to have root causes of problems explained clearly and shared freely!

---

[97] Alarmingly, it was not until 2016 that the National Institute of Health *allowed* gender specific studies to even be conducted.

Sunshine is nature's antibiotic. As a solar energy expert I think a lot about the sun, its life giving power both electrically and emotionally. Due south, the direction or azimuth of the sun, is 180° and I have adopted a 180° approach to problem-solving. I think of it as an intentional "about face" shift in perspective and I call it a Pivot Moment of Choice.

I did a little exercise in my mind with the difference between gaslighting (bad) and sunlighting (good) and here's what I found:

- Sunlighting is expansive love where gaslighting is explosive fear,
- Sunlighting is unstoppable cooperation where gaslighting is unrelenting competition,
- Sunlighting is rays in the days where gaslighting is sparks in the dark.

In that little exercise I *chose* to put sunlighting before gaslighting because it is more important and deserves a capital letter where gaslighting does not. The 180° view must be taken whenever we truly want to feel differently than we do in any particular moment.

Sometimes we need to feel the way we feel in order to accept the feeling. Feelings such as sadness, fear, or anger are not ones we are taught to welcome into our body and mind. But we cannot live without day or night, wake or sleep. We cannot have the tidal flows without the tidal ebbs. If we pursue only the flow, the day, the light and positive "masculine" things of the world, all that we ignore will come back to us as a boomerang reckoning. If we also embrace the ebbs, the dark, the scary "feminine," we can explore new and wonderfully expressive ways to find balance.

There is one other little theory I'd like to offer about 180° perspectives has to do with shame. I believe there is shame in all of our histories. And I believe the only way to heal from the shame we feel, for whatever reason we feel it, is to make peace with the truth lurking behind the shame—the instinct, the intuition, the human impulse that sparked before judgment was rendered.

Susannah Lipscomb, in a June 2020 piece in *History Today* titled *An Epidemic of Shame*[98], describes the shame inflicted on neighbors by neighbors in the 16th century Protestant church, a church community which took it upon themselves to act as "a moral tribunal." Lipscomb writes, "Guilt is easier to shrug off because you can apologise for what you've done; it's harder to apologise for who you are. Shame gnaws at self-esteem until it leaves only traces of flesh on the bone."

One aspect of shame, that has been or is being neutralized, has to do with the word slut. Slut-shaming by various names is a painful phenomenon that has been hurting women for centuries. There are many online dictionaries that define slut-shaming. I have two very different examples here to illustrate the emotion of sexuality at play:

The Geek Feminism wiki definition: "Slut shaming is the act of criticising a woman for her real or presumed sexual activity, or for behaving in ways that someone thinks are associated with her real or presumed sexual activity."

And an Urban Dictionary definition of slut-shaming (which to me reeks of defensive backhanded shaming): "Where it's wrong to call a girl a skank for showing off her tits, ass, and cameltoe in public; but a man is automatically pervert, a creep, or a potential rapist for getting a public erection after being aroused by previously mentioned skank."

Some "survivors" of such shaming have reclaimed the word slut as a positive expression of their sexiness and by doing so are neutralizing the pain; taking it out of the dark and putting some personality and sunshine on it like one might disinfect an old rug or a facemask. It is a step towards self-care. How might any shame you may be carrying be excavated, dusted off and warmed with a bit of kindness?

This line of thinking is an exercise in reframing the shame inflicted on others, particularly Karens, who are seen as "bad" and "other" and any host of shame-worthy labels. I am not at all saying to overlook or simply forgive a gross misconduct or even a present-day version of moral transgression. But is instigating the ignorant and perpetuating name calling the same as the adage, "an eye for an eye makes the whole world blind?" We can use our insights to facilitate kindness instead of

---

[98] https://www.historytoday.com/archive/making-history/epidemic-shame

fueling more emotional fire, especially if we have others by our side attempting the same. I'm leaning into a new mantra: anti-shame is my kink.

Ideas for shifting perspective may sound a bit preachy. And it might seem like I think this is easy to do; it is not. I absolutely struggle with trying to set context in difficult conversations so that my or another's feelings are protected. This is a daily practice that pays real dividends in the struggle to clarify one's words and in the experience of listening and being heard.

∞

White women who grew up like I did—with mothers whose response to questions was often, "because I said so," mothers who had to have towels folded a certain way, handkerchiefs ironed, food served piping hot, etc.—may have a fair amount of OCD, or obsessive-compulsive disorder. Needing to have to have the kitchen clean and check lists crossed off and otherwise "perfect" order before we can do something good and healthy for ourselves—like eat well, speak our Truth, go to the bathroom when we need to pee rather than hours later (the list goes on and on) may lead to extreme manifestations of stress related compulsions.

Suburban white women might have a very hard time undoing knowledge, redeveloping a voice, evaluating concerns, and understanding deeper truths about how we all inter-are because, generally, the role models have not necessarily been ones of courageous action sufficient to make lasting behavioral change. The formative matrilineal education of my demographic has largely been about how a woman should shut up, bide her time, wait for things to blow over, and put herself, her real needs, which are probably so foreign to her that everyone but her can see them, last.

Why is it so easy to name, disparage, and perhaps hate a Karen? Here are just a few answers to that question based on the research and reflection I have done so far:
1. Because what she does is wrong,

2. Because she has not stopped doing these bad things for many many generations and someone needs to take the heat for the pain and suffering being leveled on people of color across the world by white supremacy,

3. Because she has fought (or slept) her way up close to "power" (money, influence) and has not done enough good with it,

4. Because she has been programmed to hate others (and herself) and she has not yet been able to unprogram herself,

5. Because all of us have been programmed by white culture and have not yet been able to unprogram ourselves—and it is easier to hate someone else (at least subconsciously) than it is to hate ourselves.

Supposedly a Karen isn't someone who bites her tongue; she spews whatever racist, classist bullshit she thinks she sees and doesn't have a clue about filtering herself let alone really trying to understand the roots of why things are the way they are. This, my friend, is the crux of the whole meme issue. A meme speaks more loudly to the subconscious than the conscious mind.

Waking up is all about consciousness raising. Memes are shortcut marketing tools while consciousness raising is slow and steady cultivation. Memes are diabetic fast food while consciousness raising is heirloom seed small scale farming, daily harvesting and preserving, alongside family recipe meal making and eating, slowly, together.

Part Two:

Memoir

Emotional Reeducation

I've struggled most of my adult life to raise my consciousness and to say what I feel in any given moment because there are always more nuanced perspectives to consider, no matter what the situation. I grew up being told I was adorably naive, even into my twenties. Thankfully before I finished college, it became quite clear to me that no matter how much book smarts I packed into my head I could not slough off my ignorance or raise my consciousness by osmosis. I had inadequate role models for how to be in the world, how to think and feel, how to be considerate, how to assert myself calmly and respectfully, and, quite frankly, how to get pissed, advocate for something important, or even fully know how to discern the difference between true and false. So, naturally, by the time I got anywhere near clear about my own unfolding perspective in most conversations, the moment to speak had passed.

Are most middle-aged white women so different from me that they either feel completely clear-eyed about their racist and classist judgments and are in full use of their mental and emotional faculties when they act like Karens, or that they—even under the perception of extreme duress—remain so composed that none of the racist and classist cultural programming they received in their formative years escapes their lips? From the basis of all the middle-aged white women I know, I believe most of us are aware that we have unconscious biases and lack confidence that the networks we ascribe to can compassionately hold all the unprocessed ugly stuff we may want to unpack and understand.

I have also said a lot of ignorant and hurtful things over the years. I'm consciously trying to say fewer of these things. In fact, I'm not particularly motivated to write things for others to read in the current fearful climate of extreme scrutiny. While consciously trying to say fewer stupid things has obvious benefits, stifling emotions that are trying to form into opinions prevents understanding. Emotions need expression to be understood and the suppression seems to be leading many white middle-aged women to stop listening to their intuitions altogether, a rebound effect of the trolling mob surveillance state. If we are bullied to stop articulating our thoughts and feelings, we lose creative energy and we shut off and shut down. The first amendment of the U.S. Constitution, the right to free speech, is eroding as fast as the shorelines. This is not okay or healthy.

I have written millions of words in journals that are stacked in milk crates and drawers *because I couldn't find people to hold my words with me in the moments I most needed them held*—I couldn't imagine being safe enough to speak my truth. These journals are stale and the only reason I keep them is so that my children have a piece of me when I'm dead. When it came to my mother's words, I was left with nothing but a few pages in a lined notebook of anger my mother had never had the chance to express before she died two decades ago.

I've also been plagued by the desperation of wanting to be appreciated for the consideration I give to circumstances and then crushed by the cricket sounds, the lack of resonance, the nowhere-to-be-found tuning forks, the nonexistent echo to my calls—online and off. I've self-published memoir and poetry, and blogs that simply make me feel like I have put the creative energy that flows through me somewhere more respectable than in a drawer of an old desk. I've started four businesses based on needs seen and felt in the community; one was an energy efficiency training center for women coming out of correctional facilities that my business partner has been holding years after I got too depleted energetically and financially. My desire is to connect with others who are looking at the world in a similar way, to compare notes and expand our collective understanding. Maybe "the marketplace" just isn't that space?

Writing and starting businesses and posting on social media are all in the realm of a type of privilege that can always benefit from more scrutiny. The time is coming for the nervous chihuahua-like noise on social media to die down so that truth and elegance can emerge. This desperation in me and others is not going to dissolve by itself. There is so much work to do if Americans are to undo the damage brought to our collective psyches over centuries of emotional gaslighting of an unsuspecting public.

When I first thought about the Karen phenomenon, of being named alongside a despicable meme, the first thing that came up for me was a feeling of "WTF!" Then I proceeded to deny it was a thing, then I proceeded to get defensive, then I ignored it for a while, then I sat with it staring me down until it threatened to become a source of shame, which is when I started writing because I am "all full up" with sources of shame and I refuse, at least intend to refuse, to not actively block any and all new sources of shame in my life.

This chapter on emotional reeducation is intended to hold the emotional energy needed to go **Beyond Karen**, beyond the reactive, explosive emotions that rise up within us unexpectedly as human beings often ill-equipped or unpracticed in emotional management; it expands upon many ideas peppered throughout this book, like "tone down the foul and tune into the gentle," and it is an extension of the earlier chapter called Rise and Fall.

Watching the breath rise and fall is the most effective way to create the conditions in one's body and mind for breaking apart and unpacking old notions and making space for new learning and understanding. In addition to the micro and macro agreements from that chapter, I'd like to offer here a few ways in which we can make space for healing— because if you're not hurting you are less likely to hurt others.

The first suggestion of course is breathing deeply before responding to anything or anyone that evokes strong emotion. The rest I will list:

- Driving slower and leaving more car lengths between you and the vehicle in front of you. And feeling/sending positive energy toward the person(s) in the vehicle that may be too close behind you—they are obviously unable to enjoy spaciousness at the moment.
- Appreciating your feet and the earth with each step as you walk.
- Giving thanks for the miracle of water with each sip you drink (this is my favorite).

- Stretching as many parts of the body as possible to bring flexibility into her joints and tight spaces.

- Spending time each day (and through each stressful moment) in a meditative, restorative state of mind—to find the roots or kernels of your stressors—and then breathing patiently as additional nuances or colors of perspective flow into your mind and heart.

- Lowering the head below the heart (i.e. touching your toes or hanging your head off the bed, even hanging upside down) to ease into these last two ways of making space.

- Making the choice to view all time as your time—you've chosen to be doing whatever it is you are doing.

- Setting the intention to have loving thoughts, words, feelings, and actions with everyone you interact with, including the strangers you pass by (it is a blessing to be in each other's presence during this pandemic).

You know how once you set an intention for something to grow in your life, random conversations seem to take on a very specific new flavor? As I grow my desire to understand this Karen thing, I notice eerily related random things people say to me, like these:

FIRST EXAMPLE: *A 70sish stranger offering an opinion about dogs being able to run free according to their nature,* "Oh, those women are all a bunch of Karens about having dogs on leashes." Me, "Oh really, how so?" *Stranger,* "I just learned about Karens two months ago on Tik Tok and now I see that they're everywhere."

SECOND EXAMPLE: *Older woman walking a dog that Rosie nearly pulled me across the street to meet, (the only person I've met while walking Rosie who asked me my name instead of my dog's name) says,* "Oh wow, I'm Karen too. There were so few of us when I was a kid and now look what's happened to our name." I proceeded to tell her about this book, and she proceeded to tell me the nutshell version of her professional history of "catfighting" with women unable and unwilling to see the effects of the patriarchy in education.

It is utterly inspiring to notice how often we are able to dive deeply into the heart of the pain we hold with a complete stranger. It's a warp speed healing opportunity. And it is the polar opposite of the nuclear reaction that can also happen between strangers or family members when we are suddenly triggered into that same state of a cracked open heart. The random chat feels like we are behind the wheel of our healing opportunity; the sudden explosion feels like a train conductor has flipped over our car and we are skidding 100 miles per hour on our face.

∞

Maybe those who filter all their words and thoughts with a fine-toothed comb so that nothing they say will offend anyone are the epitome of communication perfection and everyone else attempting to be uber politically correct at least in public are the toned-down version. I hope not. To me, communication only approaches perfection as it agrees to messy, chaotic, unpredictable, and patient honesty. To varying degrees, verbal filters used in communications with others can be likened to compassion.

On the surface it would seem that the solution to Karening is simple—just be compassionate and kind. But as we speak, act, and even think in a way that brings our heart forward, engages our mind as fully and deeply as we are able, and even considers the spiritual dimensions of words, actions, and thoughts, not just with regards to others but also to ourselves, we begin to see that kindness and compassion is no simple feat.

Add to this personal growth practice our experiences (or lack thereof) with politics, or our societal rules of engagement, and the complexity of being compassionate becomes exponential, quantum. Fortunately Karen gives us all a frame of reference for reflecting on the art of being together, even if the examples available are limited to the public domain. On the surface, Karen is far from perfect; under the surface Karen has been striving for perfection her whole life.

The idea of perfection is intriguing—aspirational yet toxic, the north star guiding a vision yet creating countless blind spots along the journey. Perfection is one of those weaknesses cloaked as a strength, like the ideal interview "I am a perfectionist" response to "tell me about one of your weaknesses." To say we are struggling to overcome being a perfectionist is to get a capitalist salivating; Lord knows the financially attractive extractive value of a perfectionist who will work harder and longer at a thing for the free and primary payoff of their own endorphins. What a deal!

I grew up with a general disgruntled or discontented sense that one should strive for perfection, which in some way I "blame" on my mother for modeling this and in another way I blame on America for actively perpetuating the fallacy of perfection for profit. I can remember stumbling upon an article about perfection, probably in Ode Magazine (now called the Intelligent Optimist), the first subscription I ever *invested* in monthly. The article was lauding a practice of disavowing Perfection with a capital P.

If I could wave a magic wand or rub a genie lamp and get just one wish, it would be for all humans to accept themselves and each other for who they are. Of course this is complicated because we all think we are who we are purporting to be in any moment, even as we are seeking perfection.

Perhaps the phenomenon of young women physically altering their bodies to look as much like a barbie doll as possible (like the photo of real women here) and the bizarre ceremonies of marrying oneself were signs that we have taken the notion of perfection a bit too far. The "perfect" partner, job, body, dog, idea will never be "enough."

Disavowing perfection sounds like a noble, 180° turn from the obsessive-compulsive behaviors that are keeping many white people believing that they're holding their shit together independent of all the other forces of life up or down stream. And to help us let go of perfection there is even an art of imperfection that has been developed by the Japanese called wabi-sabi. A friend mentioned wabi-sabi to me when I broke my favorite piece of pottery my son had made in school. She said one practice of this art of imperfection is to emphasize cracks in pottery by gluing them back together with gold paint. In a blog called randomwire.com I found this lovely definition about the essence of natural, unpretentious perspective:

> [W]abi-sabi is not an intrinsic property of things, but an "event", or state of mind. In other words, the beauty of wabi-sabi "happens", it does not reside in objects or environments directly.

The effects of needing things to be perfect are serious. When a young white boy (especially from my father's generation) is raised to believe he is the center of the universe, that he can and should have everything he desires, that he will be successful no matter what, and that others (women) will take care of his basic needs like keeping the house clean and making meals, he is likely to grow up with a twisted sense of reality. Such a boy will likely block out all aspects of reality that do not conform to his sense of self and sense of the world, which could very well create social and emotional imbalance or narcissistic psychosis and a ripple of consequences to his less than mindful actions.

Reflecting on narcissism a while brings to me the sense that it may also be a natural boomerang or whiplash kind of response during the initial stages of self-care. If one (say a woman growing up in the 80s or 90s) learns that their voice is less important than the others' around them (say all men), they will be so other directed, other-oriented, that their self-awareness and genuine empathy may atrophy. But if another thing such a one learns is that they are expected to care deeply about all others (up to a point—and that point is clearly defined to them as they get labeled "hysterical"), the expression of caring may become mechanistic, performative, and artificial. As one programmed thusly begins to unpack these learnings, they will need to direct and reorient a disproportionate amount of their energy to the self so that the unlearning and relearning can be effective, meaningful, and lasting.

If this process of self-care looks, feels, and acts like narcissism, those friends, family members, and coworkers affected may have emotional reactions. Such reactions can likely include anger about the rebalancing of chores, tasks, and other responsibilities newly landing in their laps, on their plates, etc. Reactions can also include jealousy, which is a mix of anger and fear, over the perception that they themselves don't have the necessary conviction or chutzpah to pull off the same degree of self-care.

A quick look at trending book titles about perfection on Audible made me chuckle as I compared what I found with the type of books that trended in the 90s. After I had graduated and was getting my career going, the book titles of the day were all about how to succeed, be successful (i.e. put yourself in a box); today there are numerous books about failing, including "Failing Up" and "Failure is an Option," along with topics like, "How to Do Nothing," "Minor Feelings," "Unf**k Your Brain." Are these 90s and 2020 examples just getting to the same message with slightly different branding strategies?

∞

As I began writing the chapter about Enough, in late May 2020, my lovely, self-assured son, with political interests so vastly different than mine that we have to take great care to be respectful of each other, came home concerned about both a tick in his head and a meme that his Army-graduating friend was in hot water about. I was so grateful for this unexpected quality time with him. The tick was an easy fix; the meme was a potential landmine he was trying to help his friend navigate around as safely as possible.

His friend had shared a post about the looting that was going on at Target stores (did anyone notice the irony of the bullseye logo being "target"ed?). As a result, some acquaintances were throwing hate and my son Nathan wanted advice about the long reply he drafted in his head that would ultimately ask everyone to just be kind to each other. My advice was that his friend made a choice by sharing this post and that he might want to listen to the feedback he was getting, and that while the reply in his head was a good one, it might not be particularly helpful. But if his friend was getting hate for simply having gone into the Army for an education and deciding that he wanted to be a police officer, then yes, step in to defend your friend with kindness.

My son and I have had more red-hot angry arguments and disagreements than I could have ever imagined could be healthy. It's not healthy for my husband or daughter to witness, but it is healthy for the two of us because our differences challenge us to love each other better. When he got really chatty about things that were pulling my attention too far away from my heart's focus of writing this book, I gently told him so. Our conversation lasted maybe an hour and kept going well beyond my attempt to redirect it. At one point I shared the title I had in mind for this book, **Beyond Karen**. He had first heard "beyond caring" and I remarked that there could be a place for that energy in the book. But then he laughed, having assumed that his cool but too-old-to-be-that-cool mother wasn't aware of Karen the Meme. This led us to the subject of internet desperation and how even celebrities are trying to capitalize on the media feeding frenzy and posting YouTube videos of the brokenheartedness in Minneapolis, in a way that seemed self-serving. The fact that he and I could agree about the vacuousness of social media, despite its unparalleled potential for connecting, uniting, and bridging divides, was a real moment of growing love for each other which hopefully keeps rippling out far and wide.

Honestly, the experience of Nathan and I butting heads for so long, with the clearly defined edges or boundaries we hold for ourselves, has given both of us valuable opportunities to refine our speech. This has, over the years, made both of us formidable debaters, if only with each other. We all seem to have the opportunity for this kind of edgy growth by virtue of the significant differences of opinion we can find within our families. It is almost a de facto design of the family unit to have edginess, largely political, that allows our spirits to continue to grow.

A tense familial relationship will wear a person out, as this mother-son one has at times done to both of us. This is my child who told me at age three that he chose me to be his mommy, the one whose nighttime bedroom smelled like cookies and apple juice for years. Yet even with the critical support beams of love we have as mother and child, we often bite our tongues or walk away feeling unheard and unappreciated by each other. We name what's up and this keeps our hearts warm towards each other.

∞

At roughly the same hour that a colleague had indirectly called me out as an armchair quarterback (not his words) for sharing a MoveOn resource to our mostly white company email thread where we were discussing our Black Lives Matter sign out front and the anti-racist work we all want and need to do, my son told me that his Black best friend has asked all his white friends to tell their white friends to stop using the #BlackLivesMatter hashtag. It wasn't up for appropriation.

It is tempting for me to not pause here and attempt to feel into what people of color are going through. It is tempting for me to instead state ways in which I feel in solidarity with this awesome, awe inspiring movement of people who know how to show up for each other. But I don't and I can't feel what people of color are going through. Even though my husband identifies as a person of color, I have had far too few heart experiences with politically active people of color; and solidarity is not achieved "in theory."

I get some of it. I get the distrust and disappointment with people who are just riding the latest trend to act woke or savvy or cool, acting period. I get the frustration with others' lame too-late-ness. And I was not among a lot of my white community members joining in the local protests those first weeks. I was on the front lines protesting the murder of Eric Garner in July 2014 with the first wave of BLM protests through the regional mall, through the local Walmart. But I felt then, as I do still, like an outsider in this movement; and all I can do is keep educating myself and showing up as I am able.

Here is the mission of the Movement for Black Lives:

- We believe that prisons, police and all other institutions that inflict violence on Black people must be abolished and replaced by institutions that value and affirm the flourishing of Black lives.

- We believe in centering the experiences and leadership of the most marginalized Black people, including but not limited to those who are trans and queer, women and femmes, currently and formerly incarcerated, immigrants, disabled, working class, and poor.
- We believe in transformation and a radical realignment of power:

> The current systems we live inside of need to be radically transformed, which includes a realignment of global power. We are creating a proactive, movement-based vision instead of a reactionary one.

I absolutely love the phrase "radical realignment of power." Wherever a painful imbalance of power exists, compassionate and lengthy conversations need to happen, followed by genuine commitment to make behavioral, systemic, lasting change.

The colleague I mentioned above did something telling. Publicly he made it known that he didn't think much of my resource but privately he thanked me for sharing it and other resources I'd included. To me, he instinctively defended his intention not to dismiss me, to which I said that such public dismissiveness was such a regular and painful thing for me that even the private clarification was not enough to help me feel resolved. But then, within one minute, he sent an apology-ish message to the social email address, *without connecting with me first*, and then hours later sent an email to me individually suggesting we talk it out…

Was I being a Karen by sharing too many resources? Should I have understood that the thread was only about putting a BLM sign out front and a space for personal sharing? Would it have been more "appropriate" had I only shared 1 or 2 article *links with no content* shared very carefully so as to not seem *aggressive*? Was he, a colleague I genuinely respect, trust, and like, being a Karen? Is every insensitive thing someone says or does getting named Karen?

As I've said earlier, I believe a "Karen" is someone who is acting like a "know it all" and pushing her opinions on others with little regard for what others think, feel, or have to contribute about a topic or situation. Sharing resources in order to get props or some kind of "aren't you well informed, thank you for enlightening me" response is a white-mind competitive thing to do. And this competitive behavior has its roots in jockeying for positions of privilege in all facets of life.

It is hard to keep coming back after others' acts of insensitivity (bold or subtle), to keep rising up after the small interpersonal things like this email thread or the large meta struggles in America. I've always sought dialogue to resolve conflicts however small and still advocate for "talking feelings out" with anyone, even after an ignorant word or deed causes pain; but it gets harder and harder as the raw unhealed edges around the wounds that have scarred over continue to get poked with sharp objects.

A week prior to the BLM considerations flowing through my workplace I had reached out to my chief of police (at the time I was his "boss" as the chair of my town's select board). I asked him to post a response to his Facebook page about 75 things white people can do, given that our town is predominantly white (also one of the links I'd shared at work). He said he was inclined to wait until the investigation was over. He then posted something predigested from the state police. I interviewed him again in person and he said that he (and the state police) was of the opinion that it would all "blow over" after the election...

I am looking for those among us who are stretching. I seek to stay as flexible as possible and help others who want to be flexible in body and mind. And yet even among younger groups, like the defund the police group I joined, the bridge building between paradigms of young and old can seem, at this moment, as difficult as the bridge building efforts between Black and white or Republican and Democrat.

Rosie the Riveter

My dog Rosie (the Riveter) is perfect in the way that the canine species can be so effortlessly under the right conditions. She is a tawny and brawny, an affectionate hound dog about seven months old as I write. She sits, lays down, gives high fives and shakes paw. She has quadrupled in size in the past four months but is not afraid to roll over for a dog with a Napoleon complex. She barks firmly to intimidate just a little when a stranger comes into the yard, but then jumps on them like they're best friends when she sees we are comfortable with them. And she is great with children and other dogs.

In fact, she is so great with other dogs that she reads them in relation to her own overjoyed energy and modulates herself accordingly. If we walk by an older, slower dog who still has a good amount of pep, she seems to draw it out of them. If she meets an energetic dog with a different energy or play style, she approaches as cautiously as a puppy is able and will sit or let herself be sniffed first. If we walk by another puppy who has the same play style, they could romp and roll all day if I let her; I know this to be true because her "niece" Luna and she have now shared a few weekends together and this is what they do nonstop.

Rosie is also very sensitive. She was "diagnosed" as having special needs by the amazing shelter where she arrived with her 12 siblings and her mother Domino. The last to be adopted, we were thrilled to bring her home because we knew we were up to the challenge. Rosie had nightmares, presumably from a combination of traumas encountered in her first two months of life, from being unwanted, from being stomped on by so many siblings and having to fight for sustenance, and from traveling across the United States. She has chewed up all of our sofa pillows—right through the zipper. She has chewed up all my favorite sandals and one shoe of each of my husband's flip flops. She definitely has a mind of her own. Instead of coming when we called her, during her first few months with us, it quickly became clear to me that she was choosing to come only if what she was doing was less exciting than the prospects of getting a snack, which we are still inconsistent about.

When my son Nathan and I brought her home the first day, it was all we could do without any calming substance like CBD oil (made from cannabis) to soothe her wild nerves all the way home. The highway minutes were especially distressing to her as the noise of loud radios during traffic and the visceral swoosh and roar of big trucks rolling past shook both the car and her fragile energy. That night I lay on the floor with her for hours telling her she was okay. She couldn't even bear to be held and hated the little strands of my hair that touched her face or her ears. We are learning to be much more consistent with Rosie, recognizing that her wellbeing requires us to listen and not think we know before we know.

What does Rosie have to do with Karen? To me, Rosie is the polar opposite of Karen, the Anti-Karen. Rosie represents equal rights for women, she's a real badass in all the good ways, she has a name that could transcend race but is hard working class, not privileged and not ignorant about the trials and tribulations of the world. And my Rosie has gobs of patience and would probably tolerate being dressed up like some of the #Karen pets, once, but then she would be like nah, ain't happening again.

Rosie was named Rosie for a number of reasons. I didn't steamroll my son about the name like I had done with our last dog Shaggy. Thirteen years ago, as a child Nathan wanted Shaggy to be named Snowball, and Shaggy was a happy-medium compromise that didn't make sense to him at the time. In his twenties Nathan and I were able to have an "adult" conversation about the benefits of various names. I had put in an application for another dog named Rosie at a different rescue, but they had already taken an application for her and gave her to another family. I wasn't heartbroken despite having made fast friends with this Rosie, but the name felt right to me and was a solid choice that Nathan went back and forth with for a bit until we settled on it together.

As a feminist I loved the connection to Rosie the Riveter (and I have learned that the original Rosie the Riveter's name is Rosinda Walker, which is a very cool name). Rosie is also easy to personalize for others; my father-in-law calls her Rosa, and my mother-in-law (Mãe) calls her Rose. My husband Paul calls her Rosita and occasionally builds up her name with a singsong rhyme he learned from his mother: Rosita Caganita Carapão Sardinha Frita (which means little shit mackerel fried sardine). My daughter Sabrina calls her Rosie Posie or Baby Ro, and Nathan calls her Rosie Girl or Baby Girl. And as perfect as Rosie is, she will never be "enough" to heal the pain and loss we all endured last season after the sudden death of our beloved Shaggy. And that is okay.

Rosie is also a perfect meme name, unlike Karen. But maybe Karen is also the perfect meme for a change on the level of Rosie the Riveter, but from the opposite, unenviable direction, the road less traveled. If the people being labeled Karen, as a direct result of reprehensible behavior, get a wakeup call and take a hard look in the mirror, seek out information, get educated about systemic oppression, come to appreciate the non-hysterical, measured responsiveness that many, particularly women and men of color, have learned to compose themselves with when under emotional duress *as a survival strategy*, then Karen could portend epic change on a scale similar to Rosie.

I hope and believe that Rosie feels respected for the formidable queen she is. She sits on the sofa nearly as tall as us and, like hopefully all healthy dogs, has not one apologetic bone in her body. She cares and demonstrates her care by being affectionate, by corralling the wayward child or puppy, and by looking straight into your eyes right to your soul.

Rosie and I often explore the local trails together. On walks with Rosie, I have to listen and redirect a lot. Pulling her away from every flying insect that enters our path is not the same as letting her inhale a deeply aromatic scent that another animal left for her, but it might look the same.

"Parenting" our family pet has come to feel like an art that doubles as giving advice or recognition that I might need myself. When I tell her to settle down, maybe it's me that needs to settle down. Seems so basic in theory but in that moment when I'm feeling impatient the lesson is elusive. And then again when I'm watching her stare at a fly for five minutes impressed with her patience and focus, maybe it's my own capacity to be patient that could use recognition.

Rosie doesn't like wearing her harness on walks, or at least she doesn't like the moment when I put it on her. But she is such a smart dog that I like to think she feels like wearing her harness is like having a job, a purpose. She often whines even when she is well fed, not thirsty, and fully engaged, even out in the forest with captivating scents to explore. Guiding her and as needed, reining her in, reminds me to be more satisfied with life as it is, not as I wish it to be. It's fascinating to think about the parallels between her and me and I stay curious about what that could be so that I stay curious about what it is in myself and, at least in theory, others.

To put a finer point on the **Beyond Karen** lessons I am learning from Rosie I will give an example of playing with toys. I know this to be true with most dogs, that when you push a dog or their toys away, they instinctively come back for more. They, especially puppies, are geared for play (she is playing with and rolling around on a dead fly as "we speak"). What happens if we try to integrate this play-oriented "leadership" into our own lives? I can think about many times when I have felt that I or my toys (ideas) have been pushed away by someone. What if I reframe that to be an invitation to play? It could rally my playful side and help the potential emotional pain to fall away. At the very least it can put me back in the driver's seat of something I feel dispirited about.

Curiosity is that magical ingredient in any communication that separates a positive conversational experience (and I argue that Rosie and I do converse) from a rote and transactional one. Curiosity is often described as the key to keeping a marriage healthy and it is that essence that sparks creative ideas which give rise to art and innovation.

I believe curiosity traverses life in the direction of a bell curve. Imagining a simple X - Y graph, at the beginning, flat start of the bell curve you have apathy or absence of knowledge, then you arc upwards as curiosity colors your world view and your respond to it with various actions, but then as you try to respond to more and more stimuli, whether it is more of life's beauty or life's ugly, the experience of overwhelm closes the spigot of curiosity so that the far end of the bell curve, the end that flattens out again, is frenzy leading to apathy and absence of awareness and knowledge.

Curiosity is one of those highs we can get from life—for free. And just about anything can tempt us to dive in with the hopes of learning something new, understanding something more thoroughly, or experiencing something different and "better." For Rosie, the smell of another dog's urine gets her every time. For me, another connection or anecdote about achieving societal emotional wellness gets me hooked.

Over the years, these curiosity detours have felt like taking the "high road" or the "road less traveled." Lately I find more reasons to choose *not* to do a thing. I have a low diet of media, a form of fasting, and I indulge in, say, ice cream in small but delicious quantities less frequently than I used to (because it clearly doesn't love me as much as I love it). Choosing not to be enticed by something sensational like hyped up media may be to use the same "mental muscle" it takes to "harness" anger from, say, road rage.

Robert Frost, a famous poet and long-ago professor from Amherst College, has a 47-mile trail in his name that traverses a bit less than half of the Metacomet-Monadnock trail in Massachusetts. This is where he found inspiration for his famous poem The Road Not Taken, a poem which has helped countless people appreciate the power of intentionally choosing how to perceive our choices in life. The Road Less Traveled.

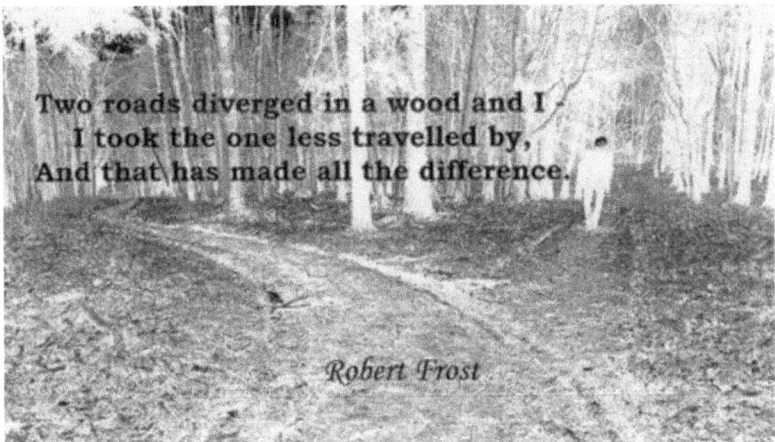

Two roads diverged in a wood and I -
I took the one less travelled by,
And that has made all the difference.

Robert Frost

I shall be telling this with a sigh
Somewhere ages and ages hence:
Two roads diverged in a wood, and I

I took the one less traveled by,
And that has made all the difference.

The appreciation of the significance of Name—of being able to name a trail, a bridge, a stadium, a street—whose name achieves significance, as well as the refusal to tolerate name-calling, is what I hope the world is waking up to for real right now. Ultimately, we may be able to shift toward a way of being that honors Name at an individual level but not at a commercial level or a manipulative and emotionally destructive level. In thinking about how big this topic is, how it personally affects everyone as we have all been called names, some have left deep scars, I again turn to the way Rosie responds to her name and our tones of voice, like all dogs, perhaps like all mammalian nature. When we call her in a pleasant tone, she comes to us with tail wagging. When we approach her too quickly to say good morning or call her name with any intensity in our voice, she puts her ears back as if to cover them as she might when a big scary truck is driving by us on a walk.

∞

On a meta level, our name is what our life stands for; all that we have aspired to and achieved, how we have interacted with others, and the ways in which we demonstrated our values. If we are so lucky as to have value in our name at the time of our death, and as a legacy beyond death, we were fortunate, our lives were lived well and our efforts successful.

I think about the power of a particular name, like the complex legacy of George Floyd, to hold the promise of change and growth, the capacity to grow love. There are George's family members and friends who have a direct appreciation of how George's life and name can hold this legacy. There are also countless strangers observing the unfolding of his legacy with an indirect appreciation; for me, watching George's brother Philonese give testimony about being robbed of the opportunity to have any kind of closure with him before he was murdered (all the while calling the white cop "Sir"), gave me a visceral appreciation. It was impossible to not lose composure. His brother's testimony is the epitome of grace, like it seems George himself was. George Floyd's name is catalyzing great change.

In the process of the riotous momentum following George's death, the one name ready to contain it all, Black Lives Matter, and the hashtag

#BLM, got saturated, perhaps watered down with overuse, making the pulse of authenticity harder for organizers to keep. Many purport that the name Black needs to be capitalized in order for white people to notice Black men and women standing up tall together.

Phrases are a whole level different, but after writing the phrase "keep the pulse" I think of the phrase "keep the peace" that is supposed to be synonymous with policing… more on that stress and the need to unpack power and authority in America later.

∞

Back to Rosie. It might be strange to think of a dog as having been diagnosed as having special needs. I have had a pet dog most of my life and had one dog with epilepsy who had to be put down after a few wonderful years with him (I was told he was brought to a farm and no matter how many times I disbelieved my father he never went back on his story). So when the rescue informed us of Rosie's diagnosis my reaction was less of concern, and more, "okay sure, whatever you say." But the world grows more subtle and sensitive every day and we are all subject to it, even our pets. Did you know there are dozens of anti-anxiety medications for dogs? The American Kennel Club recommends prevention and consultations with veterinarians and CBD oil.

In Rosie's training classes we played a bingo game which had things on it to check off to support their development and behavioral adjustments like meeting other animals, getting wet, walking in public, hearing airplanes, big trucks and fireworks. We had crossed off just about every square on the board except the fireworks … and then went to visit family for the fourth of July weekend. We stayed in a camper and did a rather poor job of social distancing, especially given the fact that we spent a lot of time on my sister's boyfriend's boat. Rosie's best friend Luna was with us when we rode out to the middle of the pond for the fireworks; Luna had no issue with the fireworks, Rosie seemed about to explode right along with them.

We got situated pretty close to the barge where the fireworks were going to be set off and it's hard to know if this was ultimately better for her or worse, the point is that her support community was there for her.

She's incredibly curious so it's likely that being able to make the connection between the launch and the noise and the mind-blowing colorful sparks in the sky was helpful. But immediately on the first launch she strained as hard as she could against her harness and the leash Paul and I had secured. Sabrina had read about dogs' tendency to bolt around fireworks and suggested we prepare for that possibility as she was with Luna. Luna was half asleep while it was all Paul and I could do to hold Rosie close and comfort her. The story we're telling ourselves is that it was best for her to experience this as a puppy so she'll be prepared and less agitated if she hears fireworks in the future.

Exposing children (and pets perhaps) to a lot of different things allows them to get a broader sense of the world as they grow up, which is part of the narrative about privilege in the world. If every child had similar opportunities to experiment with sports, music, arts, education in general, the world would be a better place. Rosie may have more opportunity to get a sense of the world than some children may get—although does being on a motorboat and watching fireworks give one a "sense" of the world? Maybe an explosive sense of a hyped-up world.

∞

As my life has become more purposeful, more on purpose, it has also become softer, easier, more privileged, and perhaps more fragile. Is this White Privilege? *White Fragility?* I'm not entirely sure and would like to talk about this, particularly the class aspect of what privilege is or is not, in a skillfully facilitated, diversely represented community. I have been able to work hard *and* have some sense of achievement alongside all the failures where others who are not white may have had to work even harder than me to have, perhaps, a lessened sense of achievement. And when I think about how *small* my sense of achievement is despite all the opportunities I have had and pursued; I cringe with sympathetic sorrow.

I think soft and easy is one definition of privilege and that we all could claim and pursue this privilege in our present life; the privilege of being intentional with each other, of deeply listening to and witnessing the thoughts and feelings emerge from whomever we are with, of setting boundaries that may be necessary when we feel we are being talked at and not treated with the level of respect we desire for ourselves, the privilege of breathing in the fresh air outside, as we are able. These may be the only privileges we can control. And I suspect that, categorically, white people are the last to understand the privilege of being intentional.

On the flip side, when life becomes a bit too soft, when access to food, to travel, to wealth and material luxuries is entirely easy and predictable, it is time to up the effort to serve, to stretch out of the comfort zone and experience other less fortunate realities.

Most of my time sheltering in place is with Rosie. She is the being I get to communicate with. And training Rosie is about listening. One example is the sometimes ordeal of putting her safely in the car for a ride. She wears a harness to keep her feeling secure and if she gets in the car and sits down, all is well. Half the time she just stands there which is annoying. I could think, "Why is she not sitting, she is resisting the routine she knows so well," which would get me frustrated. Or I could think, "Maybe each time she gets in the car is a brand new experience and she won't sit until I demonstrate patience and respect her ability to know when it's okay for her to sit." This would lead me to observe before instructing.

In the second scenario I don't give her more "credit" for knowing the drill than she "deserves" or get myself agitated. Instead, I feel curious and open hearted, which then makes her feel safe enough to sit and get seat belted. Even though a seatbelt gives her the sense of security she needs to be in a fast-moving vehicle, it may be a very unnatural thing for a dog!

Another example of patiently observing Rosie versus short-sighted reacting—the behavior modification most needed by Karens at this moment—has to do with her whining. I've noticed that she sometimes whines at the moments when I would *assume* would be moments of pure happiness for her, like while we are on a walk on a lovely day. I could think, "Geez, Rosie, *what is wrong with you*, why are you acting like a 'spoiled brat' (the phrase I often heard as a child)" which would be mean, rude and insensitive. Or I could think "Whoa, it has been a couple of weeks since Rosie has played with another of her species, she seems to be smelling the pee of other dogs on the crabgrass, rocks, plantain and poison ivy, maybe she is whining because she really needs to be with other dogs, after all, she was one of 13 siblings and may have an urgent need for canine touch that human touch can't satisfy."

What a different and intentional thought process! Here again is another lesson for me, through Rosie, in how to pause enough in relation to others to redirect habitual reactions toward patient observations.

And with COVID-19 keeping us apart, we are all hurting on some level, wanting to shake hands and hug all the people we now see primarily on our computer screens, unable to be by the side of our loved ones especially at end of life. This is no small thing.

The need for affiliation and connection is underneath most of the values-based compromises we make. We humans are nice people who sometimes do really not nice things and then justify ourselves with conscious and subconscious rationalizations to ourselves and to those with whom we have an established affinity.

Rosie—and each dog loving their human unconditionally—offers a great non-human example of how to go **Beyond Karen**. She is full of surprises and has an impressive, enviable, and steady disposition for fairness. Fairness may be a strange attribute to ascribe to a dog, but, fully aware that I am anthropomorphizing, this is what I see in her.

My American Dream

After all the data and science that proves this or that, the defensible positioning and the legal battles… After all the math… After all the he-said-she-said emotional exhaustion one encounters trying to share knowledge with others (and we all know how it feels to be in those conversations) … After the dust settles after these bombs explode—in our own bodies and minds, not just the shit storms and fires and battles… We get up. All the Karens who have been publicly shamed, and all the righteously angry doing the shaming, particularly over the Memorial Day to Independence Day 2020 period that this book explores and beyond, must eventually stand up with a new and distilled story.

Perspective comes more clearly into focus after major events, which is why the idiom "hindsight is 20-20" rings true. I believe that the reason this Memorial Day to Independence Day period was so volatile is because America has still not reckoned with its past, and these holidays are what punctuate its incomplete, distorted history. It is time for America to face a few hard truths about the Dream its governance has sold to its citizens and the rest of the world, about the media machinations and the market manipulations that have duped the innocent, about the fallacy of growth—as if the perfectly packaged greed of exponential returns could be anything but self-destructive, and about the resulting impact to every facet of nature and life as we know it.

How do we wake up from the dream? We may need to be doused with cold water, but the process is about understanding the forces at work and unpacking—separating out the unwanted effects these forces have had on our beliefs, values, and outlook on life.

To understand the root of the American Dream we go to Wall Street. And for a bit of history post-2008 market crash, this straightforward Guardian article[99] offers perspective. Why did throngs of people protest and "Occupy" Wall Street (OWS) in 2011?[100] Because enough people, a surge of the middle class, including most major unions, had had enough of the games, the lies, the corporate influence on policy, and the devastating economic and social inequality impacts from these policies and procedures including the $475 Billion Troubled Assets Relief Program (TARP), aka big bank bailout (which was necessary due to severe fiscal irresponsibility, aka greed). Many high-profile figures took supportive positions or principally supportive ones. President Obama weighed in[101], House Speaker Pelosi weighed in[102], and Mitt Romney called OWS "class warfare." But even if the OWS goals were not clear, the Occupy message, "We Are the 99%" certainly was.

In *Biographies of Hegemony: The Culture of Smartness and the Recruitment and Construction of Investment Bankers*, Karen Zouwen Ho writes:

"The 'culture of smartness' is central to understanding Wall Street's financial agency, how investment bankers are personally and institutionally empowered to enact their worldviews, export their practices, and serve as models for far-reaching socioeconomic change. On Wall Street, 'smartness' means much more than individual intelligence; it conveys a naturalized and generic sense of 'impressiveness,' of elite, pinnacle status and expertise, which is used to signify, even prove, investment bankers' worthiness as advisors to corporate America and leaders of the global financial markets. To be considered 'smart' on Wall Street is to be implicated in a web of situated practices and ideologies, co-produced through the interactions of multiple institutions, processes, and American culture at large, which

[99] https://www.theguardian.com/business/2013/dec/09/finance-gambling-volcker-rule-banks-lottery
[100] https://en.wikipedia.org/wiki/Occupy_Wall_Street
[101] https://web.archive.org/web/20130515113324/http://www.businessweek.com/ap/financialnews/D9Q6U0O83.htm
[102] https://web.archive.org/web/20140415123921/https://abcnews.go.com/Politics/pelosi-supports-occupy-wall-street-movement/story?id=14696893

confer authority and legitimacy on high finance and contribute to the sector's vast influence. *The culture of smartness is not simply a quality of Wall Street, but a currency, a driving force productive of both profit accumulation and global prowess."*

This is a lot to think about; diving deeply into and emerging out of the cultural constructs of capitalism is exceedingly complex. And yet, as someone who got drunk on the market Kool-Aid, Zouwen's words are like a balm to my soul, even only finding them all these years later.

And waking up to any deeper truths about the American Dream is hard, excruciating if done alone. Sometimes even when you think you are super clear-eyed about a thing, you might have only one eye open. Sometimes you might feel really focused but you're only using one sense impression, one sensory organ. Sometimes you can only see the clean polished streets in a city, like New York, but not smell the rats behind the scenes.

My big going it alone story is trying to infiltrate the banking world to make change from within. I did this for over six years in as many banks (all three banks I worked at had a major merger while I was there). Twice I took long and carefully researched socially responsible banking proposals to the respective chairman of the board and twice I was brushed aside, after careful consideration and obligatory compliments. With the first experience I had already put in my resignation knowing how it would turn out given how many times the meeting was rescheduled. With the second I was able to rebound by shifting gears to plan and host a regional socially responsible investing retreat paid for in part by that bank.

But this story begins in the mid 1990s when I attended formative meetings for the Business Alliance of Local Living Economies, now called Common Future and a member of the New Economy Coalition. I had just graduated with a Master of Business Administration degree and was full of piss and vinegar in the throes of a man's world. I was proud of myself for leaving my first major, mechanical engineering, because there were no other women in my classes. I was also aware that something else was missing; I was not part of the happy club.

The group of "hippies" on campus who ate vegetarian food and smelled like beans—a group of people that moved slowly and had not been infected with the plague of productivity that struck all the unawares like me—somehow telepathically let me know I was missing something fundamental. I had been infected with this plague of productivity but, like a fish in water, only realized it when I started going to these unusual BALLE meetings where notions like cooperation and the common good had supplanted entrenched notions of competition and every man for himself.

I had been so anxious about the first BALLE meeting that I stalled enough to be late and hopefully unnoticeable but wasn't so lucky. When I walked in—and I am still amazed with myself that I did given the fact that it was a perfect day in a perfect building in a perfect room with a bunch of perfect people who all stopped, including the white guy presenting, to gape at the stranger walking in late—I saw there were no seats at the table, so I sat against the wall on the floor and wished I had remembered my invisibility sunglasses. Nevertheless, my ears were wide open and what I heard struck my heart chords like nothing I had ever heard before. Truth. The unpacking of my early programming had begun.

I guess you could say the first business I started was a "franchise" for the white-men-owned Success Motivation Institute out of Waco, Texas. It was the era of Dale Carnegie workshops on How to Make

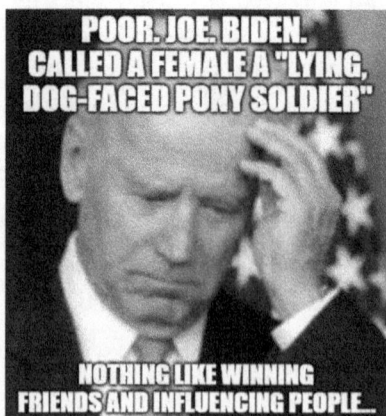

Friends and Influence People (which to me translated to "how to act like an automaton overriding all of your intuition and instincts"). I had spent more money flying to Texas than I made selling these audio/visual goal setting programs and I had also received more trauma from standing up doing memorized "dog and pony shows" in front of apathetic car and insurance salesmen (and a few women) than any job satisfaction beyond the ability to say I had a job.

It was on the airplane home from one of these damn rah rah conferences, where you get gold medallion paper certificates in dollar store photo frame awards for making appointments and leaving messages on the "cheer" hotline, that I decided to get a real job. I applied for a sales position in radio advertising and outcompeted many other candidates because I asked a simple question, "WHY?" in response to the scenario I was told to pitch. But, five years later, after losing a second term pregnancy that devastated my husband, I decided I was all done groveling for contracts from the bar owners and car dealers and general creeps that only met with me to look at my ass in a skirt.

BALLE meetings helped me imagine a better way of doing business, and about what economic justice meant. I attended a conference at Smith College and met a legendary female systems thinker and organizational behaviorist who helped me to start seeing myself in this new paradigm for real, even though I still felt like I was *under* the table instead of *at* it (or off in a corner). I still didn't get the jokes everyone laughed at and still didn't get invited to afterhours things with the cool kids, but I was in a special place and I knew it. I mustered up the courage to start a marketing agency, with my best friend Pam, a colleague from the radio station, and grew that for five years, until my mother died.

This is when I started going it alone. I had long been journaling to myself, writing out all my worries and receiving sparks of insights from God, the spirit world, higher powers; and this felt genuinely collaborative. But after my mother died, the challenging and beautiful sisterhood that I had had with my friend and business partner wasn't enough to sustain me. I couldn't name the grief, I hadn't any words for it, the prior grief from my childhood was buried too deep and was threatening to rise up. All of this, alongside the pain of presenting ideas to white men who owned companies and who took those ideas to their buddies along with the commensurate financial value of my ideas, was literally enough to make me quit my clients and my company and throw my hands up to God and ask for him to rescue me.

Three days later I was offered a job managing a bank. The woman who offered it to me had to ask me to my face a few times because I kept saying, "I'll let you know if I come across someone who might be a good candidate." The only thing I knew about banking was my own mortgage. Radio sales had been as good for me financially as it was bad for me emotionally. What I thought to myself was that banking was boring and it would be an easy 9-4pm job where I could crawl into a boring box during the day and write books on the side.

The first day on the job I had to close a loan for a real estate broker who basically read the whole thing to me and shook his head reinforcing a deep shame I was now able to put in a new context. Within days there was a gambling pool taken up to see how long I would last there, the $100 million headquarter branch of the regional bank. The shortest bet was a couple of weeks (shit, anyone can last two weeks, right?) and the longest bet was six months. I lasted in this nightmare for three years, even after my branch was "given" to the asshole who duped my customers into moving their accounts to his branch by illegally opening accounts at his branch and leaving a few bucks in the account at my branch. His antics won him a huge flat screen TV and a trip to Disney. There was even a picture in the paper about this ordeal, my hometown paper with me looking like a sad puppy with her tail between her legs and a big fat fake smile on her face.

So, I was damned if I was going to not go down without a fight. I got into banking with the notion that I was going to make change from within, be the change, infiltrate the belly of the beast and make the world a better place. I had appropriated animal totem medicine for my team so they might think in new ways about their catty proclivities, but this is what alienated me so greatly. I doubled down with the little branch I was given and took the 110th ranked branch (dead last) up to third within six months. Then, after getting into a massive car accident on the one day (it was a Friday) that my branch had back up management coverage, after 18 months straight of working six days a week and coming back to work in a neck brace on Monday, I quit to get into international banking (this was after presenting the first CEO my initial socially responsible banking proposal).

So now I've "made it." I negotiated a surprisingly good salary for myself, got a Vice President title and a company car. The international bank was hoping to get a solid foothold in America, and I was opening five new branches in addition to the four I was managing. After a few months the finances weren't so great and I was rudely fired and given a taxi ride home, on the director's premise that I had violated some pretend human resource policy because I had asked an employee how her mother was, seriously. I left with a meager settlement I had negotiated by threatening the president to go to the press about the whole asinine affair. Was I supposed to just walk away without a fight, or was negotiating a settlement a Karen thing to do? If Elon Musk can make $600 *million* a *year*, getting three months of meager cushion was, in my opinion, barely respectable.

Well, my mom used to tell me I was too big for my britches, so I stayed in banking and spent another few years of hitting ever bigger targets and blah blah blah. Until I figuratively got struck by lightning and remembered again why I had gotten into banking in the first place. To make a difference, Karen!

I reached out to a woman named Susan whom I had befriended at the networking group I'd started for the bank and told her I wanted to do something important. I mapped out a second Socially Responsible Investment strategy and presented it to the last bank I would serve. Again, I was not included in any of the discussions about my plan's merits or weaknesses. At a holiday dinner I sat next to the Chairman who told me he was impressed with my proposal and that it was sitting on the top of his desk. Within two weeks a Senior VP, the only female at that level, told me in the hallway, in passing, that my project wasn't going anywhere. That was that. I was pissed and was going to do something about it. Susan liked my idea and we developed a multi-stakeholder standing-room-only event that truly changed the regional thinking about collaborative, socially responsible investment.

But it was the *collaboration*, not my idea, that was successful. This was the first time that I was not a lone ranger, just me against the big hairy ass goal that I was going to obliterate. I have to be honest; it was not easy to let go of the reins. A few men among the twelve of us who came together to plan this event were very familiar with collaborating, familiar with the local economies paradigm shift, and could easily see for themselves the vision I had. In fact, despite the fact that I did all the corresponding and managed all the logistics, pre- and post-event, I think the whole thing could have been successful without me. I did not get real credit for the idea or the inspiration, though I did receive a lovely vase of peonies that had been on the kitchen table of one of the committee members as well as an afterthought mention in one of the press releases. The real credit went to the white guy with the most clout.

Is that okay? Personally I felt deflated and needed to lick my wounds. At the end of the day, credit was given to those who knew how to hold it. I was so grateful to have collaborated with these folks, up close and personal. The regional impact that the event had was palatable and reverberated. New organizations were founded and are still doing great things. I wasn't comfortable through the "birthing" of this event, but after the fact I realized that this was my training for emotional wellness, for learning how to plan, push and process *with* other people. I needed all of this training to come through the professional doorway because I was too guarded.

The big question is WHY? What in my mind led me to put the guards up? Eventually, after distancing myself from workspaces I'd grown alarmingly accustomed to, I realized that I was quite sore from repeated emotional bruising and battering.

Rebecca Solnit also has an answer. From her latest book, **Recollections of My Nonexistence**:

"Your credibility arises in part from how your society perceives people like you, and we have seen over and over again that no matter how credible some women are by supposedly objective standards reinforced by evidence and witnesses and well documented patterns, they will not be believed by people committed to protecting men and their privileges. The very definition of women under patriarchy is designed to justify inequality, including inequality of credibility."

Solnit goes on to explain "preemptive silencing" and the essential ingredients of voice: audibility, credibility, and consequence. She asserts that "stories should be measured on their own terms and context, rather than patriarchy's insistence that women are categorically unqualified to speak."

Truths like these don't resonate with everyone, particularly with people who haven't gotten the cold water of this particular reality splashed in their faces. And if we find ourselves in situations where the assaults, the emotional bruising and battering, keep happening, we need to find reinforcements and we need to stop the pain. Unfortunately, we often get to the point where we just can't take any more before we get the reinforcements needed to make a change. And no one in pain should ever be expected to educate or take the blinders off those doing the offending.

∞

In my most clear-eyed moments I can appreciate the fact that my perception is what leads people in my life to "cause" me pain, particularly if I label the circumstances as dishonest or disingenuous. I compare *my* perception of *their* honesty to my sense of my *own* honesty. This is impossible. I cannot even compare my *current* level of honesty with my *past* level of honesty. But in the heat of a triggered moment, in the heat of raging anger—and there is a lot to be angry about—we revert to operating from the limbic brain. This less evolved part of our brain does not apply all the layers of rationalizations and social filters we've installed to make us appear politically correct or at least socially acceptable. I believe we all need to learn how to hold "love consciousness" while experiencing pain from others' unconscious, hurtful, words and behaviors.

Many have paraphrased what Socrates implied about the more we learn the more we realize what we don't know. No matter how much I co-create (as there is nothing new to be created, just recycled and repackaged in our own unique ways), no matter how accomplished I may feel, I'm still just one expression of a species—one that pisses and shits and gets pissed and says shit. And knowing that makes all the difference.

When I consciously started to question my understanding of the various realities of the world, I found community in the fight against climate change. What I was looking for was community, united around raising feminine consciousness, but that would have to wait until later, until now.

In the early 2010s I found myself among veterans of environmental activism, people who had been coming together to educate themselves and each other about the science of global warming, glacial melting, ocean acidification, and especially about fracking and other forms of fossil fuel extraction—for decades. Education leads to activism in the most honest and authentic way and I found myself hooked. Being informed allowed my heart to break around the potential devastation that people in the scientific community model quite conservatively (many researchers have been discredited by malicious Merchants of Doubt[103]). My passion that previously had no container was now focused and purposeful. Add to focused passion a tightly woven community (even a loosely woven community), and one's call to action becomes formidable.

The subsequent years that I spent planning and participating in rallies, marches, presentations and street theater, lobbying elected officials, organizing targeted actions, campaigns and watch parties, were the years when my voice came alive. Combined with a Buddhist spiritual practice to complement a lifetime of Christian perspectives, it quickly became very clear to me that I had to change careers and somehow serve the planet more intentionally.

Anthropogenic, human caused climate change is real. I wonder about how and when the wave of climate deniers will come crashing up and out of their hypnotic slumber. I am still waking up from the American Dream and thought that I could help others wake up if I infiltrated the banking world. I couldn't. Then I thought I could sing more loudly (as Wen Stephenson suggests in his book, **What We're Fighting for Now Is Each Other**) with the climate change choir; we are very good but still not making sufficient progress. Then I thought I could dive right into the electorate and somehow move the needle toward justice. Perhaps my contributions on all fronts do make a

---

[103] https://grist.org/article/from-tobacco-to-climate-change-merchants-of-doubt-undermined-the-science/full/

difference, I suspect they do, but the evidence is not for me to know. Getting up every day and speaking whatever truth I can speak is all I can ever confirm, because my body lets me know what's what.

I feel lucky to now be a worker owner of a solar cooperative installing small scale sustainable renewable energy in my local region. Nothing is easy these days, compared to the 90s when one could make six figures selling air (broadcast advertising). But there is no place I would rather be right now in America's current political moment (it helps me feel sane to say "we're having a moment"), which now sees us in the middle of a devastating COVID-19 health crisis. My colleagues and I are all struggling to be motivated to work 30-40 hours a week given the blooming atmospheric fear, even as we are grateful to be employed. And if a group of conscious communicators who generally love their jobs are struggling this intensely, I can only imagine what a group of bankers may be feeling—or actively suppressing like a levee about to break—at the moment.

∞

As an entrepreneur I have a few thoughts about business. Most of them are negative vestiges of the physical and emotional and spiritual impacts of gaslighting, the dark underbelly of the perpetual growth mentality. Businesses do their best to keep prices levelized so that people keep spending their money unconsciously. When people spend their money consciously, they don't consume as much, and they consume things of better quality. Volume is the key to capitalism.

I once did a five-minute lightning talk about growth and in it I compared the typical 10 X return in three years that venture capitalists seek in any investment (or at least try to despite the noble slow money movement). If a human's weight grew at this rate it would weigh 4 tons by age 9. A baby grows about ten times their birth weight in the first month, but if this continued it would be my height by two years of age and 9 feet tall at age 4. Spiritual growth is the only type of growth that is infinite.

Another fanciful idea I have about working, particularly as we collectively reflect on work life balance in the midst of a pandemic, is that we should all only have to work the number of hours that our cell phone batteries keep a charge.

Wilma Mankiller, the first female chief of the Cherokee nation, shares her story in a beautifully compelling video[104] which features her book, **Every Day Is a Good Day: Reflections by Contemporary Indigenous Women**. In it she explains that the models for sustaining culture and language are desperately needed and her hope is in the current generation of native students, holding their culture and bridging it alongside other realities. Chief Mankiller also offers thoughts on what constitutes a good person. "I think a good person is someone who is very respectful to other people no matter who they are or what station in life they find themselves in, someone who will extend a hand to help other people." I so appreciate someone who can speak with full command of their truth like her. I also remember her sharing a powerful Mohawk proverb that filled my heart and gave me courage: "It's hard to see the future with tears in your eyes."

We cannot accept others' words or behaviors that are hurtful and ignorant. But instead of labeling someone a Karen, perhaps to fill an emptiness in ourselves, a need for affiliation of some kind, we can use *our* words and behaviors to first, be kind to ourselves, and second, spell out in no uncertain terms, what is and what is not acceptable, and third, be prepared to receive feedback about what is and what is not acceptable to another. This is my new American Dream.

---

[104] https://videos.oeta.tv/video/oetas-conversation-wilma-mankiller/

Speaking Woman

Maybe white cis women, by virtue of their *proximal* or associated privilege to the heteronormative order, which has flexed its powerful muscles across the planet, should *stay silent*, observing the rebalancing of power of other races and genders testing out what it feels like to be seen and heard.

Maybe by virtue of the fact that cis men do not labor and physically birth children, do not bear the pain of bringing life into the world and thus feel a depth of aliveness that could classify them as special, their subconscious mind and body are filled with jealousy. The anti-penis envy. And because of this, women should gallantly continue to hold space for men as they "lean in" to their emotional wellness.

Maybe the gentle spirit, named "weaker sex" hundreds or thousands of years ago, has evolved into a tongue-biting, other-way-looking, unventilated, self-recriminating, patriarchally complicit KAREN of America. Maybe Karen is so bound to explode it is self-evident that the act of having tamped down the voice of truth, the truth in her body-mind and e-motional nature (i.e., natural energy in motion), would have consequences so dire that hyper*visibility* to counterbalance her hyper*vigilance* seems just and right.

Maybe all the turn-the-other-cheek and religious power brokering that has given children no voice against abuse in the church, and the incessant refrains of forgiveness that completely usurp survivors' experience of pain, sadness, rage, and grief—power brokering that has fomented and teased out misogynistic injustice for centuries—will resorb back into the pagan soil from whence it came.

If sardonic notions like these, and countless others, could be inspected by open hearts and minds, perhaps we could then find within ourselves the deep roots of compassion necessary to bear witness to others when they deflect and change whatever subject we urgently wish to discuss. Deflection is behavior we can all exhibit when talking about uncomfortable subjects, along with the adrenaline-fueled fight response we experience when confronted by another's incongruent behavior. Incongruence or cognitive dissonance short-circuits our brain, sending all of our politically correct, programmed behaviors out the window.

I want this chapter to exalt women, hence the title. I want to draw more attention to evidence about countless transgressions against women over the ages, the indoctrinated subjugation of women that has *caused* the intense unrest in the world. I want to wag the proverbial finger at the *system* and howl to the moon about all manner of self-righteous indignation. I truly want to scream in a way I have never done before, not alone, in a vast sisterhood of feminine energy keening until every last ounce of despair has been wrung out of every last one of us.

I also want to live in harmony and foster peace with my husband and children, my neighbors, my coworkers and friends, my community. I do not want to be shamed for the genuine concern I have and attention I give to this ebb and flow values conflict. What I want is for divisive liberal and conservative bashing to stop; and I want mature adults to feel safe to explore and express real feelings with each other.

Women are constantly learning from each other; we are generally happy to share with and lift up one another. Women have to make up for the assumed gender deficiency that seems to have been programmed into our DNA since the dawn of religion, which, I understand from the research of Riane Eisler[105] and countless others, usurped and appropriated pagan earth-centric rituals, ceremonies and beliefs. Middle-aged American women may have more unwanted cultural constructs to reprogram than younger women, and an ideal scenario is one in which mothers and daughters do this reprogramming together by talking about patriarchal influences and *how they feel*, how these influences are experienced in various ways.

We have consciously or subconsciously learned all that our mothers could teach us about how to be in the world—for better or worse. We have learned from others' mothers, from friends and family, bosses and

---

[105] https://rianeeisler.com/the-chalice-the-blade-highlights-of-international-impact/

coworkers, and umpteen "how to" books. It is only when we hear what we already know in our body-mind echoed out in the world, preferably by multiple sources and scientific studies, do we believe we know enough about a thing, even if that "thing" is our own mind and body.

Keep planting seeds. Their subconscious mind is awake, even if their conscious mind is asleep.

Old patriarchal constructs are breaking and falling apart hard and fast. The mess, the rubble, the chaos in our midst, is a lot to deal with. We are already hyper wound up. This intensity could be due to the stress of single parenting and disgustingly low wages that barely cover the cost of energy and medicine. And it is not coincidental that the energy and medical industries, at the investor-owned level, are saturated in greed and are the epitome of wealth inequality and systemic oppression.

While the "big pharma" pharmaceutical industry has usurped and appropriated nature, absent the greed it could actually model a wonderful and respectful appreciation of nature—an aspect of biomimicry dedicated to the wellbeing of humankind. The experience of intensity could also be due to the stress of competition to do all the "right things" so that the vestiges of achieving the American Dream— which has lately been reduced to simply staying sane and alive physically, mentally, emotionally, financially, and maybe, just maybe, spiritually— can be realized.

This hyper wound-up state of being might look like sleeplessness, shakiness, agitation, crying at everything, and uncontrolled outbursts in public—the last place anyone would want to be caught out of control, especially on film. The costs of having proven, even if only to ourselves, that we are badass survivors, may well be the very thing—our sanity— that we didn't know was so precariously balanced on the edge of reason.

If we are privileged enough to have a house, we are likely either drowning in our unkempt mess of clothes, electronics and cords, boxes of things and trash, or we are fastidiously organizing our drawers, carefully folding our clothes, and constantly straightening the things that won't stay where they belong.

And of course we add to this the manufactured insanity (or PTSD) of Trump, the "WTF[106]!?" instability of our cellular devices and apps, and the rapidly thawing permafrost in the arctic and the plastification and acidification of oceans, coastal erosion, etc. (not to mention trees falling dead irrespective of storms and other extremes of nature in our communities), and our deteriorating physical, mental, emotional and financial health seems right on par. How can we not be explosive when someone does something—anything—to topple our carefully crafted composure of "I'm fine"?

Personally, I'm finding it difficult to even be in nature with what I used to understand as composure or presence. But I know that nature immersion helps me find the answer to the question of "am I really fine?", and gratitude for nature helps me find the best understanding of "true nature" I am capable of at any moment in time. When I walk Rosie, most of the time I am present with *her presence* with nature rather than my own experience of it, but that is certainly a degree better than being oblivious to both her presence with nature *and* my own. I have also found that truth tingles a bit like goosebumps.

On the way to genuinely being fine, how can we safely blow off the boiling rage and "let it all out"?

There was one moment in my life where I let it all out. Okay two. The less interesting one was in the middle of the night when I'd awoken from an intense dream in a pool of sweat. I shared the dream with Paul and the process led me to wail uncontrollably. I let myself cry even with the windows open. Guess what happened? A neighbor called the police on the woman next door to me thinking that she was a nuisance and that all the screaming had to be her creating a problem. Total bullshit.

The time that I let it all out for real took me a bit by surprise despite the fact that I was on a two-week island retreat with a group of mostly

---

privileged, mostly white, people processing deep feelings. I would have never imagined myself in this space, but what brought me there felt magical.

I have had a handful of moments like this where my intuition screamed "do it!" at me so clearly that I took a leap of faith. I had heard about a retreat center in Big Sur California from the BALLE people I'd met years prior and had dreamed about someday going there with the same dispassionate level of dreaming that one might have about having dinner with a famous person. But when I received an email about a specific retreat happening at Esalen in a few months' time, I did everything I could to get myself there. Paul was his typically supportive self and encouraged me to attend even though the topic was about Eros and we were not at all into ours at that moment. Reflecting back on this and the improved communication skills we now have, I know that this was a big part of the necessary stress we had to experience in order to grow our relationship. Because in all honesty I met someone and this someone paid most of my way to a training program on a Mediterranean island two months later.

This "story" is huge and a bit beyond the scope of **Beyond Karen**. I include it here because it is reflective of the deep "unpacking the invisible knapsack"[107] work that may be needed in most relationships. It certainly was and remains necessary in mine.

So there I was at an island retreat, letting it all out. I was sitting in the middle of a row of about seven chairs facing another row of seven chairs with people sitting in them and many others holding space with us. We were role playing mental unwellness, people who had received negligent care inside an institution and we were all (seven of us) instructed to get angry and say whatever we wanted to "at" the person, the warden, on the other side. It was fascinating to get deep into the role and simultaneously witness ourselves and each other. I made a lot of generalized "you people suck" remarks to initially get into the spirit of the exercise but it was surprising how fast and how deep we all went

---

[107] https://nationalseedproject.org/Key-SEED-Texts/white-privilege-unpacking-the-invisible-knapsack - note: Peggy McIntosh's work is most often quoted in relation to racial awareness. It also has solid application to gender awareness.

with it. I recall acting like a baby and starting to sing the alphabet and heard everyone sing it along with me at one point. Then I heard myself rage about patriarchal bullshit to the point where I was spitting. I

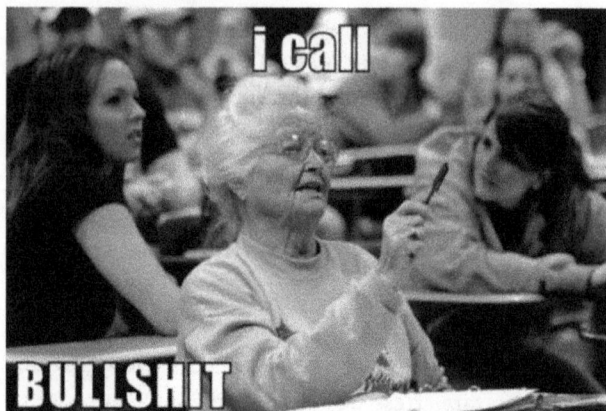

screamed about having to smile and pretend everything was okay when it wasn't, about no one caring about how I felt or what I said, and then the

game was no longer play (which was the point of the game). Because we were all screaming "nonsense" at the same time it was "acceptable." And it was damn cathartic.

In the next few chapters I explore my contention that Karens who offend customer service folks and a host of others due to their "lazy" and other ugly judgments are people who may have yet to realize the far reaches of the patriarchy. I believe in everyone's inherent goodness and that unmindful and hurtful words and actions require direct and honest feedback delivered as kindly as possible. Karen name calling is a blessing in the way that we finally have a container for all that has been packed into it, like TNT (trinitrotoluene), or better yet, like the less stable explosive nitroglycerine. But what to do with it?

We are not yet kindly and lovingly helping someone see that they are a Karen so she can get the support she needs to change. No, from the glut of YouTube videos we see people on both sides of the camera being their worst selves. Perhaps someday the kindness algorithm will out-popularize the shame algorithm that underlies the visibility and impact of online content. It doesn't seem to matter whether we are kind or despicable; when we need to learn a lesson, we're bound to learn it.

When we are admonished for not speaking perfectly, not being appropriately or perfectly sensitive to all people, especially for challenging the status quo, the potential arises for divisive fear and hate mongering. I often except men from that statement because even though men will get abused for speaking unmindfully, for being bold and courageous, for being open hearted, there is substantial evidence that women suffer the brunt of abuse for "crossing lines" drawn by judge and jury, which could be anyone. *All women know this*—ask any one of the women journalists in the Women's Media Center[108], a "nonpartisan, nonprofit organization working to raise the visibility, viability and decision-making power of women and girls in media and, thereby, ensuring that their stories get told and their voices are heard." The Women's Media Center is the bomb, literally; check out their fbomb project. If you want to know about real women addressing real issues, you want to know the Women's Media Center.

Let's go back to basics. Learning to talk.

My first language was Baby, you know, goo goo ga ga, ma ma, dada. I have no memory of this. Then I learned Man, the loud depth of voice that is heard over other voices, I also have no memory learning this, but it was quite formative. Then I learned Boy and I remember this one, it was the voice that called all the shots, named all the rules, made all the jokes, brought on all the tears. I really struggled with Girl and never did quite get that one down. There were far too few people speaking it, as if it was one of those precious Indigenous languages that people were severely punished for using. Girl seems to be coming back now, a little here and there, or at least I hear rumors about it used by the younger generations.

And then there is the language of Woman. I realized something was out of sync with me when I was in my mid 30s. My mother had already died, so right as I was becoming aware that there was a foreign language, no, another native language that was missing in my person, I had no one to turn to. My sister didn't seem to know Woman either. I don't know

---

whether or not mom knew Woman or could teach me even if she did. I certainly have my doubts. I knew and could feel this missing sensation, an emptiness in my body, some disconnect in my mind.

So I started looking for signs of Woman. I couldn't find it in bookstores. Even books like Chicken Soup for the Soul, books that sounded Woman, were written in Man with so many tautological references to Man that I thought I might be crazy to be hearing faint whispers of something, thinking it was important and worth listening to, but unable to find confirmation of my instincts or resonance or evidence, out in the world.

This went on for years until one day when I was praying for a sign, for something to prove Woman existed and that there could be a way for me to learn and understand it, by some miracle it found me. The world cracked open like my heart and searching eyes.

A younger woman I'd met in a business roundtable meeting, the one that stood out, didn't belong—you know the childhood puzzles, which of these things is not like the other—that was her. No makeup, open toed flat sandals, maybe even Birkenstocks. Honestly I thought she was wearing a burlap skirt and figured she had no idea what a razor looked like. Anyway, well, she felt a connection to me and we started talking. I think I pretended to be interested in what she was saying so others wouldn't judge me, but now that I clear out the cobwebs in my memory I am pretty sure I was trying to pretend I wasn't interested in what she was saying because to stop pretending that I was interested in the busyness of the business that absorbed my every waking moment was, now that I reflect back on that person who didn't know Woman, to entertain complete annihilation. I may have saved myself years of angst if at the time I had known Woman a little better, but I'm getting ahead of myself.

This lovely young woman said she was trusting her gut as, days or weeks later, she invited me to a Red Tent Temple. I knew this was a big deal, maybe even an answer to my prayer, but I was still skeptical and judgey and didn't want to let on that I was actually interested. Intrigued really. So the day approached and I was getting irritated about the lack of a plan. I ended up driving because I think she didn't have enough gas in her car or something. It was already dark by the time we got there and it was deep in the woods so far off the beaten path I wasn't sure if I could navigate my way home (pre GPS on all devices) if things went bad. I parked and then reparked after it was hinted that I had parked wrong and then walked into the back yard.

There were people coming in and out of a round building behind the house and off to the west and north sides adjacent to the trees called a yurt. It was really big and spacious and literally a red space full of tapestries and big pillows all over the floor, lights strung around this big open room, fluffy blankets and ribbons and percussion instruments and candles glowing. It was unlike anything I'd ever seen or even heard about. And it was 100% Woman.

I felt as though I had come home after surviving in the desert on cactus juice my whole life. I was initially hearing Man in my head, which sounded like suspicious doubt, judgment and sarcasm. But I had been searching for Woman so my heart rose up and overpowered my head. And guess what?! I could hear Woman, I understood the language!

It was a language I could feel, like the rhythm of Earth itself! The respectful sharing ------ SPACE ------ to art-i-cul-ate just the right words, the essence of feelings, of truth emerging from a special place deep inside each one of us. It was all there, an open book of wisdom. Not one Word of Man was in my head! The famine was over!

The host of this red tent temple looked and felt like a pure goddess. She was the light and emitted something I hadn't remembered seeing since college when I'd caught a glimpse of the vegetarian hippies. It was happiness. It was confidence. It was connection. I understood! I had arrived at a place ------ a SPACE ------ where sacredness existed for real.

It was such a pivotal moment. I had come to my senses, but then back at home, back at work, everyone spoke Man. But I Had To Speak Woman! I could not, I would not ignore my native tongue anymore! What could I do? I had to practice speaking Woman and hope that others would hear the faint whisper of recognition. It was not easy. Most of the time I had no idea whether or not my Woman made sense to anyone. It wasn't like learning Man when everyone would correct my slightest error. No one let me know if they heard me. I had to remember how Woman felt and Trust that I wasn't fucking it up too much. That was hard.

But it's like learning anything important; once you see and know it, you can't unsee, unknow. Over time the synergies lined up, like the blue light wisps in the Disney movie Brave. Practicing Woman was worth it; the Joy, the Confidence and Connections continued to build. And while it feels infinitely better to speak Woman with others—the exponential

positive impact of speaking Woman with others sows seeds of hope in the self and perhaps in the world. When Woman is spoken—or better yet sung—to oneself Thinking begins to merge with Feeling. It's as if the body and mind come into harmony, in tune.

And so it seems now, after years of being reunited in the exquisite language of Woman, that seeking fortune requires knowing more than Man. If we seek fortune we need only look, with care, with curiosity, with genuine and impassioned interest, questing as the children of beloved communities may still do, for the tune of unity inside ourselves. I call this quest and this tune Inner Fortune.

But, lest it seem like the author now knows the language Woman, has found Inner Fortune and all is right in the world, let's heap up onto the plate a big serving of reality. All these "languages" I describe here are all White. Many People of Color have also learned White before their own "language." I don't know the first thing about Black or Red or Yellow or even the Brown that Paul feels is his to know. We all learn

White, the language of commerce. This topic is a bit beyond the scope of **Beyond Karen** but is definitely an important unfolding to welcome into life in the present moment.

I am white, I am college educated—even if it wasn't deemed necessary *for a girl* by my father, I have had the confidence to start and grow businesses—even if they were small service businesses, I have been fortunate to be able to create space for a great deal of healing in my life—even if I did ruin my family financially in the process. And with all of that, my voice is still small and out of tune.

I have often said, with a fair amount of bitterness, that my father was like Archie Bunker, as if the character played by Carroll O'Connor on that 70s TV show was his role model. In moments with him, particularly after his stroke in his 60s, when I would try to extract his feelings about his father (attempting to help him process and find some relief from the sadness I knew he carried), he would glaze over and recall experiences of neglect and disappointment: how my grandfather never went to his football games, made a profit off his mother and sister selling them cars, and spent his afternoons in the local bar. I can see how Archie Bunker resonated with my dad's experience of his father and allowed for sufficient objective, "not me" dissociation for him to laugh at and enjoy Archie's character. I could never see the humor in Archie (I did however like the Jefferson's TV show that followed with George and Weezy "movin' on up ... to a de-luxe apartment in the sky").

I didn't miss my parents at my soccer games. And after my brother's death the alcohol was ever-present but to me seemed normal and "no big deal." Having children myself led me to intentionally unpack and redirect the patterns that I felt had been modeled. As with all important change, it is infinitely easier and more possible if not attempted alone. Some of my healing work was "lucky" and being in the right place at the right time, like the one or two Al-A-Teen meetings I went to in college, and the Mediterranean retreat I mentioned attending much later in life.

When the winds of possibility carried me to this Mediterranean island for the two-week intensive where, at one point, I role played a resident in a facility for the mentally unwell, I had no idea that I would experience and transform many of my deep-seated feelings of sadness, fear, anger and joy. I was literally held in the arms and hearts of others—

all of us being our most compassionate selves bearing witness to each other. I wish this experience for everyone on the planet.

In my most profound experience in this retreat—the one that left me, with my two partners sitting close by, laying on the floor for thirty additional minutes completely unaware that the program had restarted—I was artfully guided into my saddest childhood experience. I had a witness at my shoulders and another at my feet, thankfully both strong enough to restrain me safely. I knew this sadness exercise was going to be my most intense feeling to process and a huge wave of fear crashed over me as the dear man facilitating, the one who had invited me to this retreat, began setting the stage. I looked at him in terror and he signaled that he would be by my side. The relief of this allowed me to have a life changing healing so many years after witnessing the crushing death of my brother. Energetically I removed barrels full of sand from my body and connected it to the sandbox I'd played in alone for two years after my brother died.

The 30 minutes I lay on the floor while all other participants (save my two witnesses) moved on was not a conscious choice. Prior to this I had never allowed myself to not participate on schedule in any group activity. When I "woke" and was welcomed back, I received a second healing gift, acceptance for attending to my own needs. Kindhearted acceptance of others attending to their needs is a profound gift we can all seek to give each other. By assuming that each of us can and must be a fully integrated whole human being, body, mind and soul, we give each other permission to listen to, develop, and live by our inner wisdom.

Our early conditioning, the initial development or stunting of our voice may remain internalized over years or a lifetime. How many children have internalized their parents' divorce as their fault? How many rape survivors have internalized the horrific act as their fault? How many other survivors of a loved one's death have internalized it as their fault?

There are dozens of horrifying statistics about how often a woman or man is raped, beaten, stalked, or abused; so horrifying that to invest one's heart to think-feel about the sisters and brothers everywhere under siege is enough to stop the heart from beating. What motivates me to keep writing is the hope that enough words about hope, about options, about solutions, about being differently with each other, will tip the scales toward healing for all. Writing, talking, sharing, being with each other on purpose so that healing doesn't have to be so heavy, not an either/or choice, so that safety is the norm and expressions of fear trigger responses of all hands on deck, compassion in action, everywhere, all the time.

LOVEYouKaren

It may seem obvious to readers that the antidote to FuckYouKaren, the unconscious dribble of hate spewing out from the Karen meme, would be LoveYouKaren. It took quite a bit of internal exploration for this to become evident to me. I blindly took F-you Karen to heart, like I have taken so many similar messages spoken and unspoken to me over the years. But when we take something to heart intentionally and with care, there is a process of transformation that can dissolve hatred into love.

As I mentioned previously, one origin of the use of the term Karen as an internet meme dates to an anonymous Reddit user, FuckYouKaren, who was quite effective at compiling a hate narrative[109]. I had zero interest in going to this site; I care too much for my heart. But I do care the effects of this hate narrative and am also grateful to have been so motivated as to not only write a book, but to deeply explore my biases. I can now honestly ask myself, "How am I a Karen?"

If you are a 20s to 60s woman reading this, or a man who feels inclined to police 20s to 60s women, maybe you can ask yourself, "How might I be a Karen?"

Maybe the real crux of this more benign name calling is about not knowing how to observe people bumble along to express the things they feel passionately; to not know how to bear witness to and give space for others' inarticulate, nonverbal, and perhaps immature ways they "act out" the pain and suffering at the root of their thing... all in an effort to feel heard or seen.

Maybe we all have so much trauma and frustration over the lack of understanding and compassion we have experienced, that when two or

---

[109] https://en.wikipedia.org/wiki/Karen_(slang)#cite_note-BI-2

more people come together intentionally or coincidentally around a thing, this trauma and frustration gets activated; and one or more people have just enough inexperience in managing trauma and frustration so as to "lose their shit" and bring upon themselves the silent judgment from others, relieved that it wasn't them.

Maybe there is hard-to-express awareness of things that others in one's sphere of influence cannot or will not see—like pain, suffering, or even the God or Good in all things.

Questions like these can reek of philosophical futility, even smack of mental masturbation. To pose questions like these is a more open-minded endeavor than to be certain and "black and white" about a thing. But spinning around with grand questions can twist one's already irritable bowels. So… here's another one just for fuck's sake: what if we all simultaneously went outside and touched the earth in gratitude?

What if we all could focus on our breath at all the most important moments?

The process of transformation, creating sufficient time and space for processing emotion, ideally with someone who cares, is everything. Growing love is the process of the heart. And I am reminded in this moment that the name given to me by the monks and nuns in the Order of Interbeing, in the week of a silent retreat that I took right as my mother was dying, is Grateful Smile of the Heart. It helps to remember things like this when we need these memories, these sources of resilience and courage.

As I sat to write this chapter I "invited" my meditation bell three times—once for the Buddha or body, once for the Dharma or speech, and once for the Sangha or mind, the collective body-mind of community. Then I lit a candle to invoke bright principles and trusted my intuition and the inspiration that is so much larger than me to flow as it will. This is a practice that I have started with some conversations (and writing is a conversation) that feel bigger than what I perceive myself able to hold in the moment. It's a way of not going it alone.

When the phrase LoveYouKaren came to me, I was in the middle of making love to my husband. Instead of saying "I love you" to him, I said "you love me" to us. Without a blink he said, "of course."

Paul made love to me early in the morning on this particular day, during the hours he sleeps best, entirely because the rains pouring down on our seedlings in the two raised beds still standing and the two makeshift raised beds that had already collapsed made me want to run outside to cover them up. The terror I felt for these "poor" seedlings was real, I was sweating head to toe (which is way too easy in the summer for a woman my age in the throes of the menopause), but the seedlings are stronger than I gave them credit for.

Much after he had tried to convince me that they'd be fine, it became clear to me that my seedlings were proxy holders, stand-ins for the hearts flooded with suffering all across America, all over the world. But in the moment when he gently tried to talk me off the edge, I could only hear Man, the language, the words that never fit in my ears when my heart is flooded, the words I have heard my whole life attempting to calm me down, shut me up, silence me, block the feelings that are the essence of my life, my heart.

When hearts hurt, when they assess their circumstances looking for comfort or support and find none, they turn to their head, their minds, and somehow, they are able to spin any story that will alleviate the suffering of the moment. Hearts that have suffered alone too often, have had to spin stories for self-preservation too often, run the risk of breaking. At some point the stories might not line up and the cognitive dissonance, the emotional dis-ease, can have deep and long-lasting consequences.

There is an energetic theory to heart attack that has come to my awareness which says water has a special healing property, a fourth property in addition to its solid, gas, and liquid states called structured. Structured water is the intelligent use of negative charge, the negative ions, to hold a vessel—like an artery—in perfect shape so that the fluids passing through—like blood—are able to flow smoothly. As I write this I can see a loving archway of male and female arms overhead creating a ceremonial threshold for newlyweds to pass through. But if pain, in the form of tension, holding around the wall of an artery creates blocks, the structured water cannot form a complete or perfect circle, blood cannot flow freely and over time the stuckness interrupts flow and that artery stops functioning, goes into arrest.

How much tension are we all holding in our bodies? How much of this tension is ultimately the result of not being able to freely flow with feeling? Of noticing a thing and saying a thing only to be ignored or disregarded because the person or people to whom we are speaking and sharing our heart with cannot hear, cannot admit they cannot hear?

I know I am not alone in my experience of grief resulting from not being heard. I have not had a heart attack and from all reports it's in good condition, though my mother had *four* in her fifties. My heart has had a murmur, an irregular beat that my husband has listened to frequently for years. He says that since quarantine it has disappeared, a silver lining.

But let's get back to making love. What a loaded subject! The old phrase about what not to talk about at the dinner table—sex, religion and politics—has kept these most human, important, and sensitive subjects off the table for far too long. How many girls learned about their menstrual cycles as they started flowing—flooding their minds with thoughts that they could be dying?! It's a challenge to stay focused on intimacy because there are so many layers—like the layers of an onion that Shrek mentions to the oblivious Donkey on the pivotal journey that would change his life—to this most precious part of ourselves.

"Onions have layers, Ogres have layers. You get it? We both have layers!"

My foot is tapping and I am not a fidgeter... I am letting myself get distracted with snacks... I am breathing deeply again... Ok, here goes.

Wait. First an observation and a theory. These distractions and agitations in the body-mind are exactly what call for attention. I realize that I'm about to write something that I feel raw and insufficiently processed about and *this is the state of being* that the body-mind wants me to slow down and notice; to not to push through or ignore by getting up for snacks. Yes, breathing is always a good response. So is slow, mindful walking, slow everything (moving, drinking and eating, speed limit driving, etc.). The theory is that this moment of agitation—with oneself, with another in a tense interaction—is the <u>Pivot Moment of Choice</u>. The moment of making that 180° shift. The Pivot Moment of Choice is the conscious decision to feel and be differently in a situation, the point of returning to the self, to ease, peace, truth, balance, calm, grace, love.

There comes a time in most writing I have done, or in any creative art, after all of the initial inspiration has been expressed and when doubt and uncertainty settles in, when the work of art begins to feel like a jumbled mess. At this point of writing **Beyond Karen** I knew something deeper wanted to emerge, but I had no idea how to let it flow through. I knew that the most precious part of my life, my marriage, was somehow essential to this story. But as the weight of this Karen meme seeped more deeply into me, the fear of "going there" flooded my heart. I wasn't clear whether or not this fear was simply about exposing myself, my life, and the most important person in it, again—as I have already written a memoir and a book of poetry that has been inspired by this most important relationship (which again caused Paul and me to grow tremendously as a result)—or if the fear was about the real threat of annihilation. Can this marriage, which has been so strong, been through so much, withstand **Beyond Karen?** Will this break us? Is it worth it?

I believe so and I continue to write.

Paul and I first met in second grade and we hadn't realized it until very recently when we corroborated a shared memory. He lived next to the town swimming pool and used to climb the fence and swim while the summer campers were there. I remember one day watching this little brown boy with an afro outpacing the angry teenage worker around the pool (who quickly gave up the chase) by diving off the tall diving board where I was strictly forbidden to go. He had somehow noticed me watching and then found me in the small wading pool. He tried to get me to jump in the deep end and I said no. He then showed me around like he owned the place; he said the back grassy area was where the teenagers kissed. Ten years later, after wooing me to the senior holiday party dance floor with an incredibly romantic gesture in front of my friends—the same energy he'd had that day at the pool—sent my heart fluttering (and I'd thought it was for the first time!). Over thirty years later, the chemistry is still there.

My honey has a strange habit of streaking at odd moments. In college this may have happened more times than I am aware, but it continued even up until a couple of years ago when we were at Americade in Lake George. At least this time he wagered and earned fifty bucks to get buck naked in the middle of people walking to and from the bars (including a few children)! A similar situation happened without the wager many years ago on Halloween night. We were hosting our annual party and as the evening wore down, he decided to strip down and run up and down the street.

Is it funny? Absolutely! But it is also illegal. What would it be like if streaking didn't have to be illegal, if being exposed was not about anything sexual or demented but about being free and uninhibited? Perhaps like it used to be and still is in the rare and precious corners of the world that have been preserved from the excesses of consumerism.

There is something different about this effort to share details of my marriage in an attempt to get **Beyond Karen**, different than my first self-published memoir or poetry book, both of which felt like an emergence of my spirit that needed to be spoken, a catharsis. This is an offering and a hope for catharsis. And I have truth tears threatening to flow now because of all the unrequited offerings I have made in the world—that innocent heart like a child offering her mama a dandelion. Bless all the mamas who hold that dandelion to their chest and then bring the child in for a group hug.

My husband Paul has saved my life. I don't really tell him this, and if I have, he probably didn't think a whole lot on it because I also spend a lot of time telling him what he could be doing better. We've gotten past the "stop lecturing me" phase which has taught me to soften my tone and be more in my heart when giving advice. But my darling has a lot of blind spots that I see, and he has just started to be able to tell me about my blind spots that he sees. When this subject of being perceptive and unable to create the resonant "tuning fork" experience with Paul was raw and caused me pain to think about, I would find hope in the fair number of men I know who are able to speak both Man and Woman, able to feel out loud.

All the effort to teach him Woman, or more accurately provide him with safe enough space for him to hear and be willing to give voice to the language already inside him, has not been in vain. Over the more than three decades we have been in relationship we have navigated our way through treacherous terrain to the point where we are now, which is a deep respect for the other's ability to say what is or is not safe. This is a huge cause for celebration.

What I am about to say is in no way a critique on women who stay in relationships they feel are unhealthy. We all have our "balance sheet" of pros and cons for why we do or do not do something. I think it is very brave for any woman to leave a long-term relationship, particularly one to a man who has been the "provider" of stability. The entrenchment of heteronormativity is like an immobilizing quicksand and to rise up out of it and "go it alone" is the epitome of the phrase "to cut off your nose to spite your face." The pain of seeing, of waking up to one's own disagreement with any of the many, pervasive socio-cultural constructs in America and then not being able to change behaviors in oneself or one's relationships, can drive a person mad. A woman who has found no alternative but to leave a relationship or marriage over irreconcilable differences, particularly with the impact on her children, is a woman who is finding her voice.

Esther Perel is an author, worshipped in many queer spaces for her book **Mating in Captivity**. She posits, "monogamy used to be one person for life, now monogamy is one person at a time," and an affair is "a secretive relationship, an emotional connection to one degree or another, an alchemy." This means intimacy, not just intercourse, can be an affair. She also wisely notes that people can have an average of two or three marriages in their lifetime, often with the same partner. The most important aspect of her work for me is the clarity she offers about the nature of fidelity and the false expectation that one person can be the end all and be all for another person for life. What stung the most when I listened to one of her recent TED talks was this: "stay is the new shame." For someone like myself who believes this one precious life is all about growing in love, continuing to expand our consciousness, how can one relationship, one marriage, contain all that?

One day, one heart-centered conversation, one moment at a time.

I hope all adults are making love. I hope that people living alone during quarantine, only able to make love to themselves and virtual partners, are able to find ways to keep it fresh. I hope that all Karens are having great sex, hot, sweaty, back arching, toe curling, blinding sex that leaves them shaking, crying, full of rainbows and sound asleep for a good hour afterwards.

When Paul rolled his heavy sleepy body onto mine, knowing that I was distraught about the seedlings, it was an offering. He didn't ask. He knew my state of being and he knew and trusted that if even in the state of being I was in, if I didn't want what he was offering I would say so. And I knew that I could say so if I didn't want what he was offering, and he would be okay with it. This is what feeds my soul; this knowing that has resulted from countless hours of heart sharing and caring.

And there is so much to say about the process of getting to this point. Those countless hours might feel impossible to have with someone. Maybe there have been countless hours of grief about sex. How does one unpack that? This is the saving grace of my life. Sex with my husband has always been great and full of love even in the early years of trauma recovery.

According to United Nations data curated by the World Population Review[110], 35% of women worldwide experience sexual assault. This is a horrifying statistic. Of these roughly 1.4 *billion* women, only 10% report their assailant to law enforcement. I reported mine. I was then grossly abused—alone, without a woman by my side, without my mother—by a team of male police officers getting a rise out of my harrowing experience. And that's all I want to say about that.

There is no way to go **Beyond Karen** without holding safe space for each other—every one of us. We must trust that expressions of raw

---

[110] https://worldpopulationreview.com/country-rankings/rape-statistics-by-country

emotion have important roots, even, perhaps especially, if the expression is coming from someone who may appear *on the surface*, by virtue of their painstaking attention to their no-hair-out-of-place appearance, to have it all together. And once we learn, once we know in our bones, that feeling feelings will not kill us no matter how painful they are, if we can feel in the presence of another being who cares (even if it is a tree), we will grow more and more capable of digging into our roots and compassionately exploring roots of pain and suffering with another. Aren't you important enough to feel? Yes. 100%.

How to trust after your heart has been battered? I am a big fan of telling my feelings to Rosie. Dogs are incredibly compassionate listeners. They lick your tears away and snuggle when they know you are in pain. Try it with your pet. Just a suggestion.

There is so much more I am willing to share but I am not feeling the inspiration to do so in a book. Sex and intimacy is best shared in person! But the truer reason for my hesitation to share more explicitly is that the tenor of the world—at least online in America—seems to me to be at the very beginning stages of its capacity to grasp such details without the important corresponding nonverbal communication of interpersonal exchange. Growing love, of returning to nature, or as my friend Madeleine says, "rewilding ourselves", will advance this capacity.

The truth is that there is an intense amount of unregulated fear, dysregulated bodies and minds searching for targets for their anger, their raw and unprocessed emotion. How do we learn to process emotion when it has forever been repudiated by white culture? The sort of unfiltered women being categorized as #KarensGoWild are onto something here; in their public rants, that are hard to hear because of the racist and classist and sexist themes that get regurgitated, they are actually drawing attention to the domestication and, I believe, subjugation of their natural body-centric emotional authority. We can hear it if we listen closely.

My journey to connect more intentionally, more reciprocally, to nature began about ten years ago when I attended a three-day Nature As Mentor retreat. I wrote a post[111] about it which did not include the most profound part of the experience. After trekking alone, as we were all instructed to do, late at night about a mile into thick woods with nothing but a headlamp, I shut off my headlamp and kept it off. Silence. A tiny bit of rustling leaves. The day before we'd heard that there were four-foot-tall coyotes spotted close by and this was top of mind. But standing there while my eyes adjusted to the faint moonlight, I realized, to my astonishment, that I was not afraid. I actually felt like countless creatures around me were curiously watching me, seeing me in a way I'd never known, had never been seen before—like one unified curious mind bearing witness to me!

Nature appreciation is likely another aspect of intimacy that is hard to convey in this medium, but I believe the potential spark of deep-seated limbic cognition is worth the effort.

Akin to Peter Beinart's assertion that you "Foster women's equality in the home, and you may save democracy itself," I assert that if we learn from and model our lives around the interdependent relationships in nature, we can save ourselves. If we all work in relationships with others to fortify self-acceptance and self-love (as opposed to the narcissistic pathology of this) we will be too busy to seek affiliation by engaging in forms of online mob mentality.

∞

A few years ago, I recall being on the receiving end of a woman's anger in a college auditorium. I launched and had been leading a local chapter of Mothers Out Front and was invited to sit on a panel with other environmental activists sharing tactics for engagement. Besides being challenged by a respected peer (who was espousing anarchistic tactics) for my position to begin with attention to one's uncompromising integrity (which she took to mean "recycle and don't use plastic bags") a woman of color said something to the effect of "easy for you to say as a privileged white woman." This was at a time when $20 barely got me through the week and I would sob if I lost $5.

We can never know where another is coming from, what another is holding mentally or emotionally, or physically, unless we ask. Paul and I check in with each other with questions like, "how is your heart?" in order to cut through to what really matters in any particular moment.

Due to my working-class upbringing, I'm generally offended by attitudes of privilege and pretentiousness because they usually come through my lenses of perception as ignorant. Being in a bubble of privilege is hard to notice from the inside (like being white), unless someone outside breaks it for us. Breaking bubbles of ignorance is what cancel culture and the Karen meme is doing (again in its pure form as opposed to the media manipulation and weaponizing which is also happening).

As I have gotten a bit more comfortable, i.e. having a reliable paycheck and not living so desperately between each one, I have forced myself to learn more about hard truths of privilege and why the United States consumes 25-30% of the world's resources with about 5% of the world's population. Investigating issues like global deforestation to market exotic furniture to the grossly wealthy or to grow crops for cattle living in Contained Animal Feeding Operations, plastic oceans and toxic trash being buried in coal mines and burned with ever weakening air pollution regulations, the business of fracking and chemical proliferation, etc. etc.—help keep reality in my direct line of sight.

The thing is, as I grow my perspective, Paul must also grow his so that we can stay in balance together, as a unit. I am learning to not get myself ahead of us, and he is learning to stretch beyond his comfort zone. And none of this work is easy.

One intimate thing I can share about our ongoing efforts to stay in balance has to do with pace. Based on our many years of doing the "too much" "not enough" dance, I assert that every relationship has one partner more physically centered and one partner more mentally centered. The more physical partner will likely be more quickly ready for sex and the more thinking partner will likely be slower to shift gears. For years I overrode and shut down my swirling feelings and thoughts to let Paul take the lead. But as we have become more skillful at navigating pace, as I have grown more articulate of "where I am" at any moment in time and he has grown more curious and interested, the slower start, often called foreplay, can make for an even more satisfying experience for both of us. Gentle compromises we lovingly (not begrudgingly) make for each other lead to greater self-awareness and deeper intimacy. And as intimacy grows, our capacity to confront our ignorance follows.

The edgy, fine line of right and wrong—in thought, word, and sexual advance—is a line that every animal wants to toe, in order to grow. When we get shut down, or (hopefully playfully) slapped back, we know we've crossed it and have gone too far. Even Rosie will toe the line of right and wrong by taking something, like the handheld broom, and start chewing up the handle right in front of me! If I don't take it away and replace it with an acceptable chew toy, she'll think the broom is now fair game.

Around 4:30 a.m. one day I was lying in bed listening to the click of the fan, breathing as deeply as possible to both attempt a return to sleep and alleviate the pain of poor circulation in my arms, when the thought of house mold occurred to me. I began hoping that Paul and I didn't have lung issues from living in a damp house in the woods (3-5 a.m. are the lung hours in the Chinese medicine clock). This led me down a dark path given the dreams I'd had in the very eye-of-the-storm space the world is in with the coronavirus.

I began thinking of the deplorable, unconscionable human-caused effects of climate change and the "living" conditions so many in the human and nonhuman family are enduring, or not, across the world as a result of both this house mold idea (especially for anyone living in a previously flooded house), as well as the Sun Magazine article by Jane Goodall I had just read, *Digging Up the Roots*.

The article[112] is about the severity of grief that we feel after the loss of a person, animal, or thing. Such grief "depends on the relative contribution made by each to our physical and spiritual well-being." In the article is a sentence that took my breath away.

I am no stranger to grief. I have surrendered to vast oceans of sadness and have participated in grief ceremonies where I've cried out puddles on the floor one moment and in the next moment jumped up to dance. To not feel, to not surrender to the internal weather patterns

---

[112] https://www.thesunmagazine.org/issues/535/digging-up-the-roots

that can grow torrential, is to pollute the body with unnecessary resistance. Reading her article this particular morning I cried along with Goodall's words of recollection of the guilt in losing canine family members, "in their dog minds, did I not let them down—however hard I tried to help?" But the words that really left me gutted are these:

"Now in this desecrated area [in Tanzania], the women searching for firewood must dig up the roots of the trees they have long since cut down to make space for crops."

I wish I could say I felt sickened by these deplorable "living" conditions and have overwhelming empathy for the women digging the roots. I don't; I can't yet touch that resonance in my body–mind. Their suffering is too great for me to understand. I do however have deep sadness over the loss of nature and other species' lives. Yet larger than even this is the shame I was feeling about the related phrase that came to my mind, "digging my roots."

A few years ago, I had started writing a book by that name; it was to be a juxtaposition of soil science and genealogy. The science was inspired by a week-long international biochar symposium I had chaired and the somewhat related work I had read by the preeminent pioneer of symbiogenesis, Lynn Margulis. This topic and the excavation of my family roots which took many long hours are both worthy and I would have continued with the book if I had felt capable of doing justice to the concept. But the title had a snarky "can you dig it" double entendre to it that, alongside the reality faced by these women in Tanzania and throughout Africa and elsewhere, sickens my American self. I know the truth about "disaster capitalism" and once you know a truth, you can't unknow it, in the same way that once you cut a tree (or a forest) it cannot be uncut. (If you are actively growing your courage, read Naomi Klein's *Shock Doctrine*).

This thread, this line of thought, this stream of consciousness, brings me to a hard reckoning with the work that I do each day. On the one hand I can feel somewhat satisfied that I am not doing great harm with small scale renewable energy; on the other, I know that most of the people purchasing solar energy are white people with disposable income.

I want to do more to rebalance economic power. In fact, I have conversations with people where I still *after all the years of re-educating myself* feel incapable of speaking truth to power—like the one I had earlier on the particular day that I am writing this: A prospective customer had just cut 80 trees down, all hardwood, hoping to put solar on his roof and it was still not enough for adequate solar access. He decided he was going to try to convince his neighbor to also cut all his trees down and all I could say was that the red oaks were majestic and that cutting them down would likely not help him gain solar access. I don't think anything I could have said would have opened his mind or his heart to the immeasurable value of trees.

∞

Earlier I shared a method for moving beyond shame—to make peace with the truth behind the feeling of shame. I believe we all can do this—in the way that I hope every person who has resonant and intimate relationships is able to take that necessary first step to bear witness to shame as it rises up within them. I know from my own experience in fighting for and finally finding this ability, in friendship and in my marriage, that shame can dissolve into clarity, awareness, and action, if it is held compassionately with us by another person. We need to be held, physically and emotionally. And we are uniquely capable of holding others in this way. When we find the desire within us to be held by each other and learn to hold each other—all others—compassionately, we will move beyond the desire to shame ourselves and others; and we will move **Beyond Karen**.

One of the ways I try to grow my compassion is by learning about what "hard truths" other people are holding and I particularly appreciate learning about nature. I attended a fabulous Zoom webinar sponsored by Climate Action Now in which Harvard researcher Susan Masino shared her knowledge about the importance of forest protection; the fact she shared that resonated most with me was about the brain-wellness effects of terpenes in conifer trees. Ever since experiencing this bit of consciousness raising, I have been doing my best to breathe in these amazing terpene neurotransmitters emitted by hemlock's, junipers, spruce, and other gorgeous cone-bearing beings.

I am *extremely* fortunate to have a forest of hemlocks down the road. I put a small group of hemlock needles in between my finger and thumb and squeeze to release her aromatics; I inhale with closed eyes and the citrusy deliciousness, this beyond comprehension essence, can bring me to tears. And then I wonder this: if just a 1-inch extension of a hemlock branch connected subterraneously to countless other relatives can give so much fragrance and joy and potential for healing, what does our entire forest network provide the world? We truly have no idea.

Hemlock trees are vulnerable to infestation and decimation by the woody adelgid, a tiny aphid like insect native to Japan. Each tree may have a particular nemesis like the ash has the emerald ash borer. The trees' vulnerabilities seem akin to humans' various and unique intestinal susceptibilities. I cannot help but read this bit from a 2017 Forest Invasives report[113] about hemlock woody adelgids (HWA) from Michigan State University and make the correlation to the impact COVID-19 is having on the immune systems of humans: "Although hemlock woolly adelgids cannot fly, life stages can be blown by the wind or transported on birds, animals or even on clothing. Long-range spread of HWA occurs when people transport and plant infested hemlock nursery trees into new areas."

We can all be grateful to Jane Goodall for teaching us about the relational depths of our ape brothers and sisters. Better still, we can pray that this knowledge will wake up and stop those who would destroy their lands and lives in the short-lived selfish ambition for profiteering—which is perhaps the "hungry ghost" soul craving of those who've yet to love and feel the immense contributions made by these lands and lives.

∞

---

[113] https://www.michigan.gov/documents/invasives/Invas_annual_2017_single_crops-mc1_621632_7.pdf

When one learns discomfort, especially as a way of life, it can be hard to enjoy, appreciate, and trust the experience of comfort when it comes. The human spirit is very resilient but at a certain point—a point that the department of defense has researched and practiced so extensively that it is weaponized—it breaks down and takes functional elements of the brain away with it. We can see this with our own eyes if we are willing. We can feel and know this with our own hearts as we unpack and understand systemic racism—the roots and wages of war, of crimes against humanity. **We have to not want to overpower anyone or any species.** Women have been powered over since the idea and practice of trading girls for increased social status through marriage began. Without going into that just slightly beyond the scope of **Beyond Karen** history here, I will simplify this complex societal disorder by saying that the human spirit desires visibility and recognition, resonance and energetic vibration, so that as truth emerges in oneself it can be conspired with others and grow, honoring the essence of life itself. This desire, if pursued with radical awareness and honesty, can be achieved without any of the dire consequences (ecosystem destruction, species extinction, breakage of human spirit) we have seen in very grave examples of power seeking and acts of overpowering.

I have many philosophical aspirations which can feel out of alignment with others. There are so many layers of consciousness to a middle-aged human, subconsciousness layers like our skin that can be pulled back unexpectedly. We are like old houses with thick layers of paint on the walls, the windowsills, the stairs—treads, risers, hand rails—all of it. And one lovely Saturday when lots of plans were newly put in place, the first day off after Paul and I started dreaming of literally and figuratively moving in a new and exciting direction for our middle-aged lives, I found myself crying.

I cry a lot and I'm okay with that; there is a crap ton to cry about these days. Paul had gone to the local tire store to fix the flat that the camper trailer got on our way home from the 4th of July trip to my sister's. As soon as he left, his phone on the table buzzed that Nathan's friend who does landscaping was on his way over. I freaked out. *Why didn't Paul tell me he had gone and arranged this? I thought we were on the same page about leaving the yard alone—rewilding it as E.O. Wilson would have us do—so the birds and bees and butterflies could have enough to eat?!* The unexpected 180° energy shift reminded me of that day, maybe a year after we'd moved here, when Paul's father and uncle came over and started cutting down trees in the front yard, leaving me inside in a fetal position unable to breathe—the same day that his uncle brought Nathan a blue jay in a cage as a birthday present.

Speaking of birds, I've observed the robins that nest under our deck. Five years ago, mama Robin only made one nest then she began making two nests—this year she made three. It is alarming to know that 3 billion birds have not been born since the late 70s according to a recent study by Cornell University.[114] So mama robin is hedging her bets. The first nest hatchlings are likely to be eaten by a bird of prey (as I observed this year) and the second and third nests' hatchlings are needed so that a few offspring make it through to the next year. I cheered on one recently born baby bird as she adorably hopped along the deck up to the railing with something like an "I think I can" determination.

These tensions, between aesthetic interests of affiliation (such as family and neighbor's "expectations" of a manicured or "tamed" yard) and growing consciousness (like growing food in one's front yard or letting the wild things grow), are always at play whether we take the time to attend to them or not. These tensions take time to feel and work through, time that is hard to "justify" to ourselves, let alone others. So when Nathan's friend started brush hogging the side of the driveway with ear protection, Rosie and I watched from the deck; Rosie simply being her curious self, while I, attempting to be more like her, was unable to not think of the bees and beautiful white butterflies I'd seen feeding themselves there the day before.

Inside I put on some Gabrielle Roth (on our very old stereo) and returned to staining the stairs I'd just sanded. Paul returned and we had a moment. He asked if I wanted to go outside and put the fencing up for Rosie (she's been getting too close to a neighbor's ducks and chickens). I said, "nah, I'm good." We both stewed for a bit and later he

---

[114] https://www.birds.cornell.edu/home/bring-birds-back

called me outside to get my opinion for placement of the fence. After he'd justified his "somebody needs to get it done" stance and I justified my "responsibility to nature amid the insanity of the world" stance, we took a beat to look at each other, breathe together, soften, and move on. He kept putting the fence up and I kept staining.

Here is the prayer we say together most days:

Our Mother, Our Father, whose art surrounds us
Glory Be Your Name
Thy life essence, which thou breathes through us
Is in every present moment.
Give us this day, reverence, for your perfect nourishment
And fill us with your love, your peace, your joy,
your mercy and your grace
As we walk the path you clear for us.
Lead us into heartfelt and loving thoughts, words, feelings and actions,
And deliver us into your infinite embrace.

…then we each share a personal prayer for the day.

Life is (a) Pain

Rosie's need for a walk usually becomes obvious with incessant whining, especially when, for example, I'm on a Zoom call or in the middle of putting a client project together or experiencing a burst of creativity. I do my best to choose that she is more important. And it is often easier to care for the well-being of our animals than it is to care for our own well-being.

Twice in one week we went for a walk in the woods by a stream with very slippery rocks. One day I was on the phone and holding her leash so that she wouldn't run over to bother the people a bit down the way; the other day I was sending an email that absolutely didn't need to be sent at that moment. Both days I hurt myself pretty badly.

To say it's not a good idea to multitask is to say to someone like me, "Karen, forget everything you have ever learned about being in the world; forget all the years of observing, listening, researching, practicing, learning, and perfecting the myriad skills you have developed; forget the sense of selfhood you have defined, the insulation or armor built around your identity that helps you ward off the mansplaining, or the more politically correct descriptor I have come up with for this, hyper-contextualization. (By the way, the name Karen has been called the female version of mansplaining).

Yet with all that being said, I do know that there are moments when multitasking is just wrong. Those most salient moments are the ones in nature, the ones where the breeze, the leaves shimmering on the trees, the bubbling water, the underfoot crunch of branches fallen, even the mosquitoes are all demonstrating the essence of peaceful coexistence, all expressing the aspects of harmony and at-one-ment.

The first time I hurt myself I was barefoot, so happy to be warm enough to plunge my feet into the few inches of cold water running over the slippery rocks covered in varieties of mosses I may never fully learn. Rosie had been very patiently waiting for her walk and I'd decided to take the 20-minute Zoom call break to get in a fast but nourishing visit to the stream while calling a colleague to catch up about something. I felt sure footed and careful as I walked inch by inch but suddenly, I stepped in a precarious way and slid about two feet with my big toe slamming directly into a rock. Not surprisingly I did not drop Rosie's leash or my cell phone. My toe was bleeding and the nail was bent straight up. I got off the phone and put it away, pushed my toenail back down and breathed deeply for a few minutes, grateful to have fresh spring water flowing over it. I took quite a few extra minutes to walk slowly home and to bandage my toe, even putting ice on it and elevating it before getting back on the damn Zoom call.

The second time I hurt myself I was also on my cell phone. This is the point, the problem. I have a real issue with technology, a real love-hate relationship with it. I am so sensitive to the electromagnetic frequencies (EMF) emitted by the cell phone and the laptop that my hands burn from the tingling, my elbows ache and I have a tendency to go numb in the arms. But this is how we connect with each other; this is how I am able to work remotely. This is how we all are able to be "productive" and "drive" the economy and multitask.

I had intentionally decided to bring the phone because I'd had the ringer off all morning. I figured I could take a moment to quickly (and it's never quickly) peruse all the texts and at least a few of the more important emails of the day. One email was from a client who had shared his artistic work with me, this was beyond technology—it was an experience of technology serving connection and inspiration. Then I noticed my Gmail account had suggested I follow up with someone who hadn't responded to my email sent 6 days ago. It was SO not important that I attend to this, *especially* at the moment I followed Rosie onto the big flat rocks in the stream.

I saw the big flat dry rock that was my destination, the one I'd wanted to stand on with Rosie while looking up and down the stream. I also saw the dark green big slimy stone at the edge of the stream that I had to step one foot on in order to have enough leg span to make it to the dry stone. As suddenly as the last mishap, the last instance of multitasking with insufficient mindfulness, I slipped about two feet and fell on my back, smacked the back of my head on the stone and was duly admonished by my mother, nature. That's how it happens for me. And again I didn't drop my cell phone in the water. This time I wish I had.

After a few moments of deep breathing and gentleness I laid on the big dry flat rock, full of slime and decomposed leaves and stared up to the tree branches overhead watching them shimmer in the breeze. I'd felt my brain rattle and, having had a number of concussions over the years, tried to relax my sympathetic overdrive for maximum potential healing in the moment. I struggled and took a picture wanting to "capture" the moment with Rosie. I have so much to learn about detaching from technology—and I'm a middle-aged woman who feels more like a Luddite than a technophile so I can only imagine how hard this might be for others.

∞

Multitasking is the epitome of stressing the brain. There are two types of stress: distress (bad, distracting, chronic) and eustress (good, focusing, brief). The first is harmful and the second is healthy. Multitasking gives us the feeling of eustress but the effect of distress.

I had a dream (below) about talking to my dharma brother Josh where I was aware of a choice I had made not to multitask in order to give him my full attention. Listening to our dreams, listening to other people share their stories with our full attention, these skills are very worthy of our intention and are ways to step in the direction **Beyond Karen**.

Josh and I are sitting in a little bit of traffic in the middle of Main Street near the cinema (to our right). He was in the left seat yet I was driving and I pulled over to park near the left facing traffic because I noticed he had wanted to say something serious and I wanted to give him my full attention. He shared a bit of the pain he had experienced with "white religion" as the dominant paradigm and as he said this he put a square cloth (like a chamois) over his head. After a while of silence I peeked under to ask if he was OK. He said yes. We acknowledged how big that feeling was and he said I should write it down (for the book). Instead, I looked at him and said "what I hear you saying is that this ubiquitous white religion makes it seem like your religion is less important in a way, and is bringing up feelings of shame." And then I started sobbing as I felt the weight of that statement.

∞

One of my greatest spiritual experiences was the first time I participated in an Ayahuasca ceremony. To many practitioners, Ayahuasca is a religion. This ceremony was led by a young man who had recently been through his shamanic training and the clarity and gentleness of his words and rituals over the weekend were beautiful. I learned through this connection to Grandmother and, the next day, Grandfather, what the essence of love with nature feels like; the miracle and magic of everything living in harmony all at once.

This experience has informed much of my self-regulation efforts and has helped me see when I am in my own way, unable to be present or appreciate what, especially nature, is right in front of me. With the awareness of the essence of nature, even though I was unable to truly be present after this second fall, I squatted down on the ground over the dried leaves and branches, buried my phone in leaves for a few minutes (which I hope removes some of the toxic EMF) and waited for a moment. Then I started singing, more like sounding, and finally I felt able to be in that moment, in harmony; not too dissimilar from the Ayahuasca experience.

Some people report terror with mind altering substances and I can definitely understand that; it is as if any demons we are trying hard to not see will make themselves exceptionally colorful for us in this unfiltered state. And I can't underscore the importance of safe community and the intentionality of the ritual enough in order to reach these depths in ourselves safely. This is yet another example of the route to **Beyond Karen**, in relation to one another, on all levels, all at once.

I share all of this, the story of my two injuries in nature and being in sacred ceremony, because we are all desperate for this essential relationship, this connection to spirit and its creative and healing power.

There is no course or video or expert who will "give" us the deets on this relationship. The only way to develop it is to develop it, to state our intention and to take action. This is such an easy action and yet also the easiest to ignore. As much as I want to continue to understand what a relationship with nature is, as blessed as I am to have trees and water around me, I don't believe I will ever fully appreciate it and I struggle greatly to hold up my end of the relationship.

In continuing to imagine what **Beyond Karen** looks like, I come back to my spiritual roots. Within the past year or two I learned that Nhat Hanh, the last name of Thich Nhat Hanh, can be translated to mean "one action." Thich Nhat Hanh, or Thay (teacher), is the Vietnamese Buddhist monk who for decades has held space for millions of people to Engage with Buddhism.

I have been part of a sangha, a group of practitioners, who sit together weekly. One action is the notion of being mindfully present with the activity, the person, the feeling that is with you in this moment and not being distracted by what happened or will be happening in another moment. This spiritual guidance has given me a good foundation of understanding about mindfulness. It has helped me believe that I can keep growing in the awareness of how much is alive in every moment, in every body, in every place and space, which is in itself an act of gentle faith.

Gentle faith is what I need to continuously reflect on in order to counteract the political anger and tensions within me. When I insulate myself with distractions that keep me fooled into thinking I'm being "productive" or foods that don't support heath in the body or media that stirs up feelings of disconnection, I am susceptible to anger stirred up by the media. Such media, junk foods and distractions are everywhere. So, getting **Beyond Karen**, to me, seems to be about tuning into what is true in nature, what is a gift from nature, and what grows love in this most important relationship for life.

Over the years I have had typical and not-so-typical injuries. I've never broken a bone (though my eight-year-old self tried to break an arm, like my cousin who'd gotten a lot of attention for her broken arm, by rolling off the top of a slide).

I truly have had more concussions than I can count, some from automobile accidents (four in my late teens), one or two from playing soccer, and one from diving off a rock into shallow water. I've had a big rusty nail through my foot, tore my ACL twice, and lost both my big toenails after wearing the wrong shoes on a protest pilgrimage along a proposed pipeline route (which was finally defeated!). But it has been many years since I have had a big injury and I like to think this is because I've had a solid mindfulness practice for two decades.

In early July I embarked on a vacation day, an hour or so after a morning work call. I scheduled appointments, cleaned the house, created a spreadsheet of local and national Defund the Police resources, and wrote a lot less than I'd expected to of this book. Then I crushed my index and ring finger of my left hand by manually closing the garage door with them trapped in between two sections.

I had removed the garage door trim and fully prepped it to be painted and was excited to get to the satisfying part of the project, the low effort dramatic result part of transforming a thing. The whole experience was surreal as all shock injuries are, but I observed myself crush my fingers in the way neuroscientist Jill Bolte Taylor observed herself having a stroke (which she wrote about in **My Stroke of Insight**).

Here is my story:

I heard the crush of my two left fingers in disbelief and, after a beat, realized I needed to open the door to remove them. With a right hand flat on the door pressing up and a right foot wedged underneath pushing up, the fingers came out. I felt a shooting pain up to my left armpit and I said "fucking shit" as I ran up the steps, to the door, to the utility sink, to the water.

Why this story makes sense (to me anyway) to include in **Beyond Karen** is due to the way insights appeared over the few hours afterwards. I had been writing about perfectionism and thinking about good and bad labels we put on activities, behaviors, efforts and I remembered talking with Paul about the potential rain coming and the narrow window of time to paint the first coat on the garage door so it could dry beforehand. I mused that a permanent effort like painting was good perfectionism and an ongoing effort like cleaning was bad perfectionism.

I felt the nausea coming on fiercely and for all my breathing mindfully was unable to stop it. I managed to shut the water off before my legs buckled underneath me (immediate and extended family members will attest to my intense advocacy for water conservation) and I laid on the floor on my back continuing to watch a flood of memories about my daughter at age five being an amazing help (getting me a glass of OJ and calling her father) when I sliced my left middle finger to the bone while washing a large vase, and about watching a family member get crushed to his death. It's this one that I was feeling viscerally, even though it was just fingers I was dealing with, in that moment of suspension when adrenaline is doing all it can to help.

With plummeting blood sugar, I rallied and got up the stairs to get an ice pack for my fingers and landed back on the kitchen floor. I made little deals with myself about not wasting energy in order to get the blood sugar regulated with food: I'd just cut the tops off the carrots instead of trying to peel them, and I'd dip them in hummus. I decided the energy it would take to make toast was also a good investment and made it back to the fridge. With all that thinking going on I was in good enough shape to text Paul who was 30 minutes away and let him know what had happened. I told him I was "fine" and to do what he needed to do (he was pricing a painting job). But the nausea wasn't settling down. I laid down on the couch and realized I couldn't see from the bottom half of my eyes.

I was afraid of having a stroke given my genetic predisposition on both sides of my family, but when Paul called with a calm and dispassionate voice, I was able to rally again. I actually went back to the garage door and finished painting; and as I opened the door, learned I had left Rosie outside (and you hopefully know how much I love my Rosie). Thankfully she was sitting right there. I felt as if this accident had a purpose, a reminder to be further careful and considerate. But the real power in this experience came through the story telling, the reliving of it with Paul.

The power of story sharing is a new thing to us, even after more than 30 years together. As our daughter Sabrina graduated college, we attended a life changing Spaces Between Stories retreat with Charles Eisenstein (one of the times when we were hanging on to our relationship by all our loose threads) where we, along with dozens of others, learned good techniques for being attentive. But as a couple, holding space for each other to integrate an experience is just becoming a piece of our communication tool kit. This day I just knew I'd needed to tell him the story even though he'd already known all the pertinent details and was now there with me.

There were many insights, but I'll share two big ones. As I recalled to Paul the slice to the middle finger story and the fact that I had just reinjured an area next to the triple warmer (connecting heart, liver and kidney meridians), I touched back to a pivotal moment in my life when we drove all the way from Massachusetts to Tennessee for an Edgar Cayce family camp. There I showed a woman the scar on my middle finger and she explained the triple warmer energy in that part of the body, as well as the way in which physical injuries have emotional and spiritual impacts and emotional and spiritual injuries have physical impacts. This understanding has become so ingrained in my body-mind that I forgot how important the awareness of emotional-physical connection is in healing, in moving past, in getting "beyond" the pain.

Because Paul is learning how to witness me in states of distress without taking it personally or trying to "fix" me, I was able to let myself be more vulnerable than I was comfortable being, to be irrational and cry without justification. I ended up losing the fourth fingernail but the pain was not physical.

It has taken a great deal of patience from both of us and constantly verbalizing our commitment to each other to achieve this new ability to witness each other. The second insight hurts so badly I can barely write it here. So I will say that the surreal, slow motion, disembodied experience of hearing the crush of my two fingers is what brought back the embodied experience of my brother's death, and leave it at that.

We all know we have to see positive qualities like strength and beauty in another in order for the other to bear the negative qualities like weakness and ugliness we may experience and need to process. I believe this is true because deep feelings are messy and nonlinear, they come from unexpected directions, "triggered" by old unhealed wounds and unresolved misunderstandings and if we don't feel solid and respected in myriad ways by the partner we trust, by colleagues, by anyone intimate, the strange ways in which emotions present themselves may be so disorienting as to make us feel dysregulated even as we are trying to support and help regulate another.

∞

This brings me back to the Defund the Police effort. Whether or not this achieves its nation-wide goals, it is raising consciousness and all such calls for accountability are valuable. The policing system in the United States has been built up to infuse every type of community with strong emotion—from deep trust and dependency to deep fear and intimidation. Being able to shine light on these personal and complex often subconscious emotions is a gift of this moment in time.

On the first Zoom call to mobilize the regional Defund the Police effort, I was intrigued by the facilitators' thoughtful invitation to participants to share experiences of police brutality if one felt so moved. My first reaction was to be in witness mode. I would say that my subconscious mind was thinking something to the effect of, "I'm not someone who has justifiable anger because I am a privileged white woman and I haven't experienced police brutality."

Then, after a few people shared their stories, my own experience smacked me hard and fast. I couldn't believe that something so painful in my life was packed so far back into my subconsciousness, *and* that I disallowed myself the justification to feel anger about it. What else is back there?! And this repression I am waking up to exists even though I am someone who has actively been working at emotional healing and wellness for decades. What about all of us who have yet to find a safe and "privileged" space for our stories to be witnessed?!

∞

A white woman has written a very popular book called **White Fragility** that has helped many white people understand racism. Maybe you've read it? In her Rules of Engagement, Robin DiAngelo speaks to the intense emotional "righteous indignation" white people initially have when they consider racism as anything beyond "individual acts of cruelty [by] terrible people who consciously don't like people of color."

White people are waking up to the fact that this self-serving definition is a "cop" out; and in unpacking the generations of misinformation that has shrouded reality with grave consequences to our sisters and brothers of color, we are taking baby steps toward reparations. If rules apply well to some and badly to others, the rules are not right and just.

Righteous indignation is what white people habitually do to each other when intense feelings get expressed. And yet to have a supple and receptive mind, to be a sensitive, childlike being capable of wonder and genuine interest in each other, we must make space for expression, reactions, feedback, processing and integration. These things take time and they are anathema to the prevalent paradigm of white culture and extractive capitalism which extracts the very soul from life.

I have never not felt judged and ogled and questioned and defensive when my carefully cultivated sensitivities carry my body-mind and my mouth across some figurative line of political correctness or decorum. Is this white privilege? Yes, in a really obscure way of looking at it, these intense moments are part of the equation; I have had many opportunities to grow and learn, and I have had conditions that supported my choices. At the same time, the lack of resonance or sympathy I have experienced (when I needed it most) can feel like a never-ending panic attack or a severe allergic reaction with no EpiPen in sight.

White culture has, for better and worse, served as the overarching model of growth and aspiration for far too long and we are collectively far too immature for such a thing to not end badly. We can't just dismantle white culture despite a deep and righteous desire to do so by many—not just people of color. I believe the foundation for representative culture lies in emotional consciousness raising.

The value of consciousness raising may seem debatable. Paul, in his heart of hearts, seriously questions the value of feeling deeply, the way I do. He sees what a wreck I can be when I fall apart. But, as I said to my son one day over a quick and very meaningful lunch break chat, the thing I am most proud of in my life is that, at my age, I am still able to empathize deeply, to cry with others in pain (whether I know them or not) despite my own trauma. And the reason why this book was originally dedicated to "Karens and all the people who hate them" is because I believe in the goodness of those seeking accountability and I hold out hope for those who are being pressured to be accountable.

My heart aches for people who, like most children, have completely given their authority away to others (parents, partners, employers, professionals, etc.) and must reclaim their own voice after years of vocal atrophy. I contend that Karens, as defined by professional influencers, assert their authority vicariously through association and affiliation, not through embodied wisdom.

∞

There is no question that the words and behaviors of a Karen have the potential to activate significant psychic, emotional and physical pain.

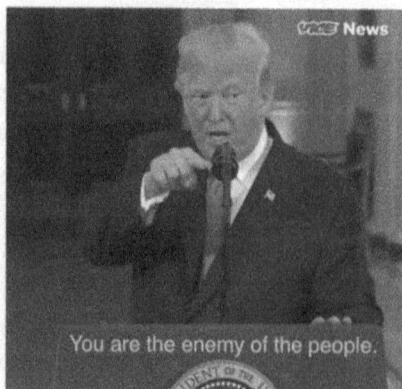

When you meet a person named Karen

You are the enemy of the people.

The most epic entitled Karen of our time, *of all time*, the former occupant of the White House, has wreaked havoc on a scale that is shaking the foundation of every living thing. It is eye opening to review the twitter feed of the Human Rights Watch establishing this administration's Timeline of Hate[115] beginning January 20, 2017.

---

[115] https://www.hrc.org/timelines/trump

This opinion of mine has been echoed by David A. Graham, writer for The Atlantic, who wrote a piece May 28, 2020 titled, "The Karen in Chief—President Trump calls the cops on those who challenge him, even if there's no actual violation, to make life miserable for them."

The United States feels like a nation of Karens[116] these days, so it's only appropriate that the president would be the Karen in chief.

When Trump gets sufficiently angry about anyone who dares criticize him, he is quick to work the referees, attempting to use the force of the law to bully the critics into submission and to try to intimidate would-be critics from opening their mouths. That's what Trump does … in preparing an executive order to punish social-media companies after Twitter dared to fact-check his words.

Alexis Grenell, a journalist who has written on gender and politics for The New York Daily News, The Washington Post and The New York Times, calls out the "53 percent [of white women] who put their racial privilege ahead of their second-class gender status in 2016 by voting to uphold a system that values only their whiteness, just as they have for decades" in her piece, *White Women Come Get Your People*. She calls these women—sympathetic to gross vestiges of the patriarchy, "who think that being falsely accused of rape is almost as bad as being raped, the kind of women who agree with President Trump that 'it's a very scary time for young men in America'"—gender traitors and women who've "made standing up for the patriarchy a full-time job."[117]

In this piece Grenell is covering the appointment of Brett Kavanaugh, the Supreme Court Justice that was confirmed even after at least seven women testified about Kavanaugh sexually assaulting them. Some women, asleep to the standards to which a Supreme Court Justice should be held, literally made and wore "Women for Kavanaugh" T-

[116] https://www.theatlantic.com/ideas/archive/2020/05/trump-social-media-scarborough/612193/
[117] https://www.nytimes.com/2018/10/06/opinion/lisa-murkowski-susan-collins-kavanaugh.html

shirts. He was also proven to have lied under oath and yet calls for impeachment go unanswered[118].

After a confirmation process where women all but slit their wrists, letting their stories of sexual trauma run like rivers of blood through the Capitol, the Senate still voted to confirm Judge Brett M. Kavanaugh to the Supreme Court. With the exception of Senator Lisa Murkowski of Alaska, all the women in the Republican conference caved, including Senator Susan Collins of Maine, who held out until the bitter end.

Grenell notes that Trump fully plays these women who are blind to their complicity.

"Ms. [Kellyanne] Conway even *weaponized her own alleged sexual assault* in service to her boss by discouraging women from feeling empathy with Christine Blasey Ford or anger at Judge Kavanaugh. Ms. Conway knows that a woman who steps out of line may be ridiculed by the president himself. President Trump mocked Dr. Blasey[119] in front of a cheering crowd on Tuesday evening. Betray the patriarchy and your whiteness won't save you."

It is time for white women to atone for their sins of complicity, for their silence in the face of illegalities and gross misconduct. Will this lead to hastening the prosecution of the morally bankrupt misogynists and "white" criminals doing the illegal deeds and perpetuating and covering for the gross misconduct?

With all the investigation and research comes the satire, some of it so unfortunately believable, particularly with this man, that it is hard to see as satire. The Stanford Daily has a satirical spinoff, The Stanford Occasionally, in which a July 2020 post[120] about Trump declaring February "Karen History Month" instead of Black History Month made my jaw drop.

I returned to a tiny poem I wrote many years ago:

---

[118] https://time.com/5677929/new-york-times-brett-kavanaugh-sexual-misconduct/
[119] https://www.nytimes.com/2018/10/02/us/politics/trump-me-too.html
[120] https://www.stanforddaily.com/2020/07/24/trump-declares-karen-history-month-calls-them-true-americans/

> Heartbreak shatters the shell around the heart
> and awakens its capacity to love.

All pain has the potential to bury us and the potential to lift us out of the ashes like the legendary phoenix. A traumatic childhood or event like losing an immediate family member early in life can break a person or break them open.

I think of my own pain of course, but also of what it must be like for people who grow up quite clear that they are so different from the views and opinions of their parents that they must run away or find themselves kicked out of their homes; people so clear that their gender identity is other than what they were born into, people so clear that their spiritual path is not what has been prescribed, even people unwilling to follow in the family heritage, or family business. We are facing the wrath, the reckoning of pain and suffering at what feels like an earth-shattering scale. We are all united—like it or not #45 included—in this global pandemic of despair.

From this line of thought I let my mind wander to some distant place where I could conjure empathy for this man. Here is what emerged:

Imagine, in a most challenging test of empathy, a scenario in which you have lived the life of the 45th president. What would it be like to be the baby-child-son of the most ruthless profit monger, the quintessential mafioso, a KKK rioter with every sort of shell game and money laundering scheme conceivable[121]? And imagine growing up exposed to the evil of all this but instead of reckoning with that truth, you bury it so deeply in your psyche, your subconscious, that your every waking action is to seek implicit and explicit daddy approval through acceptance and perpetuation of that evil? And then just imagine for shits and giggles that over and above this "deal with the devil," your childhood self in its process of individuating feels its gender identity and its spiritual path to also be diametrically opposed to the Father. What then? Wouldn't you double down to the point that you completely annihilate any hope of recovering your sanity?

---

[121] https://onepercenttakers.com/the-trump-crime-family/

Imagine the wake of destruction your Godzillan path could create. We don't have to work too hard to imagine this as it has been unfolding before our very eyes. But there is more than meets the eye in the king of the hill's crumbling exploits[122]. To me, the same reality mind games that white middle aged women have played with their psyche in order to not have a full out psychological break are in the same vicinity as the games one might have to play with themselves in the Trump family. I am looking forward to reading all about it from his niece, Mary Trump's, perspective[123]in her book, **Too Much and Never Enough**.

∞

Some comedians are expert at telling the truth slant, at bridging the pain chasm between fact and fiction. I highly recommend consuming comedy and really paying attention to the nuances of how they soften the edges of ingesting harsh reality—like Katt Williams' phone booth scene from School Dance (2014) with his baby mama trying to tell him her white, "rice skinned not light skinned" baby is his despite his 16 *consecutive* years behind bars. And then keep on keepin' on as the cascade of hard truths, like the research done by the department of defense, floods your consciousness.

A game I inadvertently found myself watching one day at Paul's sister's house left me laughing so heartily that Paul started laughing from the next room. A sweet 8-year-old girl was showing me how her game world works but could not figure out how to stop herself from dancing in the street. She danced everywhere, even while shopping in the supermarket … alone (one of many mind warps I noted). As the horror of the reality I could see behind this game settled into my awareness, the smile fell from my face. The online children's game is RoBlox (sounds like roadblocks) and the game within a game, Brookhaven, is not only

[122] https://www.cbc.ca/radio/day6/episode-359-harvey-weinstein-a-stock-market-for-sneakers-trump-s-data-mining-the-curious-incident-more-1.4348278/data-mining-firm-behind-trump-election-built-psychological-profiles-of-nearly-every-american-voter-1.4348283

[123] https://www.thedailybeast.com/mary-trump-donald-trumps-niece-is-writing-a-tell-all-book-that-details-how-she-leaked-tax-papers-to-nyt

fomenting unconscionable violence by making guns as accessible to children as penthouses with refrigerators stocked with ice cream, pizza and soda (and jobs at their disposal and house fires and car crashes with no consequence), but also building profiles of their psychographic behavior[124].

Josh Fox, Emmy-winning and Oscar-nominated filmmaker, said in an EcoWatch interview about the 2020 elections, "if you put out a racist ad and only racists can see it, it causes absolutely no controversy, but it's deeply effective in rallying people. And a lot of the time people don't even know that they're racist. So you might have things happening to folks on an unconscious level, on a deep psychological level that they're not aware of. But the internet knows. If you've got 5,000 data points on somebody, you know them on a very intimate level, you know their psychology, you know what they're afraid of, you know their sexual orientation, you know their medical history, their age, their race. So your campaign to win them over becomes very effective.[125]"

If this upsets you and you want to get to the roots of the psychographic artificial intelligence war underway, please start with a primer from Jill Lepore, **If Then: How the Simulmatics Corporation Invented the Future**. It can be really hard to not shut down emotionally and spiritually as we become educated about the sophisticated and mind-bending deception behind data mining, particularly as it is presented by the patriarchy's poster child, the pretty boy white 27 year old whiz kid Michelangelo[126] who reminds the ancient patriarchs of themselves.

∞

I once had a dream, about four years ago actually, that I had infiltrated the realm of this White House occupant, as a trusted model

---

124 https://www.familyzone.com/anz/families/blog/roblox-parents-review

[125] https://www.ecowatch.com/truth-has-changed-josh-fox-disinformation-2644813040.html?rebelltitem=1#rebelltitem1

[126] The Italian sculptor Michelangelo was 26 when he fomed David, the "perfect" man. It has been worshipped as such by the western world since the early 16th century.

of sorts (anything is possible in the dream space). I was immune to the trappings of this job and my intention was to find a way, by virtue of this insider vantage point, to take him down. Taking down corruption[127] must be a movement of movements coming clear-voiced from every direction: legal, social, familial, professional, personal.

Hopefully the time has come for a united state, a collective effort, an epic awakening to Shine Truth so brightly as to eradicate every shadow of this corrupt darkness and heal the massive collateral damage in the hearts and minds of America.

The summer of 2020, with intrastate coronavirus tensions running high and unfathomable pre-election shenanigans including the POTUS attempting to sabotage the United States Postal Service, I traveled to visit with my 16-year-old niece for half a day. We had very satisfying conversations with topics ranging from nature-based spirituality and her fascination with mushrooms to her dog and difficulties with her other side of the family.

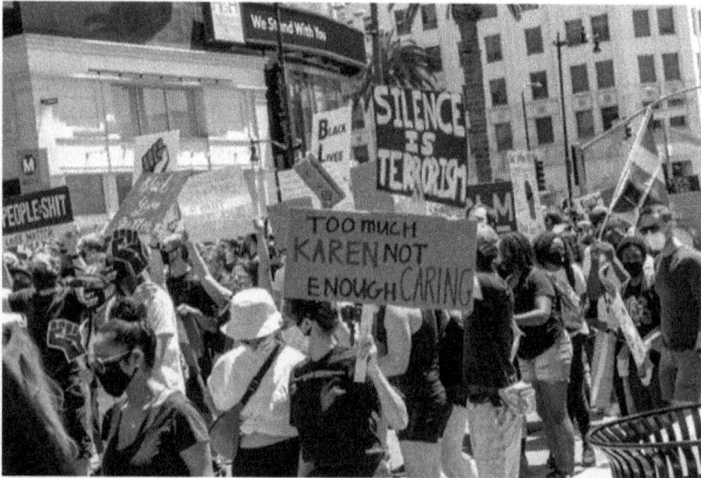

My niece was quite familiar with the Karen phenomenon and asked me questions about it that led us to talking about her family's mob mentality about politics. She shared her fear of retribution (*from her own family*) if she were to try discussing her opinions with them about

[127] https://www.globalwitness.org/en/about-us/

Trump's real record. She said that big bold announcements of support for the sitting president, who colluded with Russia to win the 2016 election, were often made when the family would gather together, almost like a gauntlet thrown on the floor for anyone to challenge. She has done a great deal of research and has never been able to feel safe speaking up about it in their presence.

I have tried to make the case for why white women are complicit in their own families, silenced and subjugated by centuries (millennia actually) of male patriarch's patronizing behaviors, explicit and implicit judgments, nonverbal criticisms and subtle, perhaps even subconscious forms of gaslighting. But why are so many men, mostly white, on (or believing they are on) the career ascent, or protecting their "assets," still perpetuating and getting away with this behavior?

Why? Because, according to research done by Women Occupying Wall Street, women do 66% of the world's work, earn 10% of the world's wages, and own 1% of the world's assets.

Think for a moment about waterfront properties. Who owns them? From what I can see, white men. I wish I could say that I understand the nature of legacy and inheritance; the determination to pass down property to future generations. I can imagine the desire to protect these assets though I believe, perhaps in my naivete, that I would worry most about the quality of the water, soil erosion and habitat health more than I would worry about how much my neighbors earn or what they look like.

Could everyone on the planet have an equal share of these idyllic spaces? What would that look like? There are 372,000 miles of coastline on planet earth, surely not all habitable. There are about 8 billion people on planet earth, surely not all interested in living on the water. In fact, as we all know, whole nations are desperately seeking solutions to the high probability that their lands will be underwater soon due to rising sea levels, which are, in no uncertain terms, due to anthropomorphic climate change. But, should all 8 billion want to live on the water, every quarter acre parcel would have to house 10 people.

The key here is not about living in close quarters. As dwellers of big cities like Mumbai might say, living together closely teaches tolerance and forgiveness of one another. The key is about allocation and use of resources. "Luxury" spaces like the waterfront properties with private acreage and thousands of square feet of living space, not to mention the "toys" for traversing said water, are A Problem. They come at great cost and require great defensive posturing which includes railing at the "welfare state."

Think back to the stories about fortresses with cannons poking through the parapet with men ready to light the fuse and pummel an invader or perhaps just an interloper. Recall the gun-toting, fortress protecting McCloskey attorneys "Ken and Karen" from St. Louis, Missouri. These are the forces of intimidation that those of us who have taken the time to reeducate ourselves about racism are up against, often in our own homes and bedrooms.

Desired use of resources only available where other people live is what wars are all about. Fossil fuels are 56 times more powerful than a horse and a horse is 10 times more powerful than a man. A 560 to 1 ratio is pretty impressive extractive value for the fossil fuel industry, wouldn't you agree? And still you can't drink oil.

In order to rise up and against this colonizing and extraction of natural resources, movements must be well organized, prepared for every sort of attack imaginable. Online shaming of Karens pales in comparison to the dog attacks and in-the-eyes pepper spraying wrought on the courageous Standing Rock protesters facing down armies and terrifying weapons. Fortunately, the Dakota Access Pipeline was shut down and the Standing Rock Sioux can breathe again, for now.

The ruling ordering a shutdown of DAPL marks the final word[128] of a March 25 decision by the same judge. That ruling found that the U.S. Army Corps of Engineers had violated the National Environmental Policy Act (NEPA) and glossed over the devastating consequences of a potential oil spill when it affirmed its 2016 decision to permit the pipeline.

---

[128] https://earthjustice.org/news/press/2020/judge-orders-dakota-access-pipeline-to-shut-down

As I was walking down the stairs to my car to return home (to my progressive college town that had been proudly Republican back when Theodore Roosevelt—the pro-lynching guy—built the national parks service and Franklin Delano Roosevelt—the man who sent 120,000 Japanese Americans to internment camps—implemented the New Deal), I told my niece that I'd spent decades working on my voice and that I wanted nothing more than for her to be fully confident in hers. I urged her to call me any time she needed to vent about oppressive family politics. I also want for all young women to have someone to call any time she needs to build her courage and test out her voice, someone to witness her truth.

Going Beyond Karen

Let me begin by saying thank you to breath, the source of inspiration, the source of life. Would that I could say thank you with every inhale—to never forget; to always remember—so that my life was a true expression of gratitude for the preciousness of this gift.

Next, let me acknowledge my matrilineal line as far back as I know it, for support.

Thank you Mary C. W., Geneva D. W., Louise O. C., Mary L. C., Albertine L. D., Bridget R. O., Bridget H. R., Emilie G. L., Marguerite G. D., Angele G. D., Theona M. G., Mary M. L., Bridget L. M., Mary H. C., Catherine K. H., Ellen K., Annie E. W., Mary L. E., Agnese (Bridget) L., Ann D. E., Elmira (Mary) P. W., Mary C. P., Marguerite G. G., Marie P. St. G. G., Marie F. P., Elisabeth H. F., Louise L. G. St. G., Marie A. F., Marie F. G. St. G., Agatha L. H. L., Jane B. W., Rebecca B., Deborah K. W.

Now I hope to be ready to hold the pain and suffering of the truth that I am an ignorant, white, middle-aged, privileged woman who, more often than is healthy, speaks and acts from a place of fear which inflicts levels of harm on those to whom she speaks. Sometimes these words are sexist, sometimes they are classist and sometimes they are racist.

Now I hope to be ready to accept that the pain and suffering held by myself and others may surprise me with its emotional rawness, may come upon me in a way entirely different than I may understand or be comfortable with, and may seem impossible to address or resolve.

This chapter opening feels, to me, a bit like the Thanksgiving Address[129] of the Haudenosaunee, who set proper context with "words that come before all else." There is so much to learn from our indigenous brethren, our wise elders.

Sometimes we can go back in order to go forward. Despite my genealogical quest, I have been able to gather very little story of my matrilineal line. Did any of these women have a voice outside the home? Were any of them properly educated? Were some of them handmaidens of French royalty, perhaps a deeply shameful experience? I wonder how many lost babies in childbirth. I have learned that many of them lost sons to fatal accidents, drowning, and war. Some of them died young, of sickness, or in childbirth. All of them had at least one job, motherhood.

"You didn't make good choices, you had good choices." This is the climactic line spoken by Kerry Washington's character Mia in the Hulu series *Little Fires Everywhere*. It comes at the moment when Reese Witherspoon's character Elena—called a "Karen you love to hate" by the hosts of the NPR podcast *Code Switch*—has completely shamed Mia over the truth of her surrogacy. No matter how equally tenacious these women are, how dedicated to their children they both are, the class and racial divide is too wide to be bridged, especially in the aftermath of the Reagan Era in which the show is set. The series ends with complete and utter devastation, not unlike the devastating failure to pass the Equal Rights Amendment following the "intervention" of Christian middle-aged white women upholding the patriarchy twenty years prior.

Remember my reference to the bumper sticker, "Think it's not Illegal Yet?" What about "Try Feeling, it's Healthy?" Maybe we Americans, or at least white middle-aged women, can allow ourselves to feel devastated for a minute. To let the physical reality of ageing, the political reality of not being equal to men in the eyes of the law, and the social reality of so many nuanced factors that have left us seeming a hell of a lot more pitiful than we know ourselves to be just sink in for a minute. Then, maybe, we can relax, breathe deeply, and be able to tell

---

[129] https://indigenousvalues.org/haudenosaunee-values/thanksgiving-address-ganonhanyonh/

our stories, our real, authentic, personal stories without all the political correctness and filters we have learned from our mothers. Just maybe?

My mother, like me, married her high school sweetheart. Her husband, my father, became a truck driver and accidentally ran over their five-year-old son, my brother (and if you've lost a sibling tragically you can appreciate the fact that watching my brother get crushed under this massive 18-wheeler two feet in front of me has left me with profound survivor guilt which underlies everything I do to make the most out of this one precious life). Sometime after that my mother became a cashier and then a very good secretary. My grandmother had married an accountant who became a successful businessman. But he had a fatal heart attack shortly after giving her five children, leading her to work at the jewelry counter of the department store on the bus route. My great grandmother, like my mother, worked tobacco in Connecticut and quite some time after her husband had died of lung disease, died in bed, in the room my mother slept in, within a year or so of my mother's father's death. My father's mother never "worked" and there is no account of any other of my grandmothers having worked.

When I reflect on the lives of the women in my matrilineal line, I feel almost nothing but grief and sadness about my perception of their lives full of cultural and religious oppression. But reflecting on these women who have come before me has been one of the greatest gifts I have given myself; it has strengthened my connection to my roots, it has filled me with a sense of cultural history that is often thin and fragile for white Americans with ancestors more intent on cultural assimilation than cultural preservation, and it leads me to believe these women have my back in a way that somehow makes up for the absence of support I experienced as a voiceless girl.

This grief and sadness leads me to feel anger in my day to day life, every time I hear men tell me things I already know, things I have put in long hours to learn the hard way, things I try to speak about but get ignored and dismissed while saying, things that I say which are then restated in their "himitator" voice, convincing them that these things were their ideas, things that have been taken, appropriated (or "a-bro-priated") and profited from.

Fun facts[130]:

- Ada Lovelace was the first computer programmer, but it took 150 years for her to receive back the credit that had been given to her male colleague.
- Rosalind Franklin's research led to breakthroughs in understanding DNA, the discovery for which her male colleague received a Nobel Prize.
- Lisa Meitner co-wrote a paper on nuclear fission with a male colleague who removed her name and went on to receive a chemistry prize from the Royal Swedish Academy of Sciences.
- Elizabeth Magie, an anti-monopolist, designed the famous Monopoly board game but an unemployed man took the idea and sold it as his.

I can stew in my anger about the ideas I have had appropriated from me, during my most abundant years—when I burned the candle at both ends while taking 21 credits a semester to get two undergraduate degrees in four years both with high honors (*Phi Beta Kappa*, having no idea what that was), yet finding no respectable employment, the years of raising a family while starting a business, the years when it seemed nothing I did was good enough, even being a mother because I was also trying to be an entrepreneur—but it was my choice to do all this, to struggle. It was my choice to believe in some "you can have it all" American Dream.

Before I had any clue about being a privileged white person, a de facto supremacist, which is hard to say but even harder to understand and atone for, I spent years stewing in anger about these and other petty things. When considering the privilege of something as "basic" as language, something that most white Americans may never give a second thought to, I can begin to understand that the ubiquitousness of the English language is a result of colonization. Baby steps like this can open the mind to more and more understandings, more genuine experiences of compassion and empathy for others with incredibly

---

[130] https://www.cnbc.com/2017/10/11/how-to-combat-hepeating-at-work-according-to-a-harvard-professor.html

powerful stories to tell in different ways and in different languages than the one we know.

Getting beyond Karen behavior is about not being hamstrung or victimized by one's pain and suffering but instead seeing all of it, *all of it*, as a portal for growth, a window for observing the learning edges in and through the everyday conversations with others, the mundane and the profound experiences of life.

I understand the isolation and loneliness in my life—of going from a middle child to an only child after my older sister moved out and I lost my brother a few months later—as a sturdy bridge of empathy to others' experiences of isolation and loneliness. It feels healthy and real and important. With respect to my learning edges around men who take, need, or simply are bestowed with most everyone's attention in small group settings, however, I am still taking baby steps. It is a constant trigger for my masculine self, which is often feeling ignored, slighted, or emasculated. But when I am able to notice that all the "airtime" a man gets to process his thoughts and insights—and not feel like it comes at my expense or explains my weaker skills of verbal expression—I am able to feel gratitude for all the times Paul has been by my side, listening to my developing thoughts and insights.

This gratitude, this 180° shift in attitude, leads me to explore other experiences of feeling listened to as well as to see ways in which I may pay it forward and be a good listener to someone else's developing thoughts and insights. Behavior shifting is what we all may struggle with as we grow and explore our learning edges. And, to the extent that we have given our authority or power to the sexists and misogynists, the racists and colorists, the ageists and any other "ists" in society, we can try on this "pain as a portal for growth" perspective; because, no matter what has caused someone to be a hater, everyone was once an innocent child. The more we practice this in real time, the less likely we will be to "lose our shit" with a hurtful emotional outburst and the more apt we will be to go **Beyond Karen**.

I spent many years focused on "business" as the key to success but was left brainwashed and depleted. These years worked me, like grist, through a mill, to separate true values I held, or "wheat," from the fluff and insubstantial beliefs, or "chaff." And even after consciously choosing to follow my inner authority to explore my feminine consciousness and develop the Inner Fortune concept that felt like divine guidance and a healing path, I still had so much more to unpack and unlearn and understand. One way I learned was through a young white man taking my concept and building a platform with it. I felt shame to have been so defenseless, but in the course of giving myself time and space to let it go, I realized that he was able to do something with it that I was not. We all have the capacity to grow from every experience, joyful and painful.

In Winona LaDuke's book **Recovering the Sacred: The Power of Naming and Claiming**, she counts many of the countless acts of disrespect, humiliation, rape and murder that white man has inflicted on indigenous people as a hard context setting from which her readers may appreciate the true depths of resilience and unparalleled capacity to overcome pain. White people can and should learn from the many ways Native people across America have worked to sustain and reclaim their sovereignty. These and other sacred models of resilience are necessary for white people to learn and understand. Karens who say things like "sacrifice the weak, reopen Tennessee" (in the COVID pandemic) are not exerting privilege, they are exposing multi-generational ignorance and racism.

It took a long while to learn how to breathe and release my anger into the ground we stand on. I am still a shallow breather, so I need reminders (like the mindfulness bell that rings on the computer every hour). Anger still gets stuck in my joints which hurt like hell as I write this, to you, human "out there" whom I envision caring about my story, whose heart I imagine glowing a bit more brightly as it breaks open to your own depths of compassion. But instead of being full of myself and thinking that I need to hold it in, I can imagine my "big" energy as an offering to the earth; I know she knows what to do with it.

Despite daily yoga for decades, a mindfulness practice and a healthy diet so my heart doesn't arrest like my mother's, despite cradling my anger with care and attention as it rises up day after day, despite having married the adorable brown kid from the town swimming pool and dedicating my heart to this man's awakening (the way he has dedicated his to mine), perhaps the way every woman before me and every woman after me has done and will do for her partner, despite all of this, I am still Karen.

I am still angry, voiceless and raw about the complete and utter venom directed over the years at me and the millions of other women who weren't able to withstand the firehose pressure—forcing them to dilute their ideas and dial down their creative sparks, water down their unique flavors, their core essence, their truth, their lives. I am still pissed off about women of my generation (particularly susceptible to Karen name calling), once backed into a corner with no viable conscious option but to accommodate the pressures to conform to the subordinate position deigned for women by men, including lewd womanizers, by "the patriarchy," "the system," to dye their hair, paint their faces, suck in, or out surgically, their guts, plasticize their bodies, hold all their muscles and their breath until their nerves rattle so loudly in their heads and their tongues curl up so dry in their mouths as to render them at best inarticulate and at worst, utterly mute, ready to snap or explode unexpectedly—paying forward and perpetuating the complete and utter venom directed at them.

∞

The energy directed at Karens can be viewed as lighthearted and "no big deal" because hey, it's just social media, it's just a joke, can't you take a joke? But taken in aggregate, over time, over a long fucking time, it is not the least bit funny; it is malicious and the chronic result of man, the masculine, powering over woman, the feminine, socially, religiously, physically, technologically, economically, emotionally, psychically, and biologically. Women have been biting the truth off their tongues so hard and for such a long time they can no longer taste the blood they've drained themselves of.

Karens, raging about half truths, possibly other people's alternative truths, must be called in, welcomed back home, into the arms of a wider, inclusive reality of care and compassion, once she has come to her senses like the wayward child who, like me, needed to experience a lot of bumps and bruises along the way.

The fear of growing, of moving beyond a stuck opinion, a stuck way of life, can feel so great as to trick the body-mind into thinking it is about to die, literal annihilation, especially if it is a massive turning point in one's life, like putting one's stories out into the world. This brings me to the beautiful "Our Deepest Fear" tapestry I have on my wall, of a poem by Marianne Williamson, the author, the former presidential candidate, the healer[131].

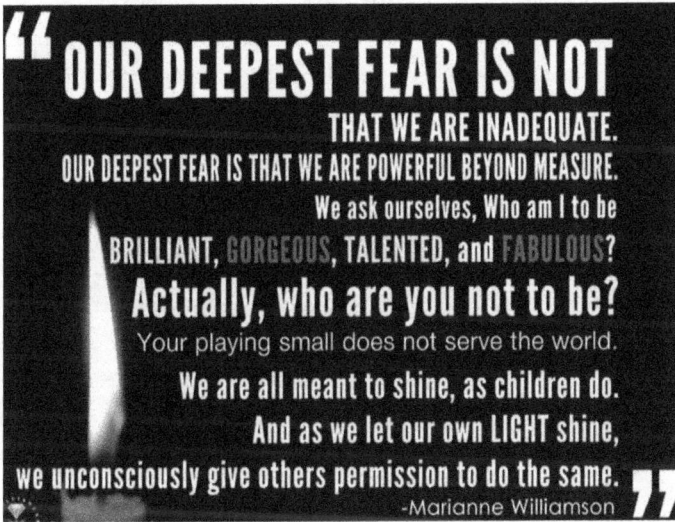

We all need hope. I find hope and spiritual nourishment from the women and men making movies and reporting news in such a way as to rebalance power and serve justice.

Feminism is a movement to levelize imbalances of power. The multi-millennial oppression and subjugation of women is killing the soul and spirit of humanity. It began with male, masculine religion to reinforce control, domination and power over women; it has led to wildfire bingeing and purging of global resources, wars and the rape, pillage and enslavement of others who were living within their means, on lands appreciated in their own natural right, not gutted and plundered and ultimately exterminated—suffocated with tar in the name of progress,

[131] http://www.sapphyr.net/largegems/ourdeepestfear.htm and
https://www.youtube.com/watch?v=rLAARJsNWHg

fucked so deep, long and hard with thousands of fracking chemicals and monster man made machines that her bones break, her blood runs dry, that no living being, not even microbes could sustain themselves, in the name of "progress"—and for what? So that women could grow as infertile as the land, unable to bear life like the poisoned, eroded, denuded soils?

My rage has led me to speak out in ways that were less than ideal, to speak up on behalf of others, mostly other women, other species, other classes and races of people—mostly to men with more power than they could responsibly manage. These people with excessive power must be held compassionately despite the horrific consequences of their willful ignorance, despite the nausea we feel about the impact of their actions, including Trump.

People blowing the whistles of alarm without the guise of humor—including those whom I have come to learn about like climate scientist Jim Hansen, the 90-plus women who finally brought 23 years of justice to the sexual predator and rapist Harvey Weinstein, the 100-plus gymnasts and their families who, after 20 years of his repeated sexual assaults on girls, served justice to Larry Nasser, as well as governmental, technical and political altruists like Chelsea Manning, Edward Snowden, Julian Assange, etc., sounding informed alarms of injustice—must be respected, listened to and appreciated and in no way, shape, or form persecuted for their courage.

In a section of Rebecca Traister's book, **Good and Mad**, called "Choosing to Hold Our Tongues," she discusses the literal and figurative trials of women at the apex of speaking truth to power: Rosa Parks, Hillary Clinton, Angela Davis, Cecile Richards, and Uma Thurman. The very real consequences to women expressing anger when utter rage is justifiable cannot be understated. Getting to the point of containing the rage that Richards sustained through a five-hour interrogation with falsified evidence about her organization, Planned Parenthood, requires an artfully woven community of support. Traister notes that Richards' containing strategy "worked to drive her inquisitors bonkers, which in turn put their spluttering, punitive frustration on display in front of a television audience." But the same nonviolent technique "is also part of the dynamic that leads us to ignore—to never even see—the catalytic power of women's rage" as it turned out for Rosa Parks, a woman "memorialized as stoic, pitied for having been exhausted, appreciated for her very refusal to show anger."

Uma Thurman was one of the many Hollywood women who helped secure a conviction for Harvey Weinstein at the height of the #metoo movement which has spawned the related #timesup movement about workplace sexual harassment. Thurman contained her anger until she was able to express it her way, which, Traister writes, "drove feminist Lindy West wild with frustration:"

> Not only are women expected to weather sexual violence, intimate partner violence, workplace discrimination, institutional subordination, the expectation of free domestic labor, the blame for our own victimization, and all the subtler, invisible cuts that undermine us daily, we are not even allowed to be angry about it.

Thurman's behind the scenes "reveal" is the sort of which we should all be aware. Our collective desire for pulp fiction makes us complicit in the twisted reality that manifests in order to produce it. Here is what Uma shares, explaining her near-death experience to New York Times reporter Maureen Dowd[132]:

"Harvey assaulted me but that didn't kill me," she says. "What really got me about the crash was that it was a cheap shot. I had been through so many rings of fire by that point. I had really always felt a connection to the greater good in my work with Quentin and most of what I allowed to happen to me and what I participated in was kind of like a horrible mud wrestle with a very angry brother. But at least I had some say, you know?" She says she didn't feel disempowered by any of it. Until the crash.

"Personally, it has taken me 47 years to stop calling people who are mean to you 'in love' with you. It took a long time because I think that as little girls, we are conditioned to believe that cruelty and love

---

[132] https://www.nytimes.com/2018/02/03/opinion/sunday/this-is-why-uma-thurman-is-angry.html

somehow have a connection and that is like the sort of era that we need to evolve out of."

Margaret Sanger, the founder of Planned Parenthood (and inspiration behind Wonder Woman), helped women evolve out of an era where people like John B. Watson were allowed to define feminism as "a form of deviance," and a feminist as "a woman unable to accept that she wasn't a man." Sanger thought women should rule the world because love is stronger than force, and she argued that the emancipation of women "wasn't a matter of ballots, it was part of a struggle that went all the way back to ancient Greece. It was a matter of liberating the 'feminine spirit'—a spirit well represented in the poems of Sappho of Lesbos."[133]

Sanger boldly put herself in harm's way, instigating arrest by handing out pamphlets about birth control in order to get media attention for her cause. And in one of her publications, *Happiness in Marriage*, she writes, "The successful husband-lover will, during every act of the love drama, seek to redirect all egotistical impulses, and, like a skillful driver, at every moment hold himself under intelligent control." An utterly revolutionary thought then, and, too often, still.

Perhaps the media "feeding frenzies" and "field days" sowing seeds of discontent (*and disconsent*) could evolve, from internalized capitalist greed keeping shareholders' and advertisers' needs in front of all others, back to the pursuit of clarity, truth, and honest education, clear sky and abundant fields every new day. This may sound a bit "pie in the sky" to the more jaded among us, but all we need to do is remember the fact that just a few short weeks after the pandemic hit and shut down the air polluting factories in China, the Himalayan Mountains could be seen, and we were all able to gaze at clearer skies.

A professor emerita of economics at the University of Massachusetts, Nancy Folbre, has had a lot to say about feminist economics. She authored *Who Pays for the Kids? Gender and the Structure of Constraint*; she co-authored *The Ultimate Field Guide to the U.S. Economy*,

---

[133] The inimitable Jill Lepore's book, **The Secret History of Wonder Woman**, is a fascinating treatise on feminism...and masculinism. Sanger's book **Woman and the New Race**, published two months after the 19th Amendment gave women the right to vote, became the philosophy of Wonder Woman.

and in her book, **The Invisible Heart**, which goes tit for tat against Adam Smith's "Invisible Hand" of the free market, she writes, "We don't have to believe that markets are intrinsically bad to acknowledge that 'who owns what' matters. We don't have to believe in decision-making by committee to fight for better rules of democratic governance. And we don't have to embrace the current policies of the welfare state to defend the principle that each of us has some obligation to care for others."

I, Karen, with the healing intention of 32 grandmothers behind me, have two things to say about that:

1. I am offering these words as a gift of my heart and soul with the intent to help stop the madness driving my fellow and sister humans to the point of hurting each other from the depths of their unprocessed emotional pain, grief, anger and myriad suffering; to stop the devastating impacts of this unprocessed emotion, this malnourished spirit and feeble undeveloped voice of truth, desperate for more words, yearning for clarity and the time and space, the love and mercy required to resolve all conflicts however large and small, and
2. I have done my time, paid my dues (which btw I have the acronym PAID to offer—Patriarchal Auto Immune Disorder), and I have earned the right, to perhaps vindicate and do right by my matrilineal line, and speak on our behalf.

I came into this world with too little protection and too great a struggle. My mother's amniotic fluid wasn't stable, perhaps due to the questionable treatment she took to avoid yet another miscarriage, and, during a long premature delivery my listless, gray and unresponsive body came out with the umbilical cord wrapped around her neck.

Come hell or high water I will not leave this world the same way. I have taken to heart the words of Louise K. Knight as spoken by the beloved Supreme Court Justice Ruth Bader Ginsberg in the film *Notorious RBG*, "I ask no favors for my sex. All I ask of our brethren is that they take their feet off our necks."

208 ∞ Beyond Karen

Feeling very subtle energetic shifts in conversations, particularly in group discussions, is an art and a skill. The feminine is much better at sensing the impact of tone and nonverbal than the masculine, beginning with the individual body and expanding, through empathy, to other group participants. Seeing patterns repeated over time and not receiving or feeling able to ask for the opportunity to clarify intention or attend to the energetic impact of what or how something was said, either privately "offline" or in a worst-case scenario, during a group discussion, can queue up in oneself like a backlog of irate customers. So instead of barking at the next person who tries to serve you across a counter, breathe and notice these tensions arising and thank the person—the innocent wick to your potential explosion—for helping you see these "little" things a bit more clearly.

My experience of "societal imbalance" (to kindly reframe the alternative definition of "patriarchy") has been boiled down (imagine with me an old cauldron that has been stirred patiently for centuries) and refined into doses of action that, hopefully, can be taken in moments of suffocating tension. The context for this action—in order to catalyze a conscious shift in behavior to stop reinforcing the patriarchy—is an appreciation of both the language and the nature of gender, a key distinction between feminine and masculine or Woman and Man:

In my experience, I have found that the feminine assumes others can see what she sees as obvious to all, as plain as day (perhaps being politely misunderstood and ineffectual). And I have found that the masculine assumes others cannot see what he sees as his unique perspective, needing explanation (perhaps until the other concedes their position).

Action: When your feminine is hypo-contextualizing (not setting sufficient context for whomever you're speaking with to follow what you are saying), consider using phrases like, "I would really like your attention for a moment," and "I see that… or I have been observing that…" Maybe, because you have specifically signaled or asked for someone to listen, the person to whom you are speaking might even respond: "Oh I didn't see that, thanks."

Action: When your masculine is <u>hyper-contextualizing</u> (setting so much context that the person to whom you are speaking feels patronized or as if most of the oxygen has been sucked out of the room), consider using phrases like, "What I hear you saying is…" and "Is there anything specific you are not clear about?" Maybe you'll notice being more "on the same page" than you had realized.

These actions are so subtle. As one approaches their edges of growth, the sharpness can feel as if it is cutting right into the heart. I notice my edges when I feel myself (energetic body) turn away from my husband, away from a colleague, away from anyone or anything I love (or at least care a lot about). Choosing to turn back toward the beloved, that in "this" particular moment looks like an ugly monster, is the hard work of growing, of letting go of constructs that have held us together, and of charting a new course forward.

I'll add here that getting support is essential in the effort to continue to turn back toward a partner, a colleague or team. I now reach out to people I know I can rely on for honest feedback and for "reality checks" about subtle context that I may need, and others reach out to me for the same. I made an agreement with a committee member to have a 5-minute check in before meetings and a 5-minute recap after meetings— what an amazing, heart-centered way to keep one's sanity.

One analogy that feels fitting has to do with flavor. We all love something tasty, we all have unique tastes, and our tastes evolve. I have been sour about a great many things in the world for a great many years. I have been a bit extreme in the sour department which can lead my husband to compensate by being very sweet in order to neutralize or balance us out. As I reframe my sourness, as I let go of the agitation, as I begin to see my wishes for the world actually take root in the world (like the formation of Supermajority.com!), I (and we) need less sweet to stay in balance. But if he isn't able to let go of the habitual sweetness, it can feel like pouring icing over a stale pastry full of curdled custard (which doesn't sound very tasty!).

Worm dream:

I dreamt about being hired to rid a vehicle engine of a snake and worm infestation, but it wasn't clear to me that we were being hired, so all we did was open the engine up. All the snakes and worms scattered. Not knowing much about them, which snakes were or were not poisonous, was unsettling. But the client was very happy. No money was offered, or if it was, Paul got it. I was unsettled because I knew that there were tiny worms still inside and they were extremely smart and resilient. These worms were fast and able to grow rapidly. One seemed to have gotten under my skin, but was simultaneously behind a glass (like Rosie was out on the porch while I washed the sliding glass door yesterday) mirroring my every move. I felt like the eradication of these tiny worms was impossible and that I was defenseless against this ubiquitous and deadly predator just waiting, calculating how and when it would eat me alive. (My heart is once again skipping beats).

I am lying in bed again, sweating during the liver hours (which, according to the ancient Chinese medicine clock is between 1 to 3 AM), as I have much too often over the past year. This worm dream is a sign that I'm worrying too much about things beyond my control. I'll deconstruct this dream in a moment, but first a stream of consciousness about blame and shame:

Paul just crept into the other room leading me to wonder if it's my tossing and turning or his, or both, that keeps us awake. This wonder, this "innocent" and instinctive seed of curiosity could easily lead either of us to blame the other. No one likes even one sleepless night, let alone a year or a lifetime of difficulty sleeping. It leads to significant health issues; it is a vicious self-perpetuating cycle where worry begets sleeplessness and sleeplessness begets worry.

If I point fingers at Paul or vice versa (which he seldom does) or if I point fingers at myself or vice versa (which he has done often) there is a whole thick layer of dis-ease that will need to be sloughed off before getting to the roots or heart of the matter. This sloughing off is where we are as a society thanks to the eruption of demonstrations against police brutality in solidarity with the Black Lives Matter movement protesting the multi-century unbearability of injustice.

The current waves of emotional mania and depression crashing everywhere I look lately is not completely unlike the physical highs and lows of a woman's menstrual moods or the sweat response in a menopausal woman. Estrogen levels help keep the immune system strong and declines can affect the body's emotional well-being; some early studies indicated that men could be 70% more likely to die of coronavirus than female counterparts and were treated with estrogen with positive results. A UK Study[134] released in July 2020 indicated that estrogen may have a protective effect but was inconclusive as to survival rates.

Male and female bodies have testosterone, and both have estrogen. Men and women can both speak the language of Man and the language of Woman. The masculine and the feminine can be unique perspectives through which to view the world. In moments of balance, we are able to touch incredible beauty in ourselves and in nature, but when we are in a manic or depressed emotional state, we lose perspective. Knowing this can go a long way toward compassionately setting a hard boundary with someone who may need a bit more perspective, which is a core skill in the art of calling someone in versus shaming or calling them out.

∞

I went to an esoteric book group a few years ago—one of those heavy lifts of time and energy where I struggled every week to get there, having read the assignment, ready to participate fully. We were reading a book about anarchy and taking drastic measures akin to Extinction Rebellion (XR) before the movement grew to critical mass.

One week there was a vegan farmer with dreadlocks who let me know in no uncertain terms how much he hated the masculine and feminine "blame game"—as if it was just some sort of excuse women cooked up. My first instinct was to bury my whole decades long experience learning about and understanding how to heal the mind-body. And I then tried for a very long time to reconcile this personal, visceral experience of throwing the baby (my ideas, beliefs, feelings,

[134] https://covid.joinzoe.com/post/covid-estrogen-hrt

truth about life, about the world) out with the bathwater (my day-to-day evolving story about the evolving relationships I was having). And all this transgressed from a harsh judgment from someone I didn't know or particularly care about. How much more intense is the effect and the challenge of expressing contrary opinions with family and friends!

Hopefully it is obvious that I have come back to these notions of inner polarity reconciliation. But please go with me down the rabbit hole my mind went down that sleepless night of the worm dream—there are so many subconscious and subterranean directions to go!

- One is the obvious (to me) nature of the dream reflecting the insidiousness of corruption in the world,
- One pathway involves the science behind the multi-dimensional female brain,
- One is the science behind not being validated and the longitudinal health impacts of validation emotionally, physically and socially, *and economically,*
- One relates to the conversation I had with my son when he came home from work telling me about exciting developments in police reform—which branches off into another subterranean direction about proposed[135] legislation Massachusetts Governor Charlie Baker introduced,
- One relates to the conversations I had with Paul about rapper Killer Mike (his uncles are police officers and infantry) and CC Sabathia (it is imperative that city kids be told how to behave around police) and Amy Cooper, and I'll stop with the last one which was related to the worm dream which got me tossing and turning and writing this in the first place,
- And lastly, the importance of following the streams of consciousness that the inner world guides us through, ideally with a partner.

---

[135] https://www.mass.gov/news/baker-polito-administration-files-bill-to-implement-police-officer-certification-system

These little tendrils of energy held in the mind-body, if followed and inspected, provide keys to subconscious angst and help us find clarity and guidance toward emotional wellness. Like anything, we can get out of balance by tipping too far toward introspection or too far toward extrospection. My guess is that societal scales could use quite a boat load of introspection before we, collectively, need to worry about having an imbalance of power favoring the feminine.

Without introspectively and objectively analyzing one's beliefs one cannot be more than a pawn or tumbleweed seeking affiliation through unexamined groupthink. To emotionally reactive "Karens" who have yet to carefully question their version of reality, have yet to find their voice, have yet to speak truth to power in the bedroom or in the boardroom, or in the emotionally charged public moments when they are most challenged to act, moments when they may feel inclined to *grab and point a gun*, I say this:

Ask yourself about the ways that ignorant, destructive, and possibly insane groupthink is accepted by virtue of complicity. Could it be...

- Because we "need" affiliation,
- Because we believe our patience will earn us credibility or respect,
- Because we believe we need more information, data, evidence before taking action,
- Because we don't think we are strong enough,
- Because we don't have a community of kindred souls who have our backs,
- Because the "leader" is our boss or we fear loss of income or reputation,
- Because we value respect and kindness and view calling out bad behavior, especially in communal or public spaces where it is most likely to occur (out of ignorance and habit), to be rude and unkind,
- Because we are concerned about retribution and need to protect our safety and well-being,

- Because we are tired of being The Adult,
- Because unmindful, ignorant and hurtful words are everywhere and calling them out is a never-ending battle we believe we will never win,
- Because we're already in pain and have been labeled or judged by others who couldn't understand our good intentions when we've previously tried speaking up?

What is it like to be in a hypervigilant mode all the time? It is literally nerve-racking. The scientific language for this is the difference between calm and hyper responsive is sympathetic (to one's own body-mind state) and parasympathetic (to everyone else's body-mind state) autonomic nervous system. The vagus nerve (ventral in the front body and dorsal in the back body) innervates the whole body and is receiving a lot of attention by individuals who study and serve people healing from trauma. What if skill building with awareness of the vagus nerve—that tells us when someone across a room, or on the other end of the phone, or even in another automobile on the road, is emotionally charged—can bridge the gaps of understanding moment to moment? Maybe it already does but we are not attending to, or embodying, this wisdom.

One day a dear friend of mine came outside to talk with me after I randomly called because I happened to be working in her neighborhood. We stood for 30 minutes in her driveway talking about the ways in which we were coping with this pandemic. We continued the conversation about trauma and recovery for three hours in a subsequent visit at my house.

Talking deeply like this with friends is an amazing gift that bears gifts of insight, like the thought that emerged from us about how different it would be if we all connected energetically before we connected verbally. What kind of skill sets would we develop in order to sense each other energetically? My friend Laura had been reading a few books simultaneously, including one on the healing properties of water and one on the history of energy. Discussing these cross connections led us to reflect curiously about human connection and agitate together about the electrification of America alongside the investor-owned utilities' doomed to fail, counterproductive-to-capitalism effort to reduce our individual and collective consumption of electricity.

Personally, I have thought a lot about all facets of energy, from the technical to the metaphysical, in part because, as I've shared, I feel the effects of touching anything cellular in my body very intensely. It burns to touch my cell phone or laptop, yet I touch them quite frequently.

I think that I am particularly sensitive to cellular energy because of the trauma that I hold in my body, both the past trauma that I had not been able to process with other people in the moments when painful interactions took place, as well as the present day-to-day trauma that exacerbates this past trauma which is also left untethered, unable to be processed with others in the moments that new painful interactions take place.

What would it be like if we held each other in such compassionate regard that we would make space—in any moment where dis-ease is identified—for those necessary words to be spoken and immediate healing to take place? No compound trauma. There is little room in my body-mind for more trauma and it looks pretty obvious to me that there is no more room in the collective body-mind of America for any additional trauma.

Practicing compassionate regard in my marriage is easy; extricating (*or exorcising!*) trauma is very hard, as I suspect it is for anyone in any relationship. It is the thing that is so hard that it has, over the past 10 years, led the two of us to consider divorce an unfortunate number of times. My desire to be healthy and fully alive is at odds with the cultural paradigm to shut up and go along, to be a good consumer which, disgustingly and insidiously, has been equated to being a good citizen, American, patriotic. We can be kinder even as we clearly define the intolerable.

∞

As I reflect on where I am at this moment in the world, working my paid job from home like so many others, working my (effectively unpaid) job as a select board member planning a spring town meeting for a small town like few others, I am clear about this: the relationships developed, or undeveloped like (missed) opportunity costs in the world of work, offer so much richness of experience and opportunity for skill building in the way the world most needs of us.

Small town municipal government has a lot of opportunity for growth in terms of the feminine nature of inclusiveness, the language of Woman (which is desperately needed as many small towns are *just now* starting to gender neutralize their leaders away from selectmen and councilmen to select board members and councilors). In terms of meeting each other energetically before verbally, in terms of checking our egos at the door and showing up with our sleeves rolled up ready to do what needs to be done, these will take collective and concerted effort.

I am a select board member, about to transition out with the upcoming election, and I wouldn't have leapt into the fray if it hadn't been for one of my closest friends who jumped in with both feet. I joined her gladly, but when she left to pursue her Passion for the Planet, I felt the loss and was not able to fill the void. This does not mean that any of the municipal relationships I have forged are less valuable, but they do take more work without female solidarity. When I do that "extra" work I am incredibly gratified; when I prepare my energy before communicating with someone who thinks differently than I do, when I open my heart up to the possibilities that might unfold, I am always surprised with the mutual joy that emerges. And yet the work, not done in an emotionally supportive environment, is truly taxing.

In one of these municipal conversations, I was sharing my desire to give certificates of service to our long-standing volunteers in town and offering gratitude to my fellow select board member. What resulted was not only an offer to reach out to potential literary agents on my behalf for **Beyond Karen**, but also the suggestion that the new Variable Refrigerant Flow system for our community center be named after me simply because I have been doggedly pursuing and managing grant funding for it. When I mentioned this to our administrator she kindly said, "Well that is a perfect example of what a Karen can do even in a small town like this."

The notion of productivity can give me a figurative rash to think about. Constant improvement in productivity is at the very core of capitalism and succumbing to its pressure keeps us in a hamster wheel, has us doing the emotional gaslighting to ourselves as we work for others. "I'm not doing enough," "I am slacking off," (perhaps by trying to be present with the natural world…) and "I'm not as productive as I used to be," waah waah.

Rosie seems to have competing energy with me around mid-morning. Just as I am in a creative or productive flow she whines to go on her walk, even if we've had a walk earlier. It's frustrating and brings up all sorts of indignation inside me. It is hard enough to get motivated to do much of anything creative or productive these days sheltering in place and it brings up the sense of putting myself last that has affected me at various points in my life. It is as if the universe tests our resolve to do a thing by throwing a great number of obstacles in the way. And the obstacles of the heart—like attending to Rosie's well-being—are much harder to fend off than my own excuses. But when I don't resist, I often find that the creative ideas are supported by the walks with Rosie. The feeling of productivity, however, is not.

So I question whether I'd rather feel productive or creative. Bottom line (this phrase is meant to get you to chuckle as the bottom line is all that matters to capitalists clenching their buttholes about productivity): we must first put on our own "air masks" before attending to others', including our bosses and anyone for whom we are employed. To think or demand otherwise is to subject or be subjected to enslavement. Spend a moment reflecting on whether or not you believe that.

I am just beginning to really understand this expanded notion of enslavement and practice it; what helps me is to do a 180° reframe of my perception of judgment—like when I "decide" someone is being selfish—by observing it as someone else doing a good job of putting their air mask on. Rosie seems to always have her air mask on and maybe her efforts are helping me keep mine on.

I have had a dog in the family my whole life. Observing dog behavior, especially with a fairly well-adjusted smart canine like Rosie, it's easy to see how responsive they are to the world around them. They perk up curiously with every odd sound, distinct scent, new movement, anything outside the "normal" regulation or modulation. My neighbor has a tiny new puppy named Pippi and my big brawny Rosie modulates herself to be gentle and patient around her new friend.

Pippi and my neighbor ventured out to a local trail well populated by off-leash dogs and their owners; they were accosted by a "Karen" who deduced that Pippi was too young to have had all her shots and was therefore not safe for the other dogs to be around. I wonder what dogs would say about this type of nose-in-your-business if they could talk. They're pretty comfortable with strange noses in their business! To my neighbor this was highly offensive, as in "mind yours!" But if this Karen had a point that was valuable to share, potentially important for the wider community of dogs' wellbeing, what about the delivery of this unsolicited vaccination opinion could have bridged the gap between intention and offense?

It appears to me, based on a host of variables I am marinating on— social and behavioral factors that "define" a Karen, actions that may reverberate negatively but may have begun with "good" intention—that the butt-insky's (and everyone, generally) need two things:

(1) to prepare their energy before opening their mouths (breathe, think about why they want to speak, why they feel compelled to speak and to whom, and to distill their message to the basics—free of as much judgment and personal story as possible unless the micro-agreement of the interaction is to share personally), and

(2) to ask for permission to offer advice (make a case for "why" this person or group would want advice, wait for permission to be granted, and be prepared to respect a clear "no" without pushing for a yes).

When one dog clearly wants nothing to do with another dog, the more eager dog will either accept the less interested dog's position or they will likely find out the hard way with a bite to the ear or an uncomfortable shakedown. The social modeling that dogs, and many other species, offer us can't be that difficult for us to learn, can it?

I'm currently sitting with Rosie on one of the rocks in the stream where I fell twice before while being on my phone when I should've been present with the running water and the earth. I will not make this mistake again (I hope). For now, I am going to attend to my beautifully patient puppy who throws her muddy body on me when she knows I need her and when she knows she needs me. She whines when she is unsettled just like I do in my mind. Maybe I can keep learning from her; I'm sure I can.

The Heart of the Matter

A journal entry:

Good morning beautiful Day!

As I wake up, I am happy because my soul is smiling at me (I'm singing a wakeup song by Buddhist nun Sister Chân Không in my head). Last night Sabrina invited me over to watch a movie. Halfway through our favorite show, This Is Us, we stopped to make cookies and I listened to her explain to me the greatest pain in her life at the moment, her sharp edge of growth. It was a gorgeous thing to witness how agile and deep her interpersonal insights are.

But it wasn't until this morning that I realized how logical it is that the need she has for her person to defend her against others' emotional assaults is so acute, given that the primary edge she witnessed as a child was me defending her and her brother against their father's insensitive and hurtful patriarchal programming. And thankfully I know Paul is able to face and appreciate this now as he reckons with the insensitive and hurtful patriarchal programming inflicted by his father (and his father …) and not defended by his mother (or her mother …).

The pain of childhood can serve us well when we can find ways through it—like what I had with an Al-a-teen group I found in college. Yesterday I was digging through some of my creative writing pieces and found the letter I had submitted to a MeToo forum during the horrendous Kavanaugh hearing that ultimately vindicated a racist misogynist and put him on the Supreme Court for life.

Here is an excerpt that follows details of two experiences of rape:

I have struggled to heal from the effects of misogyny—effects that feel like ongoing emotional rape that is both sudden and unexpected by people you want to trust; insidious and life-sapping mind fucks by people you "go along to get along with" so that you can be lucky enough to pay your bills. My dream is to heal the effects of misogyny as a series of communities communicating about it openly, gracefully, interconnected by story and hugs of understanding. Once we learn how beautiful and comfy "safe" feels, we become so much more resilient and impenetrable.

Reading this letter over was almost more than I could bear at that moment. To remember myself as innocent and fresh, capable of and happy to hold a six-foot tall friend and fellow cheerleader on my shoulders was significant. Gratitude reemerged for the effervescent big-haired ginger who became my neighbor and best friend, got me to dress up in a sexy outfit and wave pom poms at jocks, and to also challenge myself academically and shift from typing classes to calculus, and who helped break apart the foundations of my life.

I've been reflecting on my childhood trying to extract my happy memories. They're more fragile and significantly less myelinated than some of my painful ones, making them my new growth edge. I remember happiness as the feeling of having my six-foot friend Susan stand on my shoulders. Would that every child, every single child, gets this opportunity to smash the cracks in their foundations and rebuild with dynamic supports!

Paul just called to pray and listened to my happy soul story. He said he'd heard a news report about how emotional abuse is one of the things that is passed down through sperm. We celebrated our choice to have children and our ability—after a great deal of compassionate emotional battling—to hopefully alter the DNA of our son's sperm if he chooses to have kids.

End of journal entry

What I have described here, dear reader, is white privilege. Yes, it was a gorgeous moment to relax with my daughter and feel the comfort of baking cookies while having heartfelt dialogue about the discomforts in life that lead us to feel gratitude. But the heart of the matter is that I, as a white person, am able to be emotionally intense, able to traverse the continuum of joy and sadness relatively freely.

Many white people choose (subconsciously or not) to complain about their sadness or sufferings so that they don't feel the guilt of how good of a life they actually have. When many more white people come to terms with this, break our paradigms down to the point of real but figurative annihilation, we will also break down our entitlements.

As a white (and white-minded) person I have experimented with what I'm thinking about as "privilege fasting" in order to better appreciate the comforts of life that have come easy to me in this racially unjust republic of the United States. It has led me to notice how much I take for granted, including the trees I don't see all around me supporting my daily life (which really helps me gain perspective when I feel invisible about being middle-aged or whatever has me uptight in any particular moment).

At the end of the day, the "bottom line" point of this one precious life, the raison d'etre, is to evolve our spirit-mind-body through the interpersonal and interspecies forces of nature in order to be as close to in harmony, at-one-ment, with the awesome essence of all that is.

My personal lived experience opinion about why spirit-mind-body growth has seemed harder for white people to understand than Indigenous people and any peoples of color who haven't had their cultural roots decimated by white culture, is because parenting in white culture has been set on following rules that were written largely by white men instead of listening to and following the guidance of spirit and the laws of nature. When parents teach us how to see ourselves in all the myriad ways that we intrinsically and uniquely feel and are special—instead of boxing us into established and expected notions of what is special—then we unfold, blossom, and emerge into and through life more naturally, harmoniously.

Would that we could let spirit guide each precious child—every single one—through life in ways that nourish and help them feel seen, heard, and appreciated for what makes them intrinsically and uniquely special.

More Than Enough

At what point does one end a story? Everyone has a story; everyone is an amalgamation of stories, stories that matter, stories unfolding and emerging every moment of every day.

This day, only five hours in, has been so incredibly full that I must write it. Offer closure.

I woke, early am, alone in bed, wondering why Paul was not there, realizing it was because it was boiling hot and humid and he needed the fan in the other room which makes too much noise for me to sleep soundly. I dialed into the angst, that had been with me since I started writing **Beyond Karen**. I rolled over, turned on the light, and wrote, "I Am Karen." Then I got up, took Rosie outside and fed her and then went back up to make love with my sweetheart.

When we got up to make breakfast we were elated. Ecstatic and on the terrifying edge of happiness, where words cannot capture joy, where tentative hearts are so wide open that they ignore—no, are completely oblivious to—the awareness of inevitable brokenness that will come again in the future. And every word, every look, every touch is so full of truth that we float on the song carried along the spectrum of color covering every surface of everything in sight.

I made pancakes. Plain for Nathan, chocolate chip for Paul, and blueberry walnut for me. He made galãoes for the three of us. We stomped on the floor for Nathan to come upstairs to eat. He didn't want to get up so early (9:30am). We FaceTimed Sabrina and invited her to breakfast, which of course was a joke because she lives over an hour away. But I'm sure she considered it. She used to live with us, after college, as an adult, with her boyfriend, in a space made special for them. She said, "nice boobs, mom" because I had a skimpy

nightgown on and didn't care. I told her that her father had just
suggested that I maybe put something else on because Nathan was
coming upstairs (Paul had said he'd been traumatized by his mother's
nightgown boobs). I said, "I'd told dad that was his problem, not
hers." She hung up after we—so in love with her she couldn't stand it
anymore—invited her and her puppy Luna and her friend that was on
her way over to her house to all come visit.

We lit the candles and said grace and ate our pancakes while
looking at our respective computers (which we almost never do).
Paul's excitement keeps growing about his dream of having a cottage
on a lake. It was supposed to rain today, and we had planned to go
drive by a place he'd found. We both had our computers open looking
at pictures from real estate websites (him) and satellite maps (me). But
it was unbelievably perfect out. I said, "I want to work outside in the
yard and paint the deck before going to look at any dream property!"
He gently noted my tone. I thanked him for noticing. He said, "are
you being sarcastic?" and I said, "no, darling, I appreciate you saying
something."

Elton John started singing about his future laying, beyond a yellow
brick road. Ah ah, ahh ah ah ah ah[136]...

We changed into painting clothes. I appreciated the little rainbow
heart label at the neck of my tattered black tank with paint on the left
boob. (which reminds me of the time when the kids and I were driving
somewhere and one of us, maybe I, was telling a story about someone
saying, "he's got balls" which turned into a question of why don't we
say, "she's got boobs" with the same deference? For years we
substituted "she's got boobs" whenever "they've got balls" might have
been "appropriate"). I got my paint can and returned to my task of
painting the deck railings alongside Rosie who always likes to sit right
where I am. Then I hear the music.

Paul chose the Elton John Spotify channel. He clearly chose this
because of the impact the movie we had just watched had on me. I
cannot believe it took me so long to watch Rocket Man, but it was
worth the wait. I decided to move to another part of the deck where I

[136] Goodbye Yellow Brick Road, October 5 1973, © Elton John

could be closer to the speaker. I chose to put it as loud as it could go. I got back on the floor of the deck, hunkering under the bench to reach the lower part of the railings and flip my body left to right every few railings so I could get both sides painted. Then I sat up singing louder, literally crying and shaking with emotion and utter mesmerization over the magic that comes out of Elton John's mouth and hands:

Behind four walls of stone the rich man sleeps. It's time we put the flame torch to their keep.
Burn down the mission, If we're gonna stay alive. Watch the black smoke fly to heaven, See the red flame light the sky. Burn down the mission, Burn it down to stay alive; It's our only chance of living; Take all you need ….. to live inside. Ah ah[137]

Every song felt as though it was playing for me. The tears kept coming. Paul came up after cutting another piece of salvageable deck to replace the unsalvageable pieces. I walked over to him as he was telling me he chose this channel on purpose. I said I knew that and hugged him with tears still in my eyes. I thanked him and he told me to stop it, he could really get used to this. We kissed; we put our foreheads together the way the Na'vi people greet each other in the movie Avatar[138] (and the Zulu and perhaps other African peoples which the Na'vi were modeled after). He said, "I see you." I said, "I love you."

Then he started babbling about the tree behind me and the counteroffer that the couple who had come over to look at my motorcycle yesterday wanted to give me for the motorcycle my father had bought me as a wedding present. The motorcycle I am intensely struggling to part with even though I know it is time. The motorcycle that my husband and son, not me, are selling and shopping online for a replacement for me, who could care less. The motorcycle that is literally, unbelievably, somehow in his name, not mine.

---

[137] Burn Down the Mission, 1970, © Elton John
[138] https://ceasefiremagazine.co.uk/why-avatar-is-a-truly-dangerous-film/

I returned to painting. I couldn't stop my body from rocking out to the words. Oh yeah, Saturday night is most definitely alright for fighting. Can't wait to get a little action in.[139]

I didn't realize Nathan was sitting with Rosie watching me rock out wildly, while painting (not well because rocking out was way more important), watching me with the hairy legs that I no longer apologize for having (having found a happy medium of waxing less frequently after oh so many hours and moments of excessively picky legs from shaving, stubble that would literally wear out my jeans, years of tears that would flow from the stupid agony of ineffective self-epilation). The look on his face when I turned over my left shoulder was of sweetness, of full acceptance of his passionate middle-aged mother who farts when she feels like it just like he does, very much unlike her mother who wouldn't say shit even if she'd had a mouth full of it.

Van Morrison started singing one of my favorites. Something picked me up off the deck and walked me over to my son. I started dancing with him like I had danced with him when he was 15 months old and alive, after a harrowing brush with death. I had held him carefully as his head, torso, right arm and leg were all bandaged, and danced with him in the middle of the Shriner's atrium during their Christmas in July party for families suffering a loved one's burn injuries. Along with Edwin McCain, I testified to my son the fact that "I'll be the Greatest Fan of Your Life," a song we drop everything for each time we hear it, and call each other, or record the radio and text to each other, still (even though some of the words don't quite fit).

I poured love from my hands into his back as we rocked back and forth, my head on his neck, through all the lyrics, longer than would be comfortable for any young 22-year-old man, no hint of discomfort coming from him:

Oh the morning sun in all its glory, It greets the day with hope and comfort too, And you fill my life with laughter, And you can make it better, You ease my troubles, that's what you do. There's a love that's

---

[139] Saturday Night's Alright, 1973, © Elton John

divine, And it's yours and it's mine, like the sun. So at the end of the day, We should give thanks and pray to the One[140].

Then the chills:
...And have I told you lately that I love you? And have I told you there's no one above you? You fill my heart with gladness, You take away my sadness, You ease my troubles, that's what you do.

Then, as if miracles weren't happening everywhere so big you could just scream, I went back to painting. I finished all the parts under the stretch of bench, even with the chills coming, affirming all that I Am.

Elton knows that Mars ain't the kind of place to raise your kids. He says it's cold as hell ... and there's no one there to raise them anyway. He points out that (social) science is an enigma, that's just his job five days a week. He's (really) a rocket man.
And he thinks it's gonna be a long long time
Until he has to face the tension, the pain of not being seen the way he wants to be seen. Instead of trying to be both inside and outside of the box life both wants us to be in and out.
And he thinks it's gonna be a long long time
And he thinks it's gonna be a long long time.
And he thinks it's gonna be a long long time...[141]

I think it's already been a long long time.

I think it's already been a long long time.

And, dear reader, forever emerging from whatever depths of emotions you have inside you, I shall close with the words that woke me up the day I started writing this book: it's time.

---

[140] Have I Told You Lately, 1989, © Van Morrison
[141] Rocket Man, 1972, © Elton John

Index of Memes

Afterword ... and Book Circle Prompts

Derek Chauvin was tried and convicted of murdering George Floyd. President Joe Biden is now proposing the George Floyd Justice in Policing Act. Many Americans have held their breath for this judgment and for a legislative response during the past year and personally I don't want to know what would have happened if the verdict went the other way. There is a slight glimmer of hope for justice.

I am glad I have written this book and can appreciate with greater clarity the work we must all do in order to bridge the emotional spaces between us. I continue to face my own complicity, my own privilege supported by voices of those who have been able to transform anger into clear action.

Speaking of anger, like the feelings of fear, sadness, and joy, it is a tool when skillfully implemented (i.e. with compassion and respect). It is maddening to me to drive by countless "construction" projects and spy with my little eye what looks to me like large boys acting like the earth is their giant sandbox to play in. Someday I hope to be skillful with this anger and transform it into clear action.

This past year has intensified the nauseous feeling I have about the little bubbles of comfort I live and work in. Not addressing these pursuits and protections of insularity adds to the sense of complicity and the "white guilt" of an anti-racist. So I keep trying to dialogue it out.

Here are a few ways I have noticed and tried to reckon with my Inner Karen as a result of writing this book. I'd also love to collaborate with people on so many ideas not written in this book, (including ideas for experimenting with KITS, Karen Immersion Therapy in Society):

1. Really observe your energy and subtle narratives going on in your head about strangers you interact with,
2. Don't fake smile behind your mask (or at all) and do your best to match your facial expression to your authentic feeling (even if you're in sales or customer service),
3. Notice your choices around Time, Tasks, and Temperament, where there is stress, there are lessons,
4. Video yourself after a Karen experience—where you may have not been as gracefully kind or honest as you know you can be—and (when the private group is created) post to @gobeyondKaren as part of the **I AM Karen** project (I have written my I am Karen narrative but am waiting for community to build up around this before I record it).

White-minded people are in for a hard row to hoe, so to speak. We have been turning a blind eye to our racist roots for generations and need intense restructuring of belief systems about our "rights" and what is and is not equal or just. Fortunately spirit is infinitely generous as we call on her for guidance.

We know where we are energetically weak, lazy, flaccid, or comatose. We don't want reminders of this because it's really really hard. And the pain we feel is an indication we need more community, more sisterhood, more compassionate brotherhood. It's not "you and me against the world" (unless by "against" one means leaning alongside), it's "you and me with the world."

There are definite tactics and strategies the feminine spirit can and does take to get through to us in any moment—focusing on the breath, sensing what is under the hands or the feet, refining the diet, enhanced self-care, adjusting the attitude and heart-centeredness, forgiving self and others, seeking out and listening to other's stories, and wishing others well—pivotal moments of choices that can be extraordinarily effective and empowering. These and other practices allow our feminine spirit to help us let go of our grip on things that cause us stress, things we hold onto as justification of fears we believe we can't face.

I am trying to remind myself that:

- We are never too old to grow toward our dreams,
- It is never too late to choose to be different,
- It is always good to reconcile, even silently.

I hope I have expressed a "sense-able" balance of research and personal story so that your body-mind could enjoy, appreciate, and engage with all the elements that were curated for you. If there is one thing I might wish as a result, it is that you have an expanded sense of what middle-aged, middle of the road women are and bring to the world, alongside you, and everyone else.

One final note I would like to share with you, dear reader, has to do with the cover art for **Beyond Karen**. In the first stages of thinking about a cover to encapsulate this story, I imagined a picture of my bold and gentle Rosie walking down the mossy path to the hemlock forest and waterfall in the woods that we love, and have been so loved by, nearly each day while this book was written. But I worried that this image was too "soft" and would not translate or convey the depth of the overall message of transformation. I then went to the opposite extreme and printed a number of copies of **Beyond Karen** with a picture of my bruised and battered hand (blackened index fingernail and ring fingernail literally hanging on by threads after crushing them in the garage door) boldly giving the middle finger against a black background.

It took quite a bit of time and space for me to find the harmony in the process of encapsulating all that this book has meant to me into one image. The gentle feedback from friends did not resonate. But once the current cover image, like the patient feminine spirit, presented herself to me, I felt it and understood. Transformation is about solidarity, even if we can't imagine ourselves being kind in a particular set of circumstances, even if we believe we can do little more than plant a seed of solidarity in our consciousness and wait patiently for it to grow with nature's guidance. We can always set a positive intention.

May we all live in harmony.

10 Prompts for Participating in a Beyond Karen Book Circle:

1. Many Karens have been portrayed across social media but only a few were highlighted in *Beyond Karen*. Which behaviors of a Karen (either featured in *Beyond Karen* or other media) do you dislike the most? Which "Karen" do you feel most sympathy for?

2. The cover image was originally of the author's middle finger with bruised and falling off fingernails flipping "someone" off. Choosing to represent the "Beyond" vision instead of the "Karen" problem was intentional—what similar intentions have you made? Did the use of profanity or crude language in particular sections of the book stand out in any way? If so, how and why do you think you had this reaction?

3. Narcissism is a psychological disorder and is highlighted in the chapters, *The K- and F- words* and *Emotional Reeducation*. Is a Karen different than any other person exhibiting narcissistic behaviors? Does the author's implication that capitalism is at the root of narcissistic behaviors resonate with you?

4. The "culture of smartness" is highlighted in the chapter, *My American Dream* to illustrate the roots of self-centeredness in America. Do the author's experiences in finance elicit compassion or understanding about the cultural programming middle-aged women experienced in the 80s 90s and 00s? Why or why not?

5. The summer of 2020 was replete with "viral meltdowns" and videos capturing and publicizing them. Do you think that the level of "viral shaming" of Karens is fair and appropriate given her behaviors in public, her entitlements, her abuses of service workers, and her racism? Why or why not?

6. In part two, the author shares a few of her consciousness raising experiences (in business, at the Red Tent Temple, at a retreat in Mallorca). Which elements of the author's personal stories felt meaningful or inspiring to you? What are some of your 180° Pivot Moments of Choice?

7. Many experts have offered harsh critiques about the addictive nature of social media. How does the internet and the mechanics of gaining social media visibility contribute to one's emotional instability? How is this amplified when society is experiencing a crisis like the COVID-19 pandemic or the effects of police brutality?

8. The author introduces her "sensitive" family puppy to the reader as she introduces other family members. What do you think about Rosie? Does she seem like a good model for the Anti-Karen? Why or why not?

9. Karen was one of the most popular names for girls born in the late 1960s. Karen is also the name of a Burmese nation of people that have been in a brutal civil war for decades. Do you think this nation's name is a more critical factor for petitioning against the pejorative use of the name Karen than any other factor?

10. There are numerous isms in society: sexism, racism, ageism, classism, ableism. How does *Beyond Karen* treat these isms? To what extent did you identify or not identify with these treatments? What sentiments about feminism has the book left you with?

If you have hosted or participated in a book circle reading **Beyond Karen,** please post discussion highlights and photos to @GoBeyondKaren on Facebook and Twitter!

Acknowledgements

I am so glad for the enduring practice of expressing gratitude to those who support another along the conception, gestation, development and delivery processes of bringing a new book to life. My first acknowledgement is to my closest friends who hold me in their hearts and witness me as a writer. This foundation of encouragement you show me is the greatest gift in the world! Thank you Alisa, Andra, Arianna, Bob, Carla, Edith, Gloria, Ian, Jana bobanna, Jodie, Josh, Kate, Kathie, Laura, Lee, Madeleine, Marilyn, Pam, Pat, Rachel, Stephanie, Susan and many others including the dozens of friends who helped me sort through cover designs and description copy—thank you Brit for this art!

My children Sabrina and Nathaniel have been sweet cheerleaders and have both gracefully listened to their guts and challenged me when a sentence or sentiment did not sit well with them. I am so blessed to have a relationship that is as honest and transparent as a parent could ever hope for with you both. I love love love you.

My husband Paul, my sturdy oak holding me throughout my entire adult life, you hold the fears and anxieties of a new birth with me like no one else can. Thank you for wanting me to not dream so big that my heart gets hurt and for envisioning great things not just for **Beyond Karen** but for the societal shift she is dreaming.

This book would not have been as fun to make or to read were it not for the creative artists making memes. The ones in this book were shared to celebrate their work and done so in consideration of the Fair Use Doctrine relative to copyright law. The explosion of meme party games has also led to hours of family fun.

I would also like to acknowledge gratitude for the resilience of Ellen DeGeneres, J.K. Rowlings and countless individuals who have

234 ∞ Beyond Karen

endured the effects of this Karen trope in their lives, most specifically through social media and the complicated nature of cancel culture.

Victoria K. Chapman, artist extraordinaire, thank you dearly. Your gentle grace is magic.

Arianna Alexandra Collins I cannot thank you enough for your faith and confidence when I needed it most; and Madeleine Charney and Janet Steen, thank you all for your diligent and responsive feedback and editing of my anemic first draft!

I thank Elisa Nisly, Mary Bisbee Beek, Ellen Meeropol, Madeline Turner, Claudia Gere, and Shel Horowitz for their generosity of heart and wisdom. Thank you all for your incredible literary resources and insights and for pouring your talents into the world.

To all hearts and minds that invest time and energy in these words: thank you for resonating and holding the vision for a more perfect state of union in communities, families, and society at large.

About the Author

Karen Willard Ribeiro is the mother of two children, a climate defender, and a woman not afraid to dig into the weeds of difficult things. She was born and raised in Western Massachusetts where she met and married Paul, her high school sweetheart. When she is not exploring the outdoors with Rosie, the anti-Karen, she is writing, helping people understand renewable energy mechanics and policies, and experimenting with ways to simplify life for herself and her community. Karen has written a memoir, *Thirsty: Journaling to Survive, Thrive and Feel Alive* a book of poetry called *Curious: Poetic Explorations on Gender and Nature*, and she has collaborated on a few anthologies with other writers. In 2006 Karen created the multifaceted Inner Fortune journal to complement her life witnessing services and she believes that Together we can Heal the Effects of Misogyny.

www.ingramcontent.com/pod-product-compliance
Lightning Source LLC
Chambersburg PA
CBHW030242030426
42336CB00009B/211